Rach
Woodward
Nov. '89.

BUILDING FUTURES

Other titles in the **SIGNALS** *series:*

ON THE STREETS

THE GENE SHIFTERS

BUILDING FUTURES

A Layman's Guide To The Inner City Debate

SIGNALS

David Boyle

W H ALLEN

First published in Great Britain 1989 by
W.H. Allen & Co Plc
Sekforde House, 175-9 St. John Street, London EC1V 4LL

© David Boyle 1989

ISBN 1 852 27171 X

Designed by Roger Kohn

Printed and bound in Great Britain by
Mackays of Chatham Plc

This book is sold subject to the condition that
it shall not, by way of trade or otherwise,
be lent, re-sold, hired out or otherwise circulated
without the publisher's prior consent in any
form of binding or cover other than that
in which it is published and without a similar
condition including this condition being imposed
upon the subsequent purchaser.

Contents

Acknowledgements vi

Introduction 1

1 History of the Inner Cities 7

2 We Want Them Too, Next Time 31

3 Darker Corners 65

4 From Garden City to City Garden 89

5 From Yobs to Yokels 109

6 The Cultural Revolution 125

7 From Trickle Down to Bottom Up 147

8 Meet Me in St Louis 177

Notes to the text 197

Index 205

Acknowledgements

My flat gives me a wide view over London, across Brixton, Peckham towards the Docks and London's various inner city strongholds.

They look much the same as they did when I moved in, except that the Docklands must have more cranes above it than it ever did when it was a port. Looked at from ground level, though, there have been the most enormous changes in the way we think about inner cities in the last five years. I wrote this book as a way of trying to get people to talk about them – the inner cities are too important to be left to the experts and pundits.

I was privileged to be editor of *Town & Country Planning* magazine since just before the Broadwater Farm riot, and from that vantage point – better than my kitchen window – I have been able to watch the changes that have taken place.

A number of generous people have given me great support with time, advice or ideas over the different sections of the book. They include Ian Archer, Christine Bailey, Marc Dorfman, Paul Ekins, Jane Fenwick, Tony Gibson, David Hall, Dennis Hardy, John Johnson, Stephen Joseph, Robert McNulty, Janice Morphet, Steve Sharples and many others whose patience I imposed on. If it wasn't for them the book would not be nearly as accurate. But the mistakes that remain are all mine.

I would also like to thank everyone at the Town and Country Planning Association, which has for many years kept the light burning for civilized, greener cities – new and old – for introducing me to many of the ideas in this book.

Finally I must thank my publisher Susanne McDadd, for her support and encouragement. And especially Kate Cutler for her suggestions and patience while I was writing.

David Boyle
Crystal Palace

INTRODUCTION

Where there is no vision, the people perish.
                                                        Proverbs 29.18

The inner city is not so much a place as a state of mind.

As a place, it is difficult to find or pin down. It has no borders. To the sociologist it means deprivation, to the politician a symbol of blame or opportunity. To the people who live there it's just home.

Nobody finds it easy to define. The expert committee set up a decade ago by the Social Science Research Council found that some inner cities were not poor at all, while some estates on the edges of cities – like the notorious outlying estates in Glasgow – show enough inner city symptoms to need the same prescription, what ever it is. The government defines inner cities as the 57 areas covered by their Urban Programme – which include nearly a third of the population. Even so, only 45 per cent of the nation's unemployed live in these inner cities, and it is difficult to find one symptom which defines every one of the 57 varieties of places.

What we *can* say about them is that inner cities are all places that have been left behind. More accurately, they are the people who have been left behind by history and prosperity, when society and the economy moved on, when patterns of work and population changed.

The radical writer Colin Ward has imagined arriving in a strange town and asking a taxi driver to take him to the inner city: 'He might reply, "But you're there already". Or he might ask "Any particular place you have in mind? Do you want downtown, or the big shops, the business centre, the hotel belt, the red light district?" Embarrassed, you would mumble "Just take me to where the poor people live". For just as Gandhi remarked 50 years ago that India for him was an idea, not a geographical expression, so the inner city is not a place at all but a euphemism for low incomes'.[1]

An inner city is not the same as a city centre, with its ringing cash registers – though luxurious shopping districts have been built over many an inner city area. It is possible to see where the two meet in strange places like Aldgate, where the financial towers of the City of London adjoin the tower blocks of an inner city as if there was an invisible line between the two. It is even possible to find an old-fashioned coster-monger just over the inner city side of the line.

The problems are more complex than those of money, 'Poverty is . . . about rights and relationships,' said the Archbishop of Canterbury's report *Faith in the City.* 'They are about how people are treated and how they regard themselves, about powerlessness, exclusion and loss of dignity'.[2] Inner cities are full of contradictions. Visiting the Gloucester Grove estate in south London, designed relatively recently and shortly to become a Housing Action Trust, brought this home.

As you walk into Peckham, around the corner from the estate, there is a vandalized telephone box beside a wide expanse of pavement, with weeds growing up to two feet high from between the paving slabs. Rubble, old newspapers and Tennants Export cans litter the gutter. This is one of the most densely populated areas of Britain, with one of the highest rates of unemployment.

Just 50 yards away, the rubbish changes character. There is an abandoned packet of Henry Wintermans cigars, and a baggy-trousered youth passes carrying a designer label carrier bag. The houses are newly-painted, the fences mended and the window frames smooth and white.

Many of the houses have burglar alarms. But research shows that it is the nearby council tenants – especially the elderly – who are more frightened of crime than the heavily mortgaged residents of these attractive Victorian houses. Ironically, it is the owner-occupiers who are protecting themselves against a threat they perceive from the nearby estates. Gentrification has meant other changes in the area. More local people are active in voluntary committees and residents groups. 'Neighbourhood

Introduction

Watch' stickers on the doors demonstrate an awareness of the rest of the community.

It has also meant a boost for the declining shops in Peckham High Street. There are a large number of takeaways, like McDonalds, with the headquarters upstairs of the North Peckham Task Force – and they are clearly doing a brisk trade. People in the street do not look destitute. Their clothes look new. There is more money around than there was a few years ago – partly because of the incoming middle class home-owners. But the poorer people are now paying for food with credit cards, as well as their clothes: they do not actually have the cash in hand.

Those who can afford it tend to leave Gloucester Grove. But the children cycling around the estate are riding new BMX bikes. Some of the cars are beaten old jalopies – some are burnt out completely, with a mixture of rust and melted rubber around them – but many are nearly new. In a culture where marketing is at an increasingly high pressure via television and skilled poster hoardings, and when the waiting has been taken out of wanting for nearly everyone, even the poorest can buy on credit. And when they are living in close proximity to those who can afford not to wait for the 'luxuries' that have become necessities – why should they wait? The new Money Advice Centre, in a former children's home on the edge of the estate, provides evidence that many are deeply in debt.

The flats at Gloucester Grove long since lost their milk deliveries. Walking through the estate, even on a bright summer's day, the dirt, the piles of rubbish and the sheer neglect makes it hard to believe that this is home for 3,000 people. There are the burnt out and locked pram sheds, now taken over by the glue-sniffers, and the garages below the flats are no longer used. They have been filled with piles of rubbish and litter and the charred remains of small fires. When anyone lights a fire in the garages, the corridors above fill with smoke.

The lift is often out of order, and the spiral stairs are covered with graffiti in varying levels of literacy and obscenity. The fantasies spelled out on the walls, giving graphic accounts of what they want to do and to whom, produce a strong atmosphere of sexual menace. The authors presumably live on the estate.

At the end of the street, a betting shop, a Chinese takeaway, a chip shop, a pub and a brand new poster above them all advertising the flowers and colours that are supposed to be part of everyday life in the new town of Milton Keynes. The caption – tactless in the middle of Peckham – is 'Inner City Riot'.

The contradictions in the area run deep. The borough of Southwark – of which Peckham is a part – is an area of high public spending, but enormous poverty. Unemployment has actually risen by nearly 50 per cent since the 1981 riots, and was recently running at twice the national average. There has been high investment in public housing in the past, yet appalling housing conditions remains. A massive £75 billion is now thought to be the price of solving Britain's housing problems.

The contradictions extend to inner city policy. All too often attention is paid to the problems of decaying buildings and bad environments, without any thought for the main problems faced by people themselves. Solving the former may well do nothing to solve the latter, because however many shiny new buildings might transform inner city areas, there will remain people caught in a trap of low expectations and dependence on the state. Their problems will still have to be tackled under another government heading: 'unemployment', 'poverty', 'education' or 'social security'.

What makes the confusing and contradictory inner cities exciting to governments like Mrs Thatcher's, when they discover them as a political issue, is that the mistakes and historic movements that brought them into existence lie deep in the past. The responsibility for solving them belonged, until recently, to no one particular minister – so nobody can lose their reputation by failing to find solutions. Of course, it is that very confusion which explains why some governments have entirely failed to take their responsibilities at all.

When Mrs Thatcher was delivered to Conservative Central Office on June 12 1987, to claim her third successive election victory, the inner cities were at the top of her thoughts. Celebrate now, she told her triumphant party staff, but tomorrow we must knuckle down to help 'those inner cities, "Because," she went on – "we want them too, next time".' What did she mean?

Mrs Thatcher had managed to win for a third time, in spite of a plummeting Conservative vote in the cities – most of Britain's major cities outside London now had no Conservative MPs at all. She also pronounced the words 'inner cities' firmly and slowly, as if they would be unfamiliar to her audience. The fact that the remark was made to party staff indicates that it was an electoral

INTRODUCTION

statement: next time, the cities would return Conservatives. Some took it to mean that she intended to cripple, finally, the power of local government over the cities. But the Prime Minister may also have been talking about tackling problems. Perhaps this was a party leader, magnanimous in victory, admitting that there were still major problems to solve.

But the difficulty of perceiving what inner city problems actually comprise still remains. And a problem that is impossible to define is fruitful material for a democratic government. It means they can define it in any way they want, when they want – and claim success accordingly. Listening closely to Mrs Thatcher, during her 'off-the-cuff' victory remarks, she seemed to define 'inner cities' in a more personal way – as the places and people who have so far failed to accept her changes.

In this respect she is probably right. The inner cities stand for the places that, generation after generation, suffer for the changes in society that benefit others. Age after age, the enthusiasm of revolutions take their grip, and the people who get left behind tend to be found near the middle of cities, dependent on whatever charity or the remnants of the economy can provide.

As the inner city 'issues' have risen up the political agenda, and the problems that face them have grown more complex, the official solutions have also become more complicated. But new thinking is emerging in the wake of the riots, new schemes which lay emphasis on the people who actually live there.

This book tells the story of these new approaches, which are so crucial to the inner city problems of the 1990s. It tells the story of the people behind them and how these ideas are emerging out of a very different inner city debate.

1
History of the Inner Cities

As there is a darkest Africa, so is there also a darkest England?
William Booth, *In Darkest England and the Way Out*

In 1902 the American novelist Jack London, working for the American Press Association, found himself in the city which bears his name to report on the coronation of Edward VII from a 'working class point of view.'

Jack London was the well-known author of *The Call of the Wild*, of stories where people found themselves pushed to their physical limits. He wanted to see for himself the working class districts of the city, and the extremes of life they were supposed to contain. Friends and contacts would not take the idea seriously, so he consulted the famous international travel operators Thomas Cook & Son. But a trip to the East End was 'so unusual', they said.

'Never mind that', he cut in. 'Here's something you can do for me. I wish you to understand in advance what I intend doing, so that in case of trouble you may be able to identify me.'

'Ah I see! Should you be murdered, we would be in a position to identify the corpse', said the travel agent's representative, unhelpfully.

Jack London went to town on the incident. 'With ease and celerity , could you send me to Darkest Africa or Innermost Tibet,' he wrote. 'But to the East End of London, barely a stone's throw distant from Ludgate Circus, you know not the way!'[1]

Inside the 'unknown' parts of the city where Jack London ventured – hiring a private detective to keep track of him – he discovered the same two cities that so many other social adventurers and writers had found before and since: 'A West End and an East End . . . in which one end is riotous and rotten, the other end sickly and underfed'.

A century later we describe our conditions differently. Where university graduates once arrived in the inner cities as part of Toynbee Hall or the reforming University Settlement movement, they now arrive as gentrifiers and 'yuppies'. The idea of 'Darkest London' is summed up now in the phrase 'no-go areas', estates where milk is no longer delivered and where the formal economy has all but disappeared. The phrase 'inner cities' was not coined until the 1970s, but a similar set of inner city problems are recognizable through history.

The first is poverty. 'The poor are always with us', though politics and culture tend to be more aware of them at some points of history than at others, often when they feel most threatened by them. There have also always been sections of cities cut off from the sources of power, always – as the Marxist pioneer Friedrich Engels said – a 'slum area hidden from sight.'

Disease and dirt are a second inner city theme. The 13th century monks by the Fleet River, which now runs underground through central London, believed its revolting smell was killing them. The first royal commission on air pollution was set up in the same century by Edward I in 1285.

Three centuries later, the diarist John Evelyn believed that the massive increase in rickets in the 17th century was caused by atmospheric pollution from burning coal. Evelyn was driven to distraction by the way smoke from Scotland Yard obscured his view of Whitehall Palace. His campaign against air pollution included the very modern idea of moving industries out to six miles beyond the city, but it was not taken up.

The dirt mixed with the weather to bring the unpleasant conditions associated with cities now. The philanthropist Jonah Harvey amused his friends by carrying the first umbrella – not so much to keep the rain off, but to stop the dirt in the rain from staining his clothes. It has been suggested that this is the reason why umbrellas are traditionally coloured black.

Crime is the third inner city theme through history, and it spreads out to infect the city as a whole. The novelist Henry Fielding, whose novel *Tom Jones* portrays contemporary interaction between city and country people, was a pioneering magistrate in Bow Street in the 18th century. But he was in no doubt about the cause of crime: it was 'general luxury among the lower order'. The first Prime Minister, Robert Walpole, told the House of Commons in the 1730s that visiting a friend's house was as 'dangerous as going to the relief of Gibraltar'.

The rabble was pictured by William Hogarth, providing a fourth theme – disorder. It preyed upon the minds of the better off, as much a spectre for the middle and upper classes as the fear of plague. Here was the inner city at its most dangerous, a threatening urban underclass which Thomas Hardy imagined later as 'a monster whose body has four million heads and eight million eyes'.

It was to escape from these combined threats of poverty, disease and dirt, crime, and disorder, that London expanded outwards. And this geographical movement led directly to inner city problems as we know them now.

II

The London of Charles Dickens' novels, where grimy, hungry, desperate people eke out a wretched existence among the bricks and smoke, has lodged deep in the modern mind. Such dirt and degradation feel as far behind us as the pathetic helpless people he wrote about, but the association reinforces our idea that poverty means cities. It is easy to forget that Dickens was almost contemporary with the Radical MP and campaigner William Cobbett, who was travelling the countryside of southern England, exposing the grinding poverty of people on the land.

Cobbett's *Rural Rides* describe an economy that was collapsing all around him. He recognized that poverty in the countryside was bound up with poverty in the cities, and that one could not be discussed without the other. Agricultural crises in every age had led the poor to leave the land looking for opportunities in the big cities. Like starstruck youngsters flocking to Hollywood, or gold prospectors to California, the rural poor arrived hoping to emulate the rise of Dick Whittington from penniless arrival to Lord Mayor of London. But most arrived rootless in the cities, where the streets turned out to be paved with anything but gold. Without anything to sell but their labour, those who failed sank rapidly to an underclass in an inner city underworld. The French philosopher Rousseau described the same process happening in his country, where Paris became a 'Moloch that fed greedily on blood supplied by the provinces and corrupted those it did not kill.'

Officials battled to control the population of London, and as London grew, the poor became a threat to stability from *outside* the city walls, as well as from inside. Outside the city in the 14th and 15th centuries, wandering bands of beggars grew to numbers of 100 or more, and gates were watched around the clock to stop them getting in.

London at the end of the 14th century was a place of empty tenements. The Black Death had disposed of one third of England's population, and was one of at least three major events that nearly emptied the city of everyone except the poor, who suffered disproportionately, and the officials, turning back the usual pattern of growth. The others were the Great Fire of 1666 and the Blitz of 1940. London did not recover its population for another 200 years after the Black Death.

The larger population in the 16th century began to put a strain on the city's resources. There were only so many economic opportunities to be found in London, and poverty began to rise – from 1,000 on relief in 1517, the year of the Evil May Day riots against foreigners, to 12,000 in 1594.

There was also pressure on the housing stock, and the great tenements were often subdivided to fit more people in. Katherine Wheel Alley in Thames Street around 1584 had nine respectable tenements, which were shortly afterwards converted into 43.

By the beginning of the reign of Elizabeth I, when the Armada was in the Channel, London had grown to a population of 60,000 people – and it was to be 120,000 by the end of the century. Desperate officials worked to stop the growth, introducing fines by the City of London or the Crown to restrict new building, and confiscating property as a last resort. In 1580 they banned all new development except those on old foundations in a three mile belt around London – later a five-mile belt, reminiscent of our 20th century green belt policy. Later Oliver Cromwell introduced a retrospective fine.

William Shakespeare himself was among the newcomers, arriving from Stratford at the age of 23 looking for fame and fortune. By this time the inner cities were the thin alleyways behind the main streets where the rich lived, and which were regarded as places of disease and disorder. Alderman acted against the alleys in 1551, forcing people living there to pay an annual sum equivalent to their rent to the hospitals – a way of paying for the diseases they were thought to encourage. Later, in Southwark, there were fortnightly searches of alleys to clamp down on anyone taking in lodgers, or 'inmates' – a practice which was blamed for inner city poverty. It was thought that lodgers added to the squalor and overcrowding and evaded controls, leading to an even greater call on poor relief. The surveyors in Southwark were told 'to vewe that none kepe no Inmates not suffer none with childe nor no other poore'. Two parishes insisted that the poor removed their own children because of the extra burden on the rates.[2]

The parishes became determined not to accept the poor from other districts, and from the 1580s became enthusiastic supporters of the City of London Corporation's campaign against 'inmates'. Yet the alleys multipled and were identified as the source of a rise in crime.

The Great Plague and Fire a century later were all the more severe because of this unplanned growth, as some people were aware at the time. John Stows 1598 *Survey of London* found 'dwelling houses, lately builded on the banke of the saide ditch [at Bishopgate] by some Cittizens of London, that more regarded their owne priuate gaine, then the common good of the Cittie.' The filth and unsavoury things thrown in the ditch was in danger of 'impoysoning the whole Cittie'.

The year that Elizabeth I died, in 1603, found 800 cases of plague in a single massive building – four mansions which together housed around 8,000 people. Plague took hold in the new overcrowded suburbs, Although the 1665 plague was in some ways less severe than the others which hit London every 14 years or so, it was the suburbs which bore the brunt, killing over 80,000.

The first of the Great Plague deaths happened in April 1665 in the suburban parish of St Giles in the Fields. Parish officials followed the usual procedure and sealed the survivors of the family in their house, but their neighbours released them and scrubbed the cross from their door. By the Autumn two thirds of the population had fled to the country.

Building Futures

Disease remained a key theme of inner city poverty, with smallpox, dysentery, typhus and typhoid claiming victims in a series of great outbreaks that continued for two centuries.

A year later the Great Fire made 100,000 people homeless, and transformed 400 densely-packed streets into rubble – though only eight people were killed. Six years later, 20,000 Londoners had still not returned.

The struggle to control London's growth resulted in overcrowding and building on every remaining piece of green. But the restrictions – which were really on building for the poor – began to loosen in the 1630s, and the first of London's squares began to appear. The first was 'Convent Garden' – now Covent Garden – built on land owned by the Earls of Bedford behind Lincoln's Inn Fields, with encouragement from King Charles I. Like other members of the royal family since, the king had strong views on architecture.

The aristocracy were able to insist on different standards for their new squares, with leases that banned gin shops, gaming houses, brothels and schools – the latter presumably because of the noise. Covent Garden was followed by Bloomsbury in 1660 and Restoration London after the Plague began to expand westwards, to escape – as the scientist Sir William Petty explained – 'the fumes, steams and stinke of the whole easterly pyle'.[3]

The general westwards direction continues into our own time, with London house prices stretching beyond the home counties into Oxfordshire and Hampshire. The success of the London Docklands in east London may mark the beginnings of the first real growth to the east since the building of the London docks.

By the end of the 18th century, New Road – which we now know as the Marylebone Road – had become the northern boundary to London. The spreading city was speeded outwards by the new public transport and roads. New Oxford Street was forced through the slums of St Giles, where the Great Plague had started, under the Improvement Act of 1839.

The first bus ran from Paddington Green to New Road in 1829, and six years later there were 600 buses in London, carrying commuters home to the healthier outer London suburbs. The first suburban railway began in the 1830s, between Southwark and Greenwich, with one carriage disguised as a Roman galley.

Meanwhile, 40,000 refugees from the French Revolution were swelling inner London, as the middle classes began to move out to new suburbs. The homes they left behind tended to become business premises. The French were followed by other refugees throughout the next century: Irish peasants from the potato famine in the 1840s, Essex labourers from the agricultural depression in the 1870s, Russian and Polish Jews from the pogroms in the 1890s.

The inner cities as we know them now were beginning to take shape.

III

'As there is a darkest Africa, *so* is there also a darkest England?' asked General William Booth, the founder of the Salvation Army, in his book *In Darkest England and the Way Out*. The title sums up the Victorian attitude to inner city life. Darkest England – like darkest Africa – had to be discovered by middle class 'explorers', and gave rise to the same missionary problems: was this poverty simply a moral difficulty, or were there other things that could be done about it? Was the lot of the native somewhere in the Empire 'so very much worse than that of many a pretty orphan girl in our Christian capital?' asked Booth. 'Read the House of Lords report on the sweating system, and ask if any African slave system . . . reveals more misery.'

Darkest London was the London of swirling fogs described in the Sherlock Holmes stories of Conan Doyle. But London was not the only city any more – nor the only place with a problem. Other cities had grown at an enormous rate after the Industrial Revolution. Manchester grew from a market town of 70,000 people in 1800 to a city of nearly a quarter of a million in 1841. Twenty years later its population was 339,000. In Sheffield between 1831–6, no fewer than 156 new streets were built or projected.

The drawing in of the agricultural population into the centre was still the key problem, made all the worse by the state of agricultural economy and the coming of machines to replace the old forms of rural work. But through the century it was clear that although London continued to expand at a frightening rate, it was not just because of a larger population. Buses and trains were making it possible to expand the suburbs for people who could afford to live there. The old areas in the centre of the cities were being left behind as the rich ones moved out. But the social observer Charles Booth noticed that this was not helping the people left behind: 'by a strange perversion, as rents rise in the central districts, the better off are more likely to be driven away, while the poor remain.'[4]

The inner cities were less and less the centres of wealth, commerce and money. In Bethnal Green in the 1850s, half the population applied for poor relief at least once a year. Inner city problems were no longer the symptoms of over-crowding and success in the cities – they were the symptoms of failure.

The East End MP A. S. Ayrton was concerned about this growing problem. 'When these men get rich in Tower Hamlets or Wapping, or the waterside,' he wrote in the *East London Observer* in 1859, 'they go to live near the pleasant parks at the other side of the town, and have nothing to do with the poverty that has sprung from their proceedings. They go to live in those favoured regions where poor rates are trifling and leave the misery to others who are compelled to pay out of their incomes the just complement of wages withheld from the working man.'

Like their ancestors, the Victorians saw there were problems and were determined to tackle them. Unlike their ancestors, they had sufficient arrogance to believe that they could solve some of them. The early Victorian reformers were fuelled in their determination by two very different inspirations: the utilitarians shared an enlightened scientific vision of the world firmly categorized, and were determined to get the problems under the microscope. The evangelists, at the same time – fresh from their successes abolishing slavery – were determined to raise the awareness of a still complacent public.

Across the two, the novelist and journalist Charles Dickens dominates the scene.

At the beginning of his life in 1812, cities were desperately overcrowded at the centre, with unplanned, crowded and dirty factories pressed close to the houses. Transport around the cities was in its earliest stages. By 1870 when he died, the problem had gone into reverse, with the new middle classes moving to fashionable homes in the suburbs.

Dickens had first-hand knowledge of the problems of poverty. His father was imprisoned for debt, and as a boy he had had to work as sweated labour in a blacking factory. As a young man he formed the habit of wandering around London, as Charles Kingsley, Henry Mayhew and Charles Booth did after him – and saw boys like Oliver Twist and his gang crawling from one rat-infested derelict home to the next. Dickens linked poverty with slums, crime and ignorance in the same way as the moderns have.

Education was his key solution: 'I saw 30,000 children hunted, flogged, imprisoned, but not taught,' he wrote in 1850 in support of the ragged schools. The idea of contrasting these 'lost' children with the bonhomie of Christmas fare came to him at a meeting in Manchester on the importance of education, where he was sharing a platform with Disraeli. The idea turned into *A Christmas Carol*, one of the most important tracts on poverty of the last century, now remembered almost entirely for Scrooge and Marley's Ghost.

'This boy is Ignorance. This girl is Want,' the Ghost of Christmas Present tells Scrooge. 'Beware of them both, and all of their degree, but most of all beware this boy, for on his brow I see that written which is Doom, unless the writing can be erased'.

Dickens, like Dr Barnado, was partly responsible for the change in people's awareness about Victorian poverty. But this was also the result of unstinting work by individual early Victorians who stopped believing in the old solutions of fear and the occasional confrontation as the best ways of solving the problem – and bridging the massive gulf in society, as if – as Disraeli put it – they were 'inhabitants of different planets'. Something had to be done. Thomas Carlyle condemned the 'do-nothingism' of his contemporaries: 'In the midst of plethoric plenty, the poor perish,' he wrote. 'With gold walls, and full barns, no man feels himself safe or satisfied'.[5]

The average life expectancy of labourers in Liverpool at the time was just 15, compared to a gentleman in Jane Austen's Bath who could expect to reach around 55. Nor was it very surprising given the conditions of health and housing in the poor areas in the middle of the burgeoning Victorian cities – the places described by the great historian of the age G.M. Young as 'undrained, unpoliced, ungoverned and unschooled'. Young went on: 'The imagination can hardly apprehend the horror in which thousands of families a hundred years ago were born, dragged out their lives, and died: the drinking water brown with faecal particles, the corpses kept unburied for a fortnight in a festering London August, mortified limbs quivering with maggots; courts where not a weed would grow, and sleeping-dens afloat with sewage.'[6]

The overcrowding was a symptom to contemporaries of the moral threat, at a time when many thousands of families lived their whole lives in one room. But there was more to it than that.

'The traffic in children for infamous purposes is notoriously considerable in London and other large towns,' reported a Royal Commission on the child prostitution in 1871, resulting in the raising of the age of consent from just 12 to 13. It was the beginning of a long 'purity' campaign which led to the extraordinary events of 1885. The editor of the Pall Mall Gazette, W.T. Stead, bought 13-year-old Eliza Armstrong from her mother in the slums of Marylebone for five pounds in order to demonstrate the iniquities of the trade in young girls. It was an incident that led to the prosecution and imprisonment in Holloway of both Stead and Bramwell Booth of the Salvation Army. Stead, later drowned on the *Titanic*, was one of the best known campaigning journalists of the day.

Stead's crusading journalism had its roots in religious zeal at the start of the 19th century. Home-visiting and preaching were then the popular solutions to urban poverty, as was the building of churches to cope with growing city problems. Between 1809 and 1820, Parliament voted £1.5 million towards new church buildings in the cities, and more to pay the clergy to live in the inner cities. The continuing urban crisis of the Church of England came back into focus recently, when half the Archbishop of Canterbury's report *Faith in the City* in 1985 was devoted to a better church organisation in inner cities – where attendance on Sundays had dropped to below one per cent of the population.

Poverty 150 years ago seemed to be a religious issue because it appeared to be a result of the failure of moral will. Solving moral problems for the early Victorians required ample measures of soap, schooling and the Bible: get their outlook right, encourage them to save money and cut down the size of their families, and everything would come right. Some went so far as to believe, as Arnold White the son of the chairman of the Congregational Union did, that the cause of poverty was 'idleness, gluttony, drink, waste, profligacy, betting and corruption'. It was not until the more scientific surveys of Charles Booth and Seebohm Rowntree towards the end of the century that it became clear that poverty was not usually the fault of the poor. Booth, who ran his own family steamship company, began his researches because he did not believe the poor had it so bad. But he found that only 15 per cent of people below the poverty line were so because of 'idleness or drunkenness'. With earnings of less than an intermittent £1 a week, the poor were poor primarily because they did not have enough money.

History of the Inner Cities

The 19th century was a great surveying era. These were started by the Utilitarian followers of the philosopher Jeremy Bentham, and were carried out with all the zeal of the religious fanatics they so disapproved of. Bentham's followers began to search for a 'rational' poor law – a scientific basis that could distinguish between the independent 'honest' labourers and the paupers, which eventually emerged in the 1834 Poor Law. There was a horror, emerging again at the end of the 20th century, of making the honest labourer into a pauper by making him dependent on handouts.

One man who linked both the scientific and religious worlds was Thomas Chalmers, a friend of Carlyle and minister in Glasgow and Edinburgh – a professor of moral philosophy, theology, mathematics, and an evangelical preacher. His systematic visiting of his congregations was not just to uplift them, but to record them as well. Statistical societies in many cities produced a long line of reports, Royal Commissions and surveys, leading to the civil service and local government systems that we know today – but also revealing in incontrovertible form the conditions in the cities.

An early house-to-house social survey was organized by Manchester Statistical Society in 1835, and found that an incredible 12 per cent of the working class population of the city – 15,000 people – were living in airless, dark and polluted cellars. Manchester might have been 'considered a city of cave-dwellers,' said the city's first Medical Officer of Health, John Leigh, in his first report. 'It can excite no surprise that the blanched and flabby children of which they are the homes, grow up into the stunted men and women that crowd the streets of manufacturing towns.'[7]

Manchester was among the first to outlaw cellars as places to live. This was done in 1853, when the city went on to tackle the speculative slum developers, giving themselves the power to close unfit houses without compensation to the landlord. This did not entirely solve the problem, because it tended to raise the level of rents and reduce the number of cheap homes for the urban poor – a vicious circle that remains with us today.

Sanitation was the key reform of the early and mid-Victorians arising out of all the surveys. And the dogmatic energy of Edwin Chadwick, as secretary to the Royal Commission on Health in Towns, was the spur of sanitary reform. It was Chadwick, a barrister and former journalist, who achieved the public registration of deaths – their causes and numbers – and who was the architect of the Public Health Act of 1848, which gave powers to local councils over water companies, drains and refuse collection. 'Had he killed in battle as many as he saved by sanitation,' read his obituary in the *Daily News* in 1890, 'he would have equestrian statues by the dozen put up to his memory.'

It was a time when cesspits drained into the rivers, from which the water companies, without filtering, pumped drinking water to the cities. The Act coincided with a series of disastrous cholera outbreaks among the city poor. In the last three months of 1847, nearly 13,000 children died. A poignant and barely literate letter to the *Times*, signed by 54 people from the slums of St Giles, read: 'We ain't got no privez, no dustbins, no drains, no water splies, and no drain or suer in the whole place. If the Colera comes, Lord help us.'

In Manchester at the same time, Engels wrote: 'masses of refuse, offal and sickening filth lie among standing pools in all directions . . . A horde of ragged women and children swarm around here, as filthy as the swine that thrive upon the garbage heaps and in the puddles.'[8] In the whole area, he reported, there was just one 'usually inaccessible privy' for each 120 people.

Progress was slow. Chadwick and his supporters came up against official and public apathy throughout their campaign. It was not for another ten years that the 'Great Stink' of 1858 – when the windows of Parliament had to be covered in curtains soaked in lime – goaded MPs into extending local powers further.

The rise of local government, taking responsibility for so many aspects of the lives of the urban poor, is probably one of the most important developments of the last century. Local government officials began to achieve the status of civil servants, and imaginative local leaders, like the screw manufacturer Joseph Chamberlain in Birmingham, were able to push forward the frontiers of what they could do.

'Be more expensive,' the great Liberal free-trader John Bright told the boroughs in a speech in Birmingham in 1864. The new city councils took his advice, led by Birmingham's take over of sanitation, gas and street lighting, taking advantage of new laws that allowed them to borrow money. 'A corporation that is afraid to borrow is too timid to do its duty,' said Chamberlain as he took over Birmingham's gas companies in 1874. 'It is only a community acting as a whole that can possible deal with evils so deep-seated.' The rise of city councils and the 1870 Education Act, followed by free school meals, began much of the modern process of bringing light to darkest England.

At the same time came the rise of political awareness among the poor themselves, especially over the issue of housing following the launch of the Social Democratic Federation in 1882. Housing remained the responsibility of the landlords, the employers and the charities. With financial help from the art critic John Ruskin, Octavia Hill bought her first three houses in Marylebone, and in 30 years she managed to house 26,000 who could otherwise find nowhere to live.

The Shaftesbury Society began in 1844, and in 1862 the American merchant and philanthropist George Peabody was building five-storey red-brick flats in the East End; each one designed to regulate without control.

Political awareness took a new turn in 1888 with the famous matchgirl strike at the Bryant and May factory in east London – a building now being turned into the 'Bow Village' luxury flats advertised in the *Sunday Times*. The strike was stirred by the reformer Annie Besant, and was among the first of any success: 1,400 girls went on strike for four shillings a week and won. Annie Besant had recently organized an inquiry which found that there were 43,000 children in London alone who were underfed. The following year, 60,000 were involved in the Great Dock Strike for six pence an hour basic wage, and for a minimum employment time of half a day rather than an hour. With up to 16,000 pickets each day of the four week strike, the strikers marched to the West End: once going so far as to smash the windows of the Conservative Club. The East End, said Engels, had 'shaken off its torpid despair'.

There was also a new generation of committed socialists who were about to build an alternative 20th century consensus. Charles Booth's assistant Beatrice Potter, who with her husband Sidney Webb was responsible for the minority report of the 1909 Royal Commission on the Poor Laws, worked in her youth around the London docks. 'Pass from the quay and warehouses to the corners and alleys that surround them,' she wrote – 'and the mind is bedevilled with the destitution of the one place as it is in the superabundance of the other. Many come to see the riches, but few the poverty'.

IV

It became clear as the new century arrived that the historic rush of the rural population into the cities was beginning to shift into reverse. The 1901 census, taken after the end of the great Victorian age, was the first to reveal what was happening. By the 1911 census, the population of inner London was beginning to decline.

It was not a problem that emerged suddenly. In the 1880s, Southwark and London's East End could have been described as an 'industrial vacuum' as the firms there collapsed. The Cheap Trains Act of 1883 allowed all the more Victorians to live in suburbs. In 1897, *The Builder* could report that 'one cannot but be shaken with the number of waste places and corners, surrounded by bill posters and hoardings'. The people left behind as the population thinned tended to be the least able to look after themselves. And because people were leaving, the income from the rates was dropping at the same time – leaving inner city councils with less money to cope with the problems. 'The most scandalous alleys and lanes disappear to the accompaniment of lavish self-glorification by the bourgeoise', wrote Engels. 'But they appear again at once somewhere else'.

On the other hand the battle against poverty was beginning to make some progress. The number in 'primary poverty' in 1899 had halved by the end of the First World War.[9] In 1919 the Ministry of Health forced the Housing Act onto the statute books, giving local authorities responsibility for housing needs and providing subsidies for rented housing.

The LCC's Boundary Street estate in the East End, built in the 1890s, with a communal garden over the rubble from the slums, was the result of the very first slum clearance, and was one of the most advanced housing projects of its time. By the 1930s, clearance and flat-building was going on in earnest. The determination to achieve real change went hand in hand with the idea that cities did not have to be ugly and neglected. 'The Great City means beauty, dignity and a certain splendour,' wrote D. H. Lawrence. 'That is the side of the Englishman that has been thwarted and shockingly betrayed'.

The new town planning movement was increasingly influential. This was inspired by the idea of garden cities – healthy places to live, attracting the inner city poor out to new country towns in the countryside – dreamed up by the House of Commons shorthand writer Ebenezer Howard. Howard formulated the idea of the garden city as a property company and a counter-balance to

London: the urban poor could be rehoused in clean, well-planned homes in a new and healthy town, leaving space in the middle of London to improve its environment. London itself would be prevented from growing further by a green belt of countryside.

Garden cities had an immediate appeal, and Howard managed to build two, at Letchworth and Welwyn. It was left to his lieutenant, Frederic Osborn to put the idea into practical policy terms a generation later. To press for the garden cities, Howard founded the Garden City Association – now the Town and Country Planning Association – to lead a wide alliance of interests dedicated to preventing London growing any further. By the end of the 1920s, that was seen as urgent. Miles of suburbs stretched outside the cities, fed by railways and the new roads, and leaving the pockets of poverty at the centres deeper still. People wanted to leave London, and they wanted the homes with gardens that the new builders were so good at providing. They did not want to live in flats.

Joseph Chamberlain's son Neville was an early supporter of new towns, settting up the Unhealthy Areas Committee in the early 1920s. These ideas were backed by increasing numbers of people as the realities of modern warfare and aerial bombing became more apparent: a dispersed population, dotted around the country, was far less vulnerable than if they were squashed together in city slums.

In 1938, when Chamberlain flew to Munich to avert a war which was expected to start with a devastating air raid, hundreds of thousands of Londoners departed for the countryside as fast as they could. Osborn seized the opportunity: unless people could be protected with air raid shelters in the cities, they would leave faster than any policymaker could cope with. There should be no more 'cramming' of people into flats. 'To build a single further block of flats in London or any other great city is no longer a mere private crime,' he wrote a month later. 'It becomes high treason.'[10]

The Great Depression of the 30s had launched a search for new solutions to worsening old problems: the ailing industries of the inner cities were hit especially hard. By 1930, unemployment in Britain was over the one million mark.

The Prince of Wales was deeply shocked by his visit to the South Wales coalfields and told local people that 'something must be done'. The writer J. B. Priestley, touring England, compared Stockton-on-Tees to a theatre kept open 'merely for the sale of drinks in the bars'.

There were a series of violent clashes between police and unemployed, affecting nearly 30 cities in 1931. The hated Means Test, under which officials removed dole payments if it was clear that money or gifts had come in from the family from anywhere else, became the focus for campaigning, and changed the atmosphere of declining inner cities. It was an 'encouragement to the tittle-tattle of the informer, the writer of anonymous letters and the local blackmailer,' wrote George Orwell in his classic *The Road to Wigan Pier*.

In the summer of 1936, blessed by the Bishop of Jarrow, 200 people from the depressed shipbuilding town of Jarrow marched to London to deliver a 12,000-signature petition to the State opening of Parliament. When the marchers got home, they had their dole payments reduced because they had not been available for work.

The search for solutions to the twin problems of exploding cities and expanding poverty in the middle of them had intensified as war approached. Sir Montague Barlow was appointed in 1937 to head the Royal Commission on the distribution of industrial population, which came out in 1940 firmly for 'decentralization' – in the form of a programme of new towns. Sir Patrick Abercrombie's famous wartime plans for London spelled it out in detail, with a vision of a greener London of distinct communities, which is still struggling to emerge into reality. The M25 orbital motorway, finally opened in 1986, was part of the Abercrombie plan.

The war coincided with a growing momentum for social change and great disillusionment about the ability of the establishment to provide it. The King and Queen were booed when they visited the East End after bombing, and in Stepney and Liverpool, city authorities failed to cope with the ravages of the Blitz, leading to angry locals taking on much of the organization themselves. Folk memories of wartime self-help lie behind some of the demand for local power and responsibility now. But the renewal task was far too big for the cities to cope with by themselves.

The garden cities campaigner Frederic Osborn was pulled into the government by Sir John Reith – Director-General of the BBC – to start planning the reconstruction of the cities in detail. The new town development corporations emerged as the bodies to put them into effect, and were used as models in our own day for our urban development corporations.

History of the Inner Cities

When Clement Attlee's Labour government was elected by an unexpected landslide in 1945, new towns were high on their list of priorities and the search for sites began. Planning minister Lewis Silkin had his tyres slashed by angry locals when he went to see the site of Stevenage, the first new town. Protesting students crept into Stevenage Station late at night in 1947, changing all the signs to 'Silkingrad'. But 40 years on the British new towns continue to excite interest around the world – inspiring the current new country town plans by Consortium development – while the housing estates and inner city architecture of the 50s and 60s have brought odium upon the people who planned and built them.

The new towns coincided with a list of other measures that had a direct effect on the inner city environment. Green belts were already in place, planning controls emerged in 1947, and smoke control was put into effect by the 1956 Clean Air Act after the 'Great Smog' of 1952 which shut down London Transport for four days.

The big cities were left after the bombings with hundreds of thousands of homeless, and a great deal of space, part of which was used for the festival of Britain in 1951. Nearly half the homes in Stepney had been destroyed. Impatient homeless tenants in the East End began to squat in empty buildings and military camps, even luxury West End flats, taking bedding and pans to Kensington, Holland Park and Bloomsbury. Housing became an important political issue, and temporary pre-fabs on bomb sites the stop-gap solution.

When Harold Macmillan became housing minister in Winston Churchill's new government of 1951 – the first ever – he rose to prominence because he was able to meet the party's extremely ambitious promises for new homes. The battle to build afresh in a new style, demolishing and building inner cities anew, dominated the generation that followed, as idealistic councillors and officials began to believe that inner city squalor really could be consigned to the past. The Macmillan government's ambitious targets of 300,000 new homes a year were trumped by Harold Wilson's campaign promises in 1964 that they could build 400,000.

But the political battle over housing figures disguised a problem for later generations. It meant lowering standards and it meant building flats, often on out-of-town estates with few facilities or none at all. The path to high rise or system built blocks of flats was paved with good intentions, but the rotten fruits of the massive public investment remain.

V

When Prime Minister Harold Macmillan told Britain that some people had 'never had it so good' – it was clear that others had never had it at all.

The new town programme was coming into maturity and people and jobs were seeping even faster out of the cities. Between 1961 and 1975, London lost 40 per cent of its industrial jobs, most of them for good. Big redevelopment schemes made things even worse – in Liverpool, 80 per cent of jobs disappeared from one area after it was cleared. By 1978, one tenth of the whole Manchester workforce was affected by the threat of Compulsory Purchase Orders on their factories or offices. As usual, the loss of people and businesses left inner city councils with shrinking rate incomes.

The 1960s are now regarded with horror and trepidation by commentators and politicians, including Mrs Thatcher. They marked the height of an enormous redevelopment effort, with 60,000 slums cleared every year during the decade. Many of the professional and political decisions taken at the time, redeveloping vast areas, dispersing inner city communities and housing them in a style of architecture that is now almost universally reviled, are discussed as the key to today's problems. Yet they also gave birth to different movements that have also become so powerful.

The early 60s were characterized by housing campaigning. The community movement of popular anger about the condition of cities and their redevelopment began to emerge at the time – as did the voluntary sector that has risen in the 80s to rival the public and private sectors. The housing charity Shelter began its work for the 'hidden homeless' with the campaigner Des Wilson at the helm, launching a major attack on government housing policy at the end of the 1960s. Increasing evidence of the error of tower blocks was emerging from across the Atlantic, though it was ignored by many professionals at the time. Concerned intellectual Britain was becoming aware of inner city problems again, of 'deprived areas' and 'cycles of poverty', which they saw as the self-perpetuating poverty that affected generation after generation of the working classes.

There were also the beginnings of racial tension in the cities, apparent with the Notting Hill riots of 1958. A decade later, British policy-makers were looking with horror at their televisions, watching the scenes of urban violence in American cities. More than 80 people were killed in riots in 23 American cities in 1967, and Governor Otto Kerner of Illinois was given a staff of nearly 200 to report on their implications. Kerner – as Scarman did in the UK 14 years later – suggested a series of ways of creating a bigger black middle class.

By 1966 there were half a million people in the UK from the New Commonwealth, as they called it then: eight times as many as there were immediately after the war. As people moved out of the inner cities, immigrants were encouraged to take their places in the public sector jobs that still needed doing. They tended to settle in the poorest parts of the cities, as so many immigrants had done before them.

This tension between immigrants of different nationalities and origins and the people who lived there before has made the inner cities the key area of influence for the extreme right. Before the war, Sir Oswald Mosley's British Union of Fascists (BUF) made the Jewish areas of the East End the focus of their campaign in the capital, with over 1,800 meetings held there in just three months in 1936.

After the war, racial intimidation was almost the only platform for far-right groups, a message that was spread by new leaders like Colin Jordan in the 1960s and John Tyndall in the 70s. National Front candidates managed to get elected as councillors in Blackburn in 1976, and the NF fed off the failures of the Labour Party to respond to the scale of inner city problems.

But it was Enoch Powell's 'Rivers of Blood' speech that indicated a public acceptance from the establishment that immigration was a major problem. When he made his controversial speech in April 1968 he was a prominent member of the Conservative shadow cabinet, and the issue of race was high on the international agenda. It was in fiery language: 'Like the Romans,' he said, 'I seem to see the River Tiber flowing with much blood.'

The danger was strongest in inner city areas where many people from ethnic minorities had made their homes, and Powell's speech made him one of the very few senior Conservative politicians to attract a demonstration of support from the London dockers.

In a later speech, Powell went further in his portrayal of the inner cities: 'In your town and mind, in Wolverhampton, in Smethwick, in Birmingham, people see with their own eyes what they dread, the transformation during their own lifetime . . . of towns, cities and areas that they know into alien territory.'[11]

Dangerous as it was to say – with thousands of immigrant families at risk from attack – Powell was portraying what some white people in inner cities actually felt. Mrs Thatcher clearly felt this too when she made the admission that some people were afraid of being 'swamped'.

Even without any other problems, the race issue made inner cities potential disaster areas. It was in response to Powell, as well as to President Johnson's report on the American urban riots, that Harold Wilson's government announced the start of the Urban Programme to 'deal with the problems of areas where immigration had been at a high rate'. The Home Office was to administer between £20 and £25 million for the next four years, aimed mainly at providing better nurseries and child care facilities.

The Urban Programme has remained one of the government's main weapons in their inner city armoury, and it was one of three key themes emerging from Harold Wilson's government in the 60s. Another was the idea of Educational Priority Areas. If the 'cycle of poverty' was to be tackled then they had to break the vicious circles that made one generation repeat the deprived existences of their parents. A series of expert reports called for different kinds of professionalism to tackle the problems. The 1967 Plowden Report found that inner city schools were under-resourced and were often housed in the same crumbling buildings which had been put up when the 1870 Education Act enforced compulsory schooling. Priority areas should be defined, the report argued, and extra resources pumped in so that inner city children could have the added advantages of education. But ten years later, the state of inner city education was little better.

The third idea from the Wilson government was the Community Development Programme (CDP), announced by James Callaghan as Home Secretary in 1969. There would be 12 projects in five years, looking at inner city areas and involving neighbourhood organizations, to find out what the problems really were and what could be done about them.

The result was not quite as the government intended. The CDP people 'went native' and found themselves in direct conflict with local authorities and with the prevailing theories about cycles of poverty. They dubbed the best efforts of local government as 'managing poor people', and some of them argued that the forces threatening inner cities were so deep and international that only radical action from the state and trade unions could hope to counter them. The results were so radical that no final report pulling together all the CDP's findings has ever been published.

The 1970s brought the property boom, fuelling the growing community opposition to redevelopment, the energy crisis, and with it the world recession. Sites earmarked – and sometimes cleared – for redevelopment schemes simply stayed empty. Tower blocks gave way to similarly massive system built blocks that did not rise beyond three or four storeys, but which tended to be large, long and soulless. As the recession began to bite, Labour's Anthony Crosland told councils 'the party's over'.

Redevelopment began to give way to rehabilitation. But change was a long time coming: in Glasgow, the last disastrous outlying estate, Darnley, was defined as an 'area of need' even before it was finished.

More studies followed. The Heath government appointed independent consultants in 1972 to look at three inner cities and report on what the problems were. These were the influential Inner Area Studies, which looked in detail at Small Heath in Birmingham, Lambeth, and Liverpool.

Their findings were vital. In spite of peering long and hard into the roots of the inner cities, the consultants did not discover generations trapped by the problems of their parents. They found instead a lack of jobs, training and good housing, all of them economic problems. Like the Community Development Projects, they found that economic development was the key – a theme that was increasingly emphasized through the 70s and finally enshrined as sacred truth by Mrs Thatcher in the 1980s.

The Lambeth Inner Area Study of 1977 stood out from the others, suggesting that it would be a good idea to help people who wanted to leave their appalling inner city conditons for new or country towns. 'A less congested London would be cheaper to run,' they argued. They also believed that people would continue to leave cities: unless help was given, the only people left would be the poorest.

Other important governmental changes were happening behind the scenes. After making all the running on inner cities since Harold Wilson's day, the Home Office was being ousted by the new Department of the Environment (DoE). After Crosland's death in September 1976, Labour's environment secretary Peter Shore took the chair of the Cabinet committee on urban affairs – and began a series of speeches that shot inner cities up the list of political priorities. A new inner cities directorate with a staff of 50 was formed at the DoE, and he cancelled the Scottish new town of Stonehouse and moved the staff over to the GEAR project (Glasgow Eastern Area Renewal), the biggest inner city renewal scheme in Europe.

Shore represented a London inner city constituency in the East End. He resented the efforts he was expected to put towards attracting industry and people away from cities and into new towns. '20th century civilization has been based upon cities,' he told a Manchester audience, explaining his new approach. 'And if in the process of change then inner cities are simply allowed to decay – and their inhabitants to languish – the country as a whole will be the poorer.'

Shore also took on the building societies over their refusal to give mortgages for houses in some inner cities, a move which a decade later led to them leading the private sector response to the vacuum of power in city renewal. The government was also to play its part, by 'bending' the main spending programmes so that they began to favour inner cities.

He also turned his back on the big redevelopment schemes of the past. Britain had 'pensioned off the bulldozer', he told the United Nations Habitat conference in Vancouver. The *Sunday Times* responded with a major conference in Bristol with the title 'Save Our Cities', and a government white paper – crystalizing the new thinking – was published the following year.

The 1977 Inner Cities White Paper began to process that has never since been overturned, aiming to strengthen inner city economies, repair the city environment and tackle social problems. Industry and financial institutions must 'play their full part', it said. Yet it did not accept, the implications of sitting back and letting the market decide. Leaving the inner cities to their fate would 'mean leaving large numbers of people to face a future of decline job opportunities, a squalid environment, deteriorating housing and declining public servies'.

But the white paper's belief in local authorities as 'the natural agencies to tackle inner area policies' was not acceptable to the

Conservatives who took office two years later. The attitude of Mrs Thatcher's opposition to inner city councils was summed up in Michael Heseltine's speech to the Tory faithful shortly after taking office in October 1979: 'When the political barons of Labour's inner cities talk of "our people" it is . . . in the sense of people owned and controlled and directed and employed.'[12]

The white paper also recognized for the first time that ordinary people might be involved: 'Some things will be better done, or done more satisfyingly,' the paper said, 'if they are undertaken by voluntary groups and bodies'. The Inner Urban Act that followed the white paper set up 'partnerships' between central and local government to get to grips with problems in seven areas: Liverpool, Birmingham, Salford, Lambeth, Docklands, and later Hackney and Gateshead. The partnerships would be chaired by ministers and would co-ordinate all the different agencies involved. There were also 15 designated 'programme' authorities funded by the Urban Programme – increased from £30 million to £125 million – so that the partnership authorities did not take all the funds.

The new law gave powers to local authorities to attract industry to inner cities, based on pioneering work by Tyne and Wear and Rochdale, and – because of the so-called Lib-Lab Pact at the time keeping the government in office – powers to support new co-operatives as well.

There was unprecedented interest in inner cities by the end of the 1970s: since the 1930s, London had been forbidden from advertising its advantages to industry. One of the most notable aspects of the debate of the last 20 years is that inner cities have become an increasingly important political issue. In 1977, the Social Science Research Council set up a major three-year study on the problems and finally disposed of the idea of 'cycles of deprivation'.

They found inner city problems much more difficult to define than before. After all, poverty and deprivation was found in other places altogether, and there were inner cities which were rather well off. What seemed to be happening was that inner cities were suffering the same problems as the British economy, but in an especially extreme form. For this reason policies which just concentrated on areas, rather than underlying economic problems, would probably only relieve the symptoms and not the cause.

The minority Labour government only had another year after its Inner Cities Act before its defeat in a motion of no confidence in the House of Commons. When the 1979 general election arrived, only the Labour manifesto mentioned the inner cities. But their new policies came in for criticism for being 'over-bureaucratic' during the campaign. This was also the election which introduced Saatchi & Saatchi's famous 'Labour Isn't Working' poster, with a picture of a stretching dole queue: by 1979, Liverpool's 'partnership' grants for the year amounted to less than the unemployment benefit paid to Liverpudlians in one week.

So Britain's first woman Prime Minister took office and had to cope with the Liverpool dole queues herself. A new economic crisis was taking hold, with the inner cities bearing much of the brunt – the 'soft underbelly' of the British economy, as the SSRC working party put it. The chickens hatched during the post-war housing boom were also coming home to roost. Tensions created by crumbling housing and dependency on an over-stretched welfare state were reaching a danger point. The forces were coming together that would put Britain's inner cities on television screens all over the world.

2

WE WANT THEM TOO, NEXT TIME

Amid the personal tragedy and public disorder, something good emerged, because we were forced to rethink our strategy for the inner cities.
          Michael Heseltine on the riots, November 1982

Constable Stephen Margiotta left Brixton Police Station to begin his beat on Friday 10 April 1981. He little realized that he was about to witness the start of events which would break open the state of Britain's inner cities for the world to see.
   It was PC Margiotta who first spotted an injured, bleeding and frightened black youth running in his direction, with a wound between his shoulder blades nearly four inches long. Margiotta tried to stop him, but the youth slipped away, helped by three other young black men shouting 'leave him alone'. In vain he tried to explain that he was not making an arrest, but trying to help, he later told the Scarman inquiry.
   The same misunderstanding arose 15 minutes later, when the youth was discovered by two other policemen being driven to hospital by a man whose front door he had hammered on. The policemen called for an ambulance, but it was obvious now that the injured man was very ill: air bubbles seemed to be coming out of the wound, and they were afraid he might have a punctured lung. By this time an angry crowd of more than 30 people had

gathered, convinced that the police were refusing to call for help. Some believed they had hurt the youth themselves. By 6.30p.m., bricks and bottles were being thrown.

So began the Brixton riot, followed by a weekend of disorder that shocked the country. This led in turn to a summer of tumultuous violence that infected nearly every city with a significant immigrant population – and some without – during which both petrol bombs and CS gas were used for the first time on mainland Britain, and which thrust the inner city debate straight to the top of the political agenda. Except for the disturbance in St Pauls, Bristol, the year before, scenes of burning cars and buildings in a Western city had not been seen for at least 12 years. Civilization was supposed to have progressed beyond this, and the riots were a severe blow to the way Britain felt about itself.

On Saturday, the main night of the first Brixton riots, 279 policemen and 45 civilians were injured – though probably many more civilians failed to report it. At the height of the disturbance, as the Windsor Castle pub disappeared in flames, policemen facing the barrage of molotov cocktails were singing aloud to keep their spirits up, and black and white alike were calmly selecting pairs of shoes to loot from the ransacked Dolcis store in Brixton Road.

In the week of the riots there had been 784 registered young unemployed in the area, competing for just 13 vacancies at the local job centre. Racial tension was running high during the controversial and disruptive inquiry a few miles away into the deaths of 13 young black people after an arson attack in January, at an all-night birthday party in New Cross. Added to that, Brixton was in the middle of a police crackdown on street crime known as Operation Swamp 81' – which Lord Scarman called a 'serious mistake' in his report on the Brixton riots.

'Mr T', a Guyanian quoted after the weekend, summed up the general feeling in the area by telling the press that 'it should have happened a long time ago'. Mrs T, however – the Prime Minister – was telling the nation: 'Nothing, but nothing justifies what happened.' This was the main crux of the debate after the event, when the looted shops had begun to clean up and the rubble had stopped smoking. What was the cause, and did it justify anything like this violence?

To find out, Lord Scarman, a senior law lord, was appointed just four days after the start of the trouble. He went straight down to

WE WANT THEM TOO, NEXT TIME

Brixton. 'I didn't talk to anyone,' he said, watching the first efforts to damp down the tension. 'I just walked around.' Scarman was a veteran of reports on disturbances at Red Lion Square and Grunwick, and the Northern Ireland riots of 1969, and managed – against many expectations – to achieve the confidence of at least some of those who had been involved. As he settled down to his new role, newspaper reports described the warm welcome he had achieved in Railton Road, the heart of the violence. 'You come back any time, Lord Scarman,' one black lady was heard to shout after him.

Meanwhile, local community leaders were aware of the danger Brixton still faced., A demonstration to protest at police behaviour the weekend after the riot was cancelled. 'It may well be the police who are rioting this weekend,' warned the black barrister Rudy Narayan, who had helped set up the newly-formed Brixton Defence Committee. The local cinema cancelled its late showing of *Gun Crazy* and *Asphalt Jungle* – just in case they gave people ideas – and Mrs Thatcher, who was on a visit to India at the time, appeared on television wearing Indian headgear in a hurried gesture of racial bonhomie.

'You have seen nothing yet,' the ever controversial Enoch Powell told the House of Commons. He turned out to be correct. As Lord Scarman's hearing continued at Lambeth Town Hall in the centre of Brixton, British cities erupted one by one, starting on the evening of 2 July in Southall, west London – with the only one of the riots that was unmistakably racial.

Skinheads who had arrived in the area to hear a band with the unsavoury name of the '4-skins' began smashing glass and insulting some local Asians. People from all over the area gathered to drive them off, in the process burning down the pub which was featuring the 4-skins that evening, the Hamborough Tavern.

That weekend, the Toxteth district of Liverpool exploded, with rioters burning buildings down as they moved towards the city centre, reaching to within 200 yards of the Anglican cathedral. At one stage, policemen faced a stolen fleet of Unigate dairy milk floats driven at their lines. Geriatric patients had to be evacuated from hospital by taxi drivers, and found their personal belongings rifled when they were taken back. Looters, sometimes as young as five years old, queued to get to the shops, and CS canisters came out for the first time in a mainland city. By the end of the weekend, £10 million of damage had been done.

'Scenes like this can never have been seen in a British city under the rule of law this century', said the local Liberal MP David Alton – a former chairman of the city's housing committee – as the violence died down. Loudhailing demonstrators outside the Brixton hearings shouted to Lord Scarman to take account of the links between the outbreaks. Mrs Thatcher hastily changed a party political broadcast from unemployment to 'rebuilding confidence'.

There followed a series of copycat riots around the country, in Birmingham, Brixton again, Manchester, Leeds, Wolverhampton, Derby, Leicester and many others – including less predictable towns like Gloucester and Cirencester, and other smaller places where local journalists had been sent out to find disturbances, brawls or looting. One young Moss Side looter explained: 'my mum asked me to get her a wall clock'.

The disturbances petered out as the attention of the media turned to the royal wedding at the end of the month, but not before the first and only death during the 1981 riots. David Moore, a 22-year-old disabled man visiting his sister, was run down and killed by a police van during a disturbance in Toxteth on day of the wedding. But by this time the television cameras were busy at St Paul's Cathedral watching Lady Diana Spencer become the Princess of Wales.

Lord Scarman reported his findings in November, having discovered no evidence for the much-touted theories that the riots had been co-ordinated and planned. But racial disadvantage was a 'significant factor' in the riots, he said: 'Urgent action is needed if it is not to become an endemic, ineradicable disease threatening the very survival of our society'. Important sections of young black people were deeply angry with the police, and Scarman called for more sensitive policing and a familiar plea for an attack on disadvantage, particularly in the fields of education and employment.[2] Scarman finished his report by quoting from President Lyndon Johnson's call for 'an attack – mounted at every level – upon the conditions that breed despair and violence', in the US Report of the National Advisory Committee on Civil Disorders in 1968.

'We should attack them because there is simply no other way to achieve a decent and orderly society in America,' Johnson wrote after the 1967 riots in which 83 people were killed. The unpleasant truth that there were parallels between the two events – separated by nearly 20 years – was beginning to dawn on government ministers.

II

Michael Heseltine became Secretary of State for the Environment after Mrs Thatcher's election victory of May 1979 with a reputation to keep.

He had hoped to get the job of industry minister. But as spokesman on the environment since 1976, he had an interest in the inner cities, together with a strategy and determination to attract people back to live there. His appointment as Secretary of State, with a staff of over 50,000, did not take him, as he put it, 'entirely unawares'.

Heseltine intended to make the inner cities places 'where the private investor is prepared to put his money'. His idea was to bring public and private sectors together, so that public authorities could 'open their doors'. 'We have inherited from the previous government a complex machinery for urban aid,' he declared. 'I think the government must continue to be involved – though with the minimum of paperwork and fuss, and I intend to simplify procedures.'

As the 'darling' of the Conservative Party conference, and the man who had wielded the House of Commons mace in protest at the Labour government's guillotine on the Shipbuilding Bill, Heseltine had indulged in a certain amount of 'fuss' in his time. He was MP for rural Henley-on-Thames, and a self-made publishing and property millionaire with a combative style. He would need it: the task before him in the inner cities was immense.

Labour's 'partnership committees' in designated inner city areas were the main tool that Heseltine inherited for tackling the problems. Each one was chaired by a minister. Heseltine took the chair of the Merseyside committee because he thought it was the greatest challenge.

It was on a background of conflict between central cost-cutters and uncompromising local radicals that the riots hit government policy. Heseltine was appalled by the riots in the middle of his term of office. 'Walking around the streets of Liverpool afterwards I saw what living in the inner city really meant,' he told planners in a review of his achievements at the end of 1982.[3] 'But amid the personal tragedy and public disorder, something good emerged, because we were forced to rethink our strategy for the inner cities.

We were forced to think more deeply about the needs of the people living there.'

His Cabinet paper 'It Took a Riot', written shortly after the riots, infuriated his colleagues. But the evidence that there was a real change because of the riots is strong. Heseltine had trimmed inner spending in the year of the riots back to £158.2 million – £23 million less than the year before. By 1982/3 it had shot up to £190 million. And it was during his spell as 'Minister for Merseyside' that his new strategy began to emerge, using his chairmanship of the Merseyside Partnership as the engine. As the Toxteth riot burnt, he asked the Prime Minister for three weeks off from his other duties to take Merseyside as part of his portfolio. The veteran London MP Ian Mikardo dubbed the appointment 'like sending the arsonist down to the scene to find out the cause of the fire.'

Heseltine faced a cynical response as he arrived in Liverpool, announcing cautiously that he had 'no pot of gold to spend'. The Liverpool 8 Defence Committee, formed to represent local people, walked out of its first meeting with him, claiming that he was only interested in talking to 'middle class so-called representatives'. He also excluded policing from his lines of inquiry, whereas Scarman had made it central to his.

When Heseltine visited the area for the first time as 'Minister for Merseyside', the district covering Toxteth had 18,000 registered unemployed. By October there were 20,000. Heseltine realized that high profile action was needed fast, but also that it would have to be followed up by unprecedented interest from the Cabinet if there was the be any real impact on the problems. 'I never tried to pretend that a general economic decline, that stretched back 70 years, could be reversed in seven months,' he said later.[4] Yet he was moved by the conditions he saw. 'They're dreadful. Dreadful,' he said after a walkabout in Toxteth. The television pictures of the minister day after day, working late into the night, talking and listening on Merseyside, made Heseltine an instantly recognizable political figure. He may have also given the government a caring profile that they badly needed.

At the end of the three weeks he announced a series of small but significant measures, including a maritime museum for Liverpool and an international design competition for homes and a school on a long derelict site by the Anglican cathedral. The housing charity Shelter cynically dubbed them 'instant riot palliatives'.

Aware all the time of the danger of raising too many hopes, and yet running the risk of making the whole effort seem completely empty, Heseltine decided to invite the heads of the country's top financial institutions on a bus tour around the worst housing estates. After three days of telephoning around, only two had agreed to come. Luckily one-up-manship won through, and when Bank of England governor Robin Leigh-Pemberton was definitely to be among the guests, Heseltine was able to fill his bus.

'I suggested that we have tea at the Adelphi to discuss what we had seen and every face fell at my innocent suggestion,' Heseltine wrote. 'You could see that they were convinced that this was where the big touch came ... I said, "I have two things to say to you. First I do not want any money." The smiles had to be seen to be believed. Then I said, "I want one of your brightest managers to come and work in my department with us for a year."'[5]

Two organizations were set up as a result. Eric Sorenson from the DoE's Manchester regional office headed the Merseyside Task Force, and the whiz-kids seconded from the world of finance formed the Financial Initiatives Group (FIG), which began to look at some of the American ideas for attracting investment. This led eventually to the Urban Development Grant idea and to the Building Society Act of 1986, which expanded their powers in housing 'stress' ideas. The FIG was eventually wound up and transformed into Inner City Enterprises, aimed at finding funding for projects that were normally avoided by banks.

The Urban Development Grant (UDG) was for schemes worked up jointly by local authorities and the private sector, so that the council could claim about 75 per cent of the costs. UDG was based on the successful American formula (UDAG) that laid the foundations for private sector involvement in Baltimore and Boston. Tom King, Heseltine's junior local government minister, approved the first £300 million batch of successful schemes early in 1983, discounting fears that it would break laws about what local authorities could spend their money on. One of the first was a £324,000 grant for footballing and social facilities destroyed by vandals at the Merseyside Kirkby Football Club. Alliance spokesman David Alton described the grants as 'candy floss'.

The task forces, in Merseyside and other areas, brought together public and private agencies to provide small business premises, training centres, housing estate refurbishment schemes, projects to reclaim derelict land, and agreements with contractors to employ local labour. The shift of emphasis from planning to business had begun in earnest. Within seven years it was a minister from the Department of Trade and Industry – not the Department of the Environment – who had been given responsibility for regenerating the cities.

The Mersey Task Force was judged to be a moderate success a year after it was set up, by the House of Commons environment committee's inquiry on urban renewal on Merseyside. But it was a success among a 'plethora of agencies, powers and accountabilities, seeking contrasting objectives'. This was confused further, they pointed out, by the conflict between the government's spending controls and their inner city renewal push. Some areas were still losing more in penalty because their rates were too high than they were gaining in grant. It was to be a recurring theme.

III

Heseltine's inner city regeneration strategy was intended to avoid these confusions by sidestepping the local authorities, and cutting back on local authority spending.

The previous Labour government had been forced to comply with the will of the International Monetary Fund, and had been exercising financial restraint for two years. This meant that they had already started over-seeing local government affairs and spending in more detail. But Heseltine launched himself into a more serious battle between central and local government, a struggle that has become a permanent feature of the Thatcher government.

The confrontation was not so much between Whitehall and town hall – though that was largely how it was perceived – but with what the government saw as high-spending, undemocratic, left-wing city authorities. These happened mostly to be the authorities covering inner city areas, so it was difficult for ministers to escape giving the impression that it was the inner cities and the poor who lived there who were the target for the government's strictures and mistrust.

'By 1979, local government had become a barely-controllable free-wheeling employment machine,' Heseltine said in his autobiography *Where there's a will*. Within weeks of taking office, the Conservatives had made it possible for council tenants to buy their own homes. It was a highly popular move, reflecting the belief among many tenants that local authority housing was bureaucratic, paternalist and inefficient. The worst parts of the inner cities were not affected – few could either afford or face to own their poorly maintained flats – but it was those areas that provided the main opposition. The cities realized that move would polarize their housing: the better stock would drift into private ownership, while the worst would remain their responsibility. Meanwhile their problems of homelessness continued to increase.

1981 was a bad year for the government at the polls as well. As their popularity ratings fell, Conservative administrations were overthrown in four of the biggest northern cities, and in the GLC. The spotlight fell on a growing clash between alternative methods of tackling inner city problems.

There were a series of measures to impose spending limits on councils. Finally the government stepped in, and with the 1982 Local Government Finance Act made illegal the whacking supplementary rates demands sent out by some London authorities. Rate-capping followed, limiting the rate rises of selected councils – nearly all of them Labour-controlled in inner city areas – in the face of what were some of the worst backbench revolts faced by the government since the war.

In spite of Heseltine's rhetoric about freedom for local government, he maintained that there was a 'clear duty for the government to assert itself'. This led to the setting up of the urban development corporations in the London Docks and on the banks of the Mersey – organizations with special powers to regenerate their areas – made possible by the Local Government Planning and Land Act 1980.

Heseltine had first become aware of the derelict land in London owned by the Port and gas board, when he flew over the Docks in 1973 on his way to what was to have been the third London airport on Maplin Sands in Essex. 'At first I could not believe what I saw,' he said later. 'The route down-river traversed some of the most valuable acreage in the world – yet pressing close against the clamour of the City's square mile lay the emptiness and hopelessness of hundreds of acres of deserted docks, wharves and warehouses.'[6]

In fact there were 6,000 acres, handed over to the London Docklands Development Corporation (LDDC) in 1981. The Merseyside Development Corporation only had 900 acres with other small pieces in Birkenhead and Bootle.

A 13-man board was appointed to run the LDDC, chaired by Nigel Broackes of the property giant Trafalgar House, with Ber-

Building Futures

mondsey's Labour MP Bob Mellish as his deputy. The LDDC and the other development corporation in Merseyside were modelled on the new town development corporations devised by Lord Reith. They had powers to acquire and develop land, but planning powers were divided confusingly with the local authorities.

The docks began closing in the 1960s – West India Dock had never operated to full capacity. Throughout the 1970s, a series of alternative regeneration plans were drawn up and thrown out. The way ahead was signalled in 1980, with the redevelopment of St Katherine's dock near Tower Bridge as a mixture of expensive flats with a marina. It was clear that close proximity to the City of London gave the whole area great potential.

The future of the riverside Coin Street site, outside the LDDC area and opposite the Embankment, was already being fought out bitterly between office developers and community groups. The 1979 inquiry took nearly a year, and was eventually won by the community. The developers' option expired and the GLC intervened and sold the valuable site to a group of self-builders for £1.

Meanwhile the young LDDC had completely abandoned the hard-won 1976 Docklands Strategic Plan, worked out by the local councils to provide a mix of industry and social housing. The borough of Tower Hamlets had spent £3 million buying the London Docks just four years earlier. The LDDC was taking over much of the land downstream accumulated for council housing by the various local authorities for new homes, but were providing only between ten and 20 per cent for public housing. The Joint Docklands Action Group dubbed it the 'Second East End Blitz'. Heseltine was met by demonstrators when he arrived to open the first private development, in Beckton in February 1982. By then 14,000 families in the area were registered as homeless.

Who was the Docklands development for? The problem of where the local people fitted into the scheme became vital. 'We are not a welfare association,' said Broackes.

London's property boom gathered pace and Docklands homes approached South Kensington prices. Yuppies and windsurfers had taken over the deserted docks. When the massive and controversial Canary Wharf office development was unveiled, more than 70 restaurants had been included in the plans. The Docklands Light Railway was taking shape, and there was even a private preparatory school planned for the new affluent population.

We Want Them Too, Next Time

A series of national newspapers were also moving into the area, although most of the papers had bought sites or made plans before the LDDC was set up. But it was a different world for the original residents, some of whose homes were compulsorily purchased for a meagre price that put them out of the property market anywhere near where they had been brought up.

For in spite of the economic boom and the fractured opposition, the chances that success in the Docks would trickle down to the original docklanders became increasingly remote. By the end of 1987 homelessness was up 120 per cent and unemployment in the area was higher than it had been when the corporation began its work.

The housing problem was especially acute, given that 40,000 people lived in the LDDC area. In 1985 the London Research Centre found that 30 per cent of Dockland households had an income below £2,600 a year. At the same time, LDDC was building only eight per cent of their homes for shared ownership and only 15 per cent for rent. Many were set at 'affordable' prices – which only one in 20 of the population could afford. One of the Docklands boroughs, Newham, which was spending £3 million a year paying for bed and breakfast hostels for the homeless, believed that only one in 30 of local people could afford to buy a home.

The other complaint that dogged the LDDC was its lack of accountability, and as the local authorities withdrew from the board, the problem intensified. No meetings were held in public until 1986, no agendas were issued, and even the London Chamber of Commerce found it difficult to be included in consultations. Members of the board were there as individuals, not representatives, and they were not allowed to discuss anything with their council colleagues. Vital decisions affecting people who lived in the area were being taken by a small group of people, meeting in secret. An all-party trio of MPs – including Bermondsey's new MP Simon Hughes – went to deliver these complaints in the summer of 1985, and to ask for the same rules about open government in local authorities to be forced on the LDDC as well. Nobody met them when they arrived to deliver their 'Memorandum'.

The Enterprise Zone in the Isle of Dogs complicated matters further. EZs had been thought up by Professor Peter Hall of Reading University and the University of Berkeley, California: he dubbed the idea the 'Hong Kong solution'. Sir Geoffrey Howe announced EZs in his budget speech, and 11 run-down areas were designated between 1981 and 1982, and given the benefits of not having to pay rates for ten years or to apply for planning permission.

The Isle of Dogs zone was the last to be put set up, and doubts were raised early on about its success. The private sector was attracted, but after two years the figures showed that 40 per cent of the firms and 62 per cent of the jobs moving to the Isle of Dogs had actually come from somewhere else, and often not very far away. A report by consultants found in 1982 that the loosened planning had not been very important in attracting the private sector, and that much of the economic activity would have occurred anyway, though there was evidence of higher output and employment. Later studies found that the benefits came mainly from the subsidies, rather than from the lack of planning regulations.[8] By 1987 only ten per cent of the new jobs in the Isle of Dogs had been filled by people who lived there already, and the government made it clear they were not planning any more Enterprise Zones.

Dudley Enterprise Zone in the West Midlands was a case in point. Although it had created jobs, the closures going on at the same time meant that there was a net gain of only four jobs by the end of the first year. Meanwhile, they had lost a working farm, snapped up by developers for warehousing with only a 20 year life, without any means of preventing it.

In Liverpool the Merseyside Development Corporation had got off to a slower start than its London counterpart, but were aware of the great problems they had to face. 'The corporation recognized that it cannot succeed alone,' said MDC chief executive Basil Bean.

In fact it had to. Labour-controlled Liverpool City Council, locked in conflict with the government, refused to fill its place on the board. Merseyside Council soon found itself facing abolition, and even Tory-Controlled Wirral did not find its relations with the corporation very easy. The Liverpool International Garden Festival and the refurbishment of the Albert Dock were the early successes that paved the way.

The city council, under the minority Liberal administration, had considered a garden festival in 1980. Then the Tory MP Philip Goodhart told Heseltine how bomb sites in Germany had been turned into gardens after the war: there had been an important festival in Hanover in 1951. Heseltine was considering the different claims of Stoke and Liverpool when Toxteth erupted in 1981, so Liverpool got the first, and their five-year plan had to be compressed into one year overnight. Former landscape Institute president Hal Moggridge described the site as 'a disgusting combination of all the worst qualities of inner city urban dereliction.'[9]

The festival attracted 3.3 million visitors in 1984 to see the gardens, the working Yellow Submarine, and one of the most ambitious rock and water gardens put together since Victorian times. But there was uncertainty about the site after it closed, when Transworld Leisure went into liquidation after taking it over. 'The permanent benefit is less easily measured,' admitted Heseltine later.

In fact the instant hype of the festival was a large part of its purpose, in presenting an image of a rapidly improving Liverpool to the outside world. As interest from private companies became the cornerstone to the government's ideas on regeneration, so the marketing side of regeneration became more important. Company decision-makers had to be convinced they were investing in an upward wave.

In a letter to inner city authorities just after the riots of 1981, Heseltine called on them to go for 'as much visual impact as possible.' He added at the end: 'Some priority will still need to be given to projects which improve facilities and services for those who are . . . disadvantaged'. The traditional role of inner city revival still had to be kept in mind.

This is the contradiction behind the government's approach to the inner cities, Heseltine's included. There was always a danger of the means becoming more important than the end – the marketing of the cities as investment opportunities becoming more important than the truth about the cities themselves. The rebuilding of the environment could bypass the very real and deep-seated problems of the people who live there.

Yet Heseltine had – and has – a genuine interest in the problems not shared by all of his successors, and his impact on inner city policy since the early 80s has been enormous. His ability to bang heads together, and his determination to spend time on the Mersey were clearly effective in the confusion – so much so that there were fears that the work would disintegrate once he was not there. Heseltine was becoming aware of the need not just for jobs, but for citizens to take responsibility – a Thatcherite theme of the late 80s. That meant businesses should begin to take responsibility for provincial cities, rather than sitting in ivory towers in London. These concerns became sharper once he was outside the government, after his spectacular resignation as Defence Minister over the Westland Affair, but they were present before. 'Great employers who used to provide the lifeblood of the town,' he said of one northern city, 'have been replaced by branch managers with narrow powers of decision.'[10] Clearly his spell on the Mersey was formative.

IV

There was no real debate about Mrs Thatcher's intention of abolishing the GLC and the six metropolitan county councils covering many of the inner city areas before or during the 1983 general election. Mrs Thatcher said later that she decided on abolition finally on 8 May, nine days after announcing the date of the election. To put this onto the statute books – one of the most controversial pieces of legislation produced during the Parliament – she appointed former industry minister Patrick Jenkin. But Jenkin did not have the obvious interest in the problems of the inner cities which had driven Heseltine.

His two years in the post, before he was dropped from the Cabinet in 1985, and Kenneth Baker's time after him, were dominated by the battle between Whitehall and local councils – particularly those from the inner cities, who were arguing for the right to spend money on their massive local problems in their own way.

The Greater London Council provided the main ammunition for the government's campaign against local government excess. A radical Labour administration had taken control in May 1981, and the controversial left-winger Ken Livingstone ousted the existing leader Andrew McIntosh at the first group meeting after polling.

'Mr Livingstone waited in the wings for the voters to return the sheep's clothing before he, the wolf, jumped out,' the *Daily Telegraph* intoned. In fact, as Livingstone points out in his autobiography, the press had known about his plans for a good nine months. But now Livingstone increasingly became the personification of everything the government and press disliked about local councillors. When the ruling Labour group voted to decline invitations to Prince Charles' wedding in July 1981, the storm began to break. The *Daily Mail* even recalled one of their leading foreign correspondents to cover life at County Hall. The saga led to the courts for the GLC's radical 'Fares Fair' transport policy, and eventually to the GLC's abolition five years later.

'Every minority cult and creation which the mind can imagine' was encouraged by the GLC and other Labour London councils, according to Mrs Thatcher's outspoken henchman Norman Tebbit. In fact controversy over the GLC's funding of controversial voluntary groups, like Lesbian Line, was an effective smokescreen for much of the debate about conditions in London and other cities.

From County Hall, visible from the Houses of Parliament across the Thames, flew the giant banner numbering London's unemployed as a constant reminder to MPs. By 1983 Livingstone had the fourth biggest personal cuttings file at the Press Association: he remarked that his administration at the GLC was a 'rehearsal for the kind of problem a Bennite government might face.'

It was the height of influence by the new left in the Labour Party, and a new young breed of enthusiastic full-time councillors were suddenly in control of a series of London boroughs. The average age of the Labour councillors on the GLC – handling a budget bigger than that of many nations – was just 27.

Horrified by the ambitions of Livingstone and others like him, ministers launched themselves into the fight to abolish the metropolitan county councils and the GLC, just 23 years after Sir Keith Joseph had moved its creation in the House of Commons. 'We have measured the GLC for its concrete overshoes and in 1986 over the parapet and into the Thames it goes,' Lord Bellwin told the Conservative Party Conference in 1983.[12] Yet the government had misjudged the popularity of the move – especially in London. By the time rioting returned to Brixton in the summer of 1985, the GLC appeared to have won the argument. Most consultants had cast doubts on the idea that abolition would save money, one poll had put 74 per cent of Londoners against the idea, and an expensive series of skilful poster's had swung opinion round. Worse, the government faced an uphill task getting the bill through Parliament unamended. Among the concessions forced by the House of Lords was that the Inner London Education Authority should stay an elected body. It is to disappear instead in 1991.

The success of the GLC's campaign did not save the council. On the evening of 31 March, a tearful Livingstone sang 'We'll Meet Again' to an enthusiastic rally, and the GLC and the other county councils covering the major cities disappeared. The deep problems of the inner cities remained.

Building Futures

A new power to prevent councils from 'irresponsible' spending, the Rates Act, had become law in 1984. By then, spending controls and rate-capping had left high-spending councils with few places to turn. A group of Labour authorities ready to defy the legislation had come together, and by Christmas relations between them and the government had reached stalemate. There was an acrimonious end to a meeting with ministers from different departments of state. The chairman of the Labour-controlled Association of Metropolitan Authorities, Jack Layden – now Sir Jack, was furious that the Treasury had failed to send a minister.

But by the beginning of 1985 the heavy atmosphere lifted slightly. Jenkin had been advised that to be sure of winning a series of High Court actions brought by local authorities with spending controls, he had to bend over backwards to show himself ultra-reasonable. He had previously agreed to meet councillors from only one local authority at a time, but finally said he would meet a delegation from 18 Labour authorities – including Derek Hatton, the Militant deputy leader of Liverpool.

The final date for talks came and went three times in January alone. A mass refusal by rate-capped authorities to set a rate – which would be against the law – seemed likely. What could the government do? They could bail out the councils and ignore the problem, or they could suspend their authority and send in Whitehall commissioners instead, which might have been the confrontation the rebels wanted. The possible consequences for rebel councillors was harsh. Not only could they be barred from holding public office for five years – difficult enough for an obsessive young full-time councillor – but they could also be made financially responsible for any money lost by the council as a result, and that could bankrupt them and their families.

March 6 was declared 'Democracy Day' by the rebel authorities. But divisions had already emerged among the London councils, and the common front was already falling apart. By the end of the month six councils had fallen by the wayside and set a rate.

When the deadline arrived for the GLC to set a rate in March 1985, it was met by a compromise with just ten minutes to spare. The budget was only slightly above their spending limit, and Labour leader Neil Kinnock condemned the 'self-indulgent posing of the far left'. The battles within the councils over whether to set a rate were often bitter and sometimes involved riotous public demonstrations. Southwark had to delay one meeting for 48 hours. When Greenwich councillors finally set their rate after an all-night sitting in June, only Liverpool and Lambeth were left in defiance of the government. Both were by then at risk from the district auditors. Liverpool's rate was not sufficient to cover its budget, including a huge house-building programme, which would put it £25 million in the red, attracting government penalties of £80 million. Only foreign banks were willing to carry on lending to the city council.

By September, Liverpool's financial disaster could only be averted by sending redundancy notices to 31,000 council employees – from road-sweepers to teachers – to avoid running out of funds the following week. It would have saved them a wage bill of £5 million a week. But the strategy split the Labour movement, and the various trade unions concerned prepared to lobby the Labour Party conference the following month. The conference ended with Kinnock's famous denunciation: 'You end with the grotesque chaos of a Labour council – a Labour council – hiring taxis to scuttle round the city handing out redundancy notices to its own workers'.[14] Support for rebel councillors from a new Labour government was clearly far from certain. The following year, Hatton and 46 other Liverpool Labour councillors were banned from office. There was a brief interlude with the city in the hands of the Liberals, before a non-Militant Labour administration was returned in May 1987.

Labour councillors in inner cities who were defying ministers were sustained in the hope that a Labour government would be elected shortly to bail them out – both of their debts and of the legal stranglehold imposed on them. So the disappearance of the metropolitan counties in 1986, and the reappearance of the Thatcher government a year later, spelled defeat for the rebel councils and confusion for the new local authority left. They had also lost some of their most prominent leaders into the new Parliament, like Ken Livingstone and David Blunkett from Sheffield. By the end of their second term of office, Mrs Thatcher's government had all but defeated the inner city local authorities.

V

By the time Kinnock had made his speech, a second wave of inner city riots had hit British cities, throwing the debate out of gear and making the relationship problems between central and local government seem minor by comparison.

The riot in Handsworth, in inner city Birmingham, came as a 'complete surprise' to the police and authorities. The disturbance began when a young black driver was given a parking ticket, and ended with two Asian brothers left to die in their blazing post office in Lozells Road. It also happened in an area praised for its excellent police-community relations during the 1981 riots, a pioneer in 'community' policing. Perhaps it was less surprising considering that Handsworth had an unemployment rate of 35.8 per cent at the time of the riot, and that there had been a recent police crackdown on drugs.

The anti-Asian tone of the riot was emphasized by the press – stressing that this was a riot between different minority racial groups. But the evidence does not bear this out. The shops that were looted happened to be owned by Asians because most of the shops were, and the local Asian temple was left untouched. But still local Asians demanded better police protection from the new Home Secretary Douglas Hurd when he visited the area – before he was hustled sharply away in a police van when a mob broke through the police cordon. The disturbances were also 'no surprise' to former police superintendent David Webb, one of the pioneers of 'community policing' – which involved organizing more policemen on the beat and a high involvement with schools and community groups. He had resigned because he claimed that the police authorities were not moving fast enough towards his community-based methods.

By the end of September, Hurd was facing a second riot in his first month as Home Secretary, in Brixton again. This time the press found themselves almost as unpopular as the police, who had sparked off the riot in the early hours of 28 September when they broke down the front door of Mrs Cherry Groce to search her home for her son. In the minutes afterwards, Mrs Groce was shot, and a rumour that she had died during the afternoon set off two days of rioting, where the police struggled to control the streets around Brixton police station.

This was a very different Brixton to the Brixton of 1981. Male unemployment was 17.5 per cent – half that of Handsworth. And the run-down houses of Railton Road, the scenes of so much violence four years before, were now well-painted and increasingly expensive.

It was the Tottenham riot, at the Broadwater Farm estate in north

WE WANT THEM TOO, NEXT TIME

London, that was the most memorable of the 1985 disturbances. This was the first riot where shots were fired at the police, and the first where a policeman died – PC Keith Blakelock, hacked to death after he stumbled when the police lines drew back. The events were sparked off by another police raid that backfired: this time Mrs Cynthia Jarrett collapsed and died during the raid on her home. The violence began as the police tried to seal off the estate. PC Blakelock died on his journey to hospital on a fire engine – ambulancemen could not get through – with a knife that had been plunged up to the hilt into his neck.

The after effects of what was probably the bitterest of the 80s riots included rival demonstrations outside the local Haringey Borough Council offices, both supporting and protesting against the reported remarks of the controversial black council leader Bernie Grant that the police had been given a 'bloody good hiding'. The council spent 'considerable sums of money in trying to create a good atmosphere on the estate . ... only to be spoilt by the actions of the police,' Mr Grant declared.[15]

But whether or not Grant condemned the actual violence, a poll conducted after the riots showed that 26 per cent of British blacks shared his views that the riot was justified. As many as 64 per cent still believed that blacks were worse off than whites. The atmosphere was not improved by the remarks of the chairman of the Conservative Party, novelist Jeffrey Archer, in the ensuing debate about unemployment, that 'a lot of it is getting off your backside'. But the debate that followed was interesting because it looked ahead to the new strands and modifications in inner city ideas that were to follow.

The first of these was the interest in Mrs Dolly Kiffin, the community and youth leader on Broadwater Farm – one of the first genuine neighbourhood leaders who had not been appointed by officials from outside. It was clear just how important a figure she would be in the reconstruction of the estate. Few spokesmen for riot neighbourhoods had emerged with any public profile before, and the press was unclear how to treat her. She had obviously sympathy for the rioting youths, yet just as obviously, she was one of the few people who did not just care about the people on Broadwater Farm – she did something about it.

Her work had begun in 1981 in an almost single-handed protest against a police station being built on the estate. After the plan had been fought off, and the Broadwater Farm Youth Association set up, she managed to get hold of a disused fish and chip shop, and began to organize young people serving meals to the old.

Broadwater Farm also fuelled a new interest in the desperation of the people living in badly-designed estates. The riot was less than a month before the spectacular – and botched – blowing up of the Northaird Point, a 21-storey tower block in Hackney. The 19-year-old tower cost £400,000 to explode, though only the bottom half collapsed, but saved £4.5 million in repairs. Its destruction was a symbol – not just of the failure of tower block and system-built mass housing – but of the wide agreement that it *had* failed.

Finally, the 1985 riots seemed to signal a shift in the inner city debate. There began to be an acceptance by sections of the political left that the situation was too urgent to wait for a change of government: *some* of the government's thinking about encouraging private investment inner city areas – and the need for places to look after their image – had to be taken on board.

The reaction of Birmingham Labour MP Jeff Rooker to the Handsworth riot seems to accept some of these assumptions: 'The police did not start this riot,' he said. 'It is unfair that a few 100 people hell-bent on criminality have slurred the area'. Labour-controlled Lambeth Borough Council's report *Developing Brixton* was published a month before their riot – but it had quite a different tone from Lambeth's confrontational stance of 1981. *Developing Brixton*, the brainchild of planning committee chairman John O'Malley, said this: 'We recognize that we will require much assistance from the private sector and will do all we can to co-operate with the business community to ensure that Brixton and its people get the modern facilities they deserve.' It was sent to 200 developers, showing an acceptance of the role of the private sector in helping Brixton.

The Archbishop of Canterbury, meanwhile, had set up his Commission on Urban Priority Areas two years before, under former MSC chairman Sir Richard O'Brien, and chose this moment to launch it. A great deal of its findings, published as *Faith in the City*, were about the future of the Church of England in inner cities, where attendance had fallen to 0.85 per cent.

But the report also condemned government economic policies as 'inflexible and dogmatic'. 'Social disintegration has reached the point in some areas that shop windows are boarded up, cars can't be left in the street, residents are frightened either to go out themselves or to ask others in, and there is a pervasive sense of powerlessness and despair,' the report said.

The government realized immediately the damage the document could do them. 'Sources close to ministers', the phrase used to disguise unattributable remarks, suggested that *Faith in the City* was a Marxist document. 'Nobody in their right mind would ever class me as a Marxist,' said O'Brien.

VI

'We want them too, next time,' Mrs Thatcher said of the inner cities as she claimed her third general election victory in 1987, an election that left her with no Tory MPs in Manchester, Leicester, Bradford, Liverpool, Glasgow or Newcastle.

But how was she to achieve this? A panoply of grants, deregulations, freeports, enterprise zones, simplified planning zones and other special measures were now stitched onto the policy pattern of 'partnership' areas sketched out by the previous Labour government. No guiding strategy or object was apparent. The TCPA's influential report on the inner cities *Whose Responsibility?* referred to 'a series of piecemeal measures that do not add up to a co-ordinated whole'.

These piecemeal measures were also being operated on a background of continuing reviews of public expenditure. A secret review of inner city spending began in April 1984, looking at the objectives of the Urban Programme. In August the following year, 29 councils were excluded from the programme, so that it could concentrate on the worst areas. Yet another review, conducted by Hurd as Home Secretary and Baker as Environment Secretary began in the November following the riots.

Two key problems were emerging for the government. One was that so many government departments were now involved in the inner cities. Apart from the Home Office and the Department of the Environment, there was the Department of Employment, the Department of Trade and Industry, the Department of Health and Social Security, the Department of Transport – and of course, the Manpower Services Commission. Each had different responsibilities and different objectives. Some of them were clear, some of them not so clear, some of them were actually hidden.

Baker was particularly interested in how to co-ordinate them, and the watchword 'integration' began to emerge. Another initiative, to integrate action on the ground, was the launch of the City

Action Teams (CATs) – a wider-based version of the task forces – organised by Eric Sorensen, back from the Mersey as one of Whitehall's youngest under-secretaries. Local authorities suspected that this was more hype: 'They are pretending the government is doing something, when in fact it is doing nothing apart from holding press conferences,' said Manchester City Council leader Graham Stringer.

After the 1985 reshuffle, the CATs' reported to Lord Young, the new Employment Minister. Young was a key protagonist in the Cabinet battles to sort out which government department controlled inner city policy: should the government channel its resources through local authorities or through new agencies? Lord Young was among those who did not trust the local authorities.

There was a feeling in the government that councils were unpopular and would make a good target in the coming election. But who was running inner city policy? Who was keeping the peace between battling ministers? Mrs Thatcher announced that she was 'at the helm' of inner city policy, and after the election was chairing an inner cities Cabinet committee. But when Heseltine suddenly resigned as Defence Minister it became clear that a high-profile inner city expert was trying to carve out a niche for himself as a potential Conservative Party leader. In a speech in April, he criticized the government's 'neglect', calling for an English Development Agency to be set up along the lines of the one in Scotland. A year later, he was still hammering home the same message: 'This government has proved there's no hurdle to stop us rebuilding the urban areas. If you take the extremes – Glasgow, London, Liverpool – it's being done. But I want a national strategy'.

During the 1987 general election Heseltine travelled the country, and his themes included the regeneration of the cities of the north to protect the rural communities of the south.

Mrs Thatcher's apparently off-the-cuff speech, in the early hours of her election victory, spelled out her clearest commitment yet to inner cities. She told the press: 'Where you have initiative, talent and ability, the money follows' – a motto adopted by the new Teeside Development Corporation for their corporate identity. Teeside was the biggest UDC yet, covering 19 square miles, and had been among five announced by environment secretary Nicholas Ridley at the end of 1986, with a budget of £150 million each for the next five years.

We Want Them Too, Next Time

Lord Young appeared to have won the upper hand in the policy struggle. New agencies were high on the government's list, and support for local authorities rather lower. As Secretary of State for Trade and Industry after the 1987 election, Lord Young now had the lead role in the cities. But there was no sign of the expected Inner Cities White Paper, and the argument about co-ordination was far from over. The blight would remain unless there was co-ordination in the inner cities, BAT Industries chairman Patrick Sheehy told the CBI conference in Glasgow in November.

The white paper kept on being postponed. Anonymous ministers were quoted as saying that it lacked focus or coherence, and Labour industry spokesman Bryan Gould claimed that Whitehall was experiencing the 'most prolonged and bitter bout of wrangling that civil service insiders can remember. The Department of Trade and Industry has been given the lead role but with almost no resources to implement Lord Young's schemes,' Gould told a London audience. 'On the other hand the Department of the Environment, which does have the resources, is headed by . . . Nicholas Ridley, for whom any public expenditure is a grievous and bitter personal defeat.'

Mrs Thatcher was coming under pressure to appoint one Cabinet minister with overall responsibility for the inner cities. Eventually she decided to appoint the industry minister Kenneth Clarke, against the wishes of the Department of the Environment. The white paper itself appeared in a different guise in the Spring of 1988. Instead of a HMSO-style collection of dry policy suggestions, there was a glossy brochure outlining the government's intentions, launched at a major press conference in Westminster. It was called *Action for Cities*, and marked the highest profile ever given to inner city policy. Arrangements for the launch were kept under wraps until the last moment, and journalists were telephoned at home before Sunday lunch the day before.

Mrs Thatcher led in six ministers to provide the conference with some firm chairmanship. The inner cities were not 'unrelieved gloom', she said: 'I know from my own visits that this picture is utterly false'. Nor was she defensive when she declared 'I don't think there is a single new policy here'. The package was about co-ordination and concentration of resources – and it was also about the business community, at whom the exercise was mainly aimed. Kenneth Clarke was launching a series of working breakfasts around the country, and he hoped businessmen would join him in a rediscovery of Victorian business philanthropy. There was no defence from the opposition's charge that this was a 'high-gloss re-launch of the status quo', except, perhaps, that *Action for Cities* was not intended to break new ground, simply to co-ordinate the £3,000 million of government money that went towards the inner cities every year.

The new measures were nearly all extensions of old policies into new areas: City Grant to replace the old Urban Development Grand and Urban Regeneration Grant, a new UDC for Sheffield's Lower Don Valley, more CATs, new training facilities, new City Technology Colleges, a new streamlined grant system, and an extension to the area covered by the Merseyside Development Corporation. More interesting were the 12 planned 'school-industry compacts', where local companies would guarantee jobs and training for schools in their area that had reached an agreed standard of achievement and attendance – based on a pioneering idea from Boston.

Action for Cities left out of the picture the work of the growing voluntary sector, and of course the local authorities, neither of which were mentioned at all. This was in spite of the picture on the cover, which showed the successful Salford Quays redevelopment scheme in Manchester. Democrat environment spokesman Simon Hughes pointed out that Salford Quays was a partnership scheme between local business and the city council – achieved with no involvement from central government at all.

The school-industry compacts were not the only inspiration from America. Heseltine had been looking for ideas there as environment secretary, and Kenneth Clarke also crossed the Atlantic after his appointment as inner cities minister. But there was some doubt whether Clarke and the other ministers really had their minds open to some US lessons – like the importance of local autonomy, political diversity and the commitment by companies to the progress of their own cities.

At the time, housing was reaching the top of the agenda of the inner city debate. Soaring land prices made new low-income housing there all the more difficult to build, and homelessness had risen in the city by around 700 per cent since 1970. Mrs Thatcher was known to be worried about the approaching 20th anniversary of *Cathy Come Home*, the heart-rending TV drama of the homeless, shown to such a wide effect in 1966. At the same time, the number sleeping outside each night in London alone had risen to 2,000.

But the political debate about the kind of housing that should be provided had run aground. Very few would now deny that the tower and system built housing of the 50s to 70s had been anything other than a disaster. Liverpool under the minority Liberal administration had saved the money for blowing up these disasters by selling off uninhabitable flats to developers as penthouses. Even under the Militants, Liverpool, which had one of the most ambitious house-building programmes in the country, were sticking firmly to low-rise homes with gardens. Other cities were in an equally difficult position, strapped for cash, and inheriting some of the worst housing estates in Western Europe, together with a growing problem of homelessness. Yet councils were not allowed to spend more than a fraction of the money they raised by selling their housing stock, which meant that public house-building was dwindling. The homeless then had to be housed in expensive bed and breakfast accommodation, costing Tower Hamlets – for example – some £18 million in one year alone.

Labour leaders had badly misjudged their response to the sale of council houses. Over 1 million had been sold to tenants, who could at last escape the petty restrictions about who did repairs, how high hedges could be, what colour the front doors, whether they could have pets, that had bedevilled the tenants of local authority housing. Many Labour cities put everything in the way of tenants owning their own homes, ridiculing their wish to do so. But beyond that, rightly or wrongly, councillors were reaping the rewards of the apparent failure of public housing, summed up by the writer Colin Ward: 'Why is it that on one side of the street the council is demolishing old houses as unfit for human habitation and replacing them with flats which nobody likes . . . while on the other side of the street, identical houses are being bought and improved by those despised gentrifiers, and given an indefinite new life?'[19] In some ways the right to buy has brought a mixture of classes to inner cities that other policies had failed to achieve. But the social price is high.

Into this bag of questions came the government's proposals to widen the private rented housing sector, letting tenants decide on their own landlord, and also their plans for Housing Action Trusts (HATs). HATs were the solution for the run-down inner city estates, mini-UDCs responsible to Parliament with powers to encourage employment projects. They were based loosely on Heseltine's Stockbridge Village Trust on Merseyside, set up in 1983. But Stockbridge was only partly successful. Abbey National and Barclays failed to provide the full finance for buying the estate for the new trust, and Knowlsey Borough Council – who were selling it – had to provide a mortgage of £2.5 million.

HATs are intended to exist for a limited amount of time. Environment minister Nicholas Ridley is hoping that housing associations can carry the flame for social housing. The danger is that under new rules, the housing associations must raise half the money for their developments in the City – which will mean rent rises which could put them outside the range of the tenants who really need them. Nor is it clear whether the housing associations can gear themselves up to cope with carrying the whole responsibility for social housing in time.

When the first six HATs were announced in 1988 it was clear that they were not, in fact, the very worst estates in the country. All of them had received public money before under one or other government scheme. Perhaps the government was determined that its pioneer HATs should be seen to be successes, which may be why the appalling Hulme estate in Manchester successfully lobbied against being included in the scheme. There was a mixed reaction from the tenants – some of whom felt they were better off under the local authority devil they knew, and fearful that HATs would simply do their flats up and then move them out. It is clearly a high-risk strategy, but the political fall-out will not be fully felt until the 1990s.

VII

GLASGOW'S MILES BETTER was a marketing slogan that summed up a new optimism – not just for Glasgow – but for other of the most run-down British cities. By the end of 1988, the government's marketing strategy appeared to be paying off, in the sense that people believed that the inner cities were showing signs of improvement.

The impetus for Glasgow's turnaround was given by the ruling Labour Party's disastrous defeat in 1977, when the old-style councillors were pushed aside as the party lost control of the poverty-striken outlying estates to the Scottish Nationalists. The new people in charge began to worry that the city's rough, gloomy image was a key problem. Glasgow was known throughout the world as the city of the Gorbals and drunken knifings on a Saturday night – an image that the new Provost, Michael J. Kelly, knew to be out of date. A former economics lecturer, Kelly's four years as Provost put the city on the regeneration map, and it was he and advertising man John Struthers who came up with the 'Miles Better' idea in 1982. The smiling yellow Miles Better faces were soon to be seen on car stickers and posters all over the country, except in Edinburgh where the rival city banned them from their buses.

Also responsible for the changing image was the lesser known head of the city's public relations department Harry Diamond, dubbed by the local press as the man with the 'toughest job in Scotland' when he was appointed in 1975. Pleading for more staff four years later, he told councillors that the reputation of the city had not been so low for 800 years. 'We must do something to show the world that we are not morally, physically and spiritually bankrupt,' he told them in a council report.

The new gallery for the Burrell collection, opened in 1983, was an important gesture towards a new kind of Glasgow. Sir William Burrell had been a major local ship-owner in the Edwardian days when 200 portrait painters were at work in the city. The Burrell Collection was followed by the Scottish Exhibition and Conference Centre, the 1988 International Garden Festival – leading up to Glasgow's designation as European City of Culture 1990, joining Athens, Florence and Paris as holders of the title. But there was also some success in run-down eastern Glasgow, which had once been a byword for squalor, its population drifting down from 509,000 in 1948 to just 45,000 30 years later. The Glasgow Eastern Area Renewal (GEAR) scheme had been set up for a ten-year period back in 1976, investing £315 million in housing, health and social services, and working through community councils to bolster the confidence of residents. Among the successes they claim is the new Gateway store, designed with pyramids, and known as the 'Valley of the Kings', which is a potent symbol of the change: the Parkhill Shopping Centre is the largest in Scotland, and it replaces the Beardmore steel mill which once employed 17,000 people.

The success of GEAR must be largely down to the co-ordinating work of the Scottish Development Agency, but also - as Professor David Donnison argues – the people who live there. 'The fact that the area chosen for renewal was inhabited by some 40,000 beligerant people who compelled the agency to set up an office in the east end and deal frankly with them was another advantage,' he said in a study of Glasgow's turnaround.[20]

Community self help and co-operative housing has taken root in the city more than anywhere. By 1985 there were 40 housing associations running 10,000 homes. But is Glasgow such a success story? The Child Poverty Action Group reckons that one in three people in Strathclyde are on or below the poverty line. Glasgow is still high on the list of the unhealthiest places in Britain. Its unemployment is falling, but is still around 20 per cent and among the worst in Europe. Up to 15 per cent of the housing stock is below a 'tolerable standard', and Glasgow has been – as housing committee convenor Bailie Jim McLean has said – 'on the threshold of the worst housing crisis this century,' Some of Mother Teresa of Calcutta's nuns now run a soup kitchen in the heart of the city centre. 'In many ways Glasgow *is* miles better,' one of them was quoted in a *New Statesman* article. 'But in many ways it is worse. There is great, great poverty here.'[21]

Yet there does seem to be a new confidence in Glasgow people that the 'answer lies in their own hands,' as Professor Robin Boyle has explained. 'With sufficient commitment and financial help from both public and private sources they may be able to improve their own living conditions, independent of local politicians and their bureaucrats.'[22]

Arriving at Glasgow Central station now, the visitor is immediately confronted by the extraordinary rehabilitation of the station forecourt. Behind the 30-year-old advertising hoardings were walls of wood-panelling which are now restored, and which make Central Station one of British Rail's most impressive. And as Kelly himself says, the slogan is not that Glasgow is 'best', just that it is 'miles better'.

There is optimism in the air about inner cities – not only Glasgow. The economic success of London's docklands, for example, has rubbed off on other schemes. When the new UDC schemes were announced in 1987, land values rose in the areas immediately in anticipation of success. Private developers are now aware that profits are to be made in the most run-down cities, and many more expensive conferences aimed at developers are hammering home the same message: 'Enterprise in the Inner Cities' organized by a wide range of organizations, was launched in the Barbican in October 1988 and aimed to visit three other cities in the following two years.

The shift in the balance between public and private is one of the most striking changes in the 1980s. Just before *Action for Cities* was announced in 1988, the 11 biggest construction companies joined forces as British Urban Development, under Mrs Thatcher's former adviser Hartley Booth. Local authorities have generally grasped the nettle of working with the private sector, and in some cases the old Labour mythology of cloth caps and dole queues has found itself dumped in favour of marketing and upbeat image-making for their cities. Here they were at one with local entrepreneurs: 'I'll have succeeded when we finally bury the Jarrow march as a piece of history,' said MetroCentre developer John Hall. One by one the boroughs in the London Docklands area came to terms with the UDC on their doorstep, agreeing to developments in return for promises on low cost housing or jobs.

By the end of 1985 local government minister William Waldegrave could tell the Tory Party Conference that: 'What we have to do is to show that if you put private money – and good design – and planning on a human scale together, you can turn the tide in the cities'. It seemed to be a basis for agreement.

Inner city consensus seemed to be in sight. The CBI, representing Britain's businessmen, demanded public spending as 'pump-priming' in the inner cities. Meanwhile, their historic rivals at the TUC were telling the National Economic Development Council that inner city problems were too big for the government alone, and were a responsibility for business as well.

Another reason for optimism was that cities were in fashion, not just to invest in, but to live in as well. From London to Glasgow, young people without children have been chosing to buy inner city flats. Consequently the population of London and other major cities stabilized in the mid-1980s – where in the 1960s London had been losing people at the rate of 100,000 a year. Even the Isle of Dogs is now fashionable and gentrified terraced homes have changed the character of many run-down districts. This is a major success for the Conservatives within the terms they have set for themselves, Mrs Thatcher's dream of 'we want them too'.

But many problems remain unresolved: most importantly, the question whether regeneration is best attempted by central or local government. The present government has ridden over the traditional independence of local authorities, using their unpopularity both as an excuse to bypass them, and setting up new agencies in the inner cities. Between 1982-6 the block grant to local authorities went down by a quarter, and the financial restraints have made problems worse – especially when inner city councils were losing in 'penalties' almost the same as they were gaining from the Urban Programme. All this was part of a continuing struggle with the left wingers, who were alive and well in city government as they were almost nowhere else. 'Where for ideological reasons they try to obstruct us,' warned Kenneth Clarke as inner cities minister in 1987, 'let me assure you that we will not allow them to get in the way.' Would the government have behaved the same if the major cities had been controlled by Conservatives?

Public subsidies of over £700 million were given to the London Docklands alone by 1987. Would the whole renewal process have worked in the same way – or been more efficient – if councils had possessed the powers of co-ordination which were given to UDCs or CATs? We will never know. But we can guess that what the policy-makers gained in efficiency, they lost in civic pride – which as Glasgow has shown can be a powerful force in rescuing cities from the brink.

This is one lesson Mrs Thatcher should have borrowed from the USA: that local autonomy means local pride, which has been the basis of revival for some American cities. Clamping down further on the powers of local authorities will mean that they can contribute nothing to the public-private partnerships that the government professes to believe in. At the 'Enterprise and the Inner Cities' conference in October 1988, developer Godfrey Bradman warned the government not to implement their proposals for reducing councils' involvement with companies. Yet by the following year, they were limiting the rights of councillors to set up and run companies, as Birmingham was doing to regenerate the 'Heartlands'. In fact, Ridley's Local Government and Housing Bill questioned whether cities needed to keep an interest in the companies at all once the project had begun.

Another important question is begged by Mrs Thatcher's words 'we want them too, next time'. Who is the regeneration for? Were the early UDCs really aiming to improve the lives of the underpriveleged in the Docklands or Merseyside – even in the long term? Or did the ministers ignore the rebuilding of the inner citizens in their haste to rebuild the fabric of the inner cities? In those terms,

WE WANT THEM TOO, NEXT TIME

London Docklands have been a phenomenal success – but if the poor are moved out, the problems are simply moved elsewhere. Conservative-controlled Westminster was accused of just that when their radical council house selling policy left hundreds of empty homes and 10,000 on the tenants' waiting list.[23] They abandoned another scheme to put homeless families outside the borough, amid allegations that they were removing people who might vote against them.

The idea that the economic benefits of success trickle down through society to the poorest have been firmly discredited by Professor Brian Robson of Manchester University, and the rest of the formidable ESRC inner cities research programme. The House of Commons employment committee agreed. 'UDCs cannot be regarded as a success,' they wrote in 1988, 'if the buildings and land are regenerated, but the local community are bypassed and do not benefit.'

But the latest UDCs seem to be changing. Local authorities are showing more involvement, and the corporations are more interested in working with local people. Even the LDDC has become aware of its lack of involvement with local people, producing a glossy brochure with their 1987/88 annual report entitled *Working for the Community*. 'The LDDC has always recognized that regeneration is not purely about the physical provision of buildings, but the encouragement of a healthy, thriving and balanced community. A place where old and new residents can live in harmony side by side,' said chairman Sir Christopher Benson. But the security guards on the fortified new estates, and the signs marking private riverside walks on passages that used to be used by locals, are not good omens for the future. In other parts of London, the London Residuary Body – the successor to the GLC – was busy selling off low cost homes, built and allocated by the GLC in Covent Garden, as expensive private flats.

Housing continues to be a major problem. The number of new homes being built in central London, for example, fell by 60 per cent in the five years after 1982. Kenneth Baker and housing minister John Patten combined to help building societies put more money into home-building, but even new housing association homes have been going down since 1984. The new Local Government and Housing Bill stops councils from spending more than a quarter of the money they earn from selling council houses. The rest must be put aside to finance future debts.

BUILDING FUTURES

The third big question follows on from this. It is the question of ideology versus pragmatism. The Thatcher government has been accused endlessly of letting its ideology get in the way of practical solutions. The government's dislike of local authority power is part of this ideology, as is the chosen image of turning their back on the past. Yet most government initiatives have been built firmly on ideas that were emerging before they came to power in 1979. It was, after all, the Labour secretary of state Peter Shore who decided to end the new towns programme and invest in the inner cities instead.

The list of 'borrowed' ideas is a long one. The Scottish Development Agency and Glasgow GEAR scheme they borrowed – with some misgivings – from the previous Labour government, together with the task force idea. The first economic development unit was actually set up by Bradford City Council in 1979. Urban development corporations were suggested years ago by the Town and Country Planning Association, and the previous Labour government used new town legislation for urban areas, as UDCs do now. Co-operative solutions for housing estates were tried by the Liverpool Liberals in the late 1970s. Even the selling of council houses was done before: Westminster City Council, under Labour control between 1974 and 1979, sold over 95,000 of them to their tenants.

Another question concerns marketing hype. Marketing has been vital in restoring confidence, but there are dangers lurking in its over-use. Encouraging companies to invest in the inner cities means little progress if only the most visible pieces of derelict land are tackled, or only the most obvious exteriors of the estates. Nor does it help if it means obscuring the truth that the inner cities still contain some of the most intractable problems of loneliness, poverty and crime.

Finally there is the question of the problems associated with success. There is still too little co-ordination, and businesses that want to get involved in regeneration are – as Professor Robson says – 'confused with an alphabet soup of acronyms of the innumerable schemes and programmes'.[24]

An important framework of co-ordination has disappeared with the metropolitan county councils. And if planning and other government co-ordination is undermined in the rush to build anything in the inner cities, more problems are likely to be stored up for the years ahead. Without the GLC, planning in London is now a compromise business: a great city is effectively out of control. Architecture critic Martin Pawley described the explosion of London – where 50 per cent of all homes in the centre are second homes or investments and 20 per cent belong to international companies – as a bad dream: 'Imagine all the American architects with their psychological training taking the little English planners out to lunch. Imagine *Evening Standard* readers commuting 250 miles every day. Imagine faxes tripping down wires; currency dealers being measured for suits at their workstations. Imagine rows of unregistered BMWs and Porches, prowling VAT men, armed policemen, thousands of tourists each making a feature video, freelance wheel clampers, sponsored litter bins; one-room flats at £1,000 a week. Imagine all this in London and then wake up in a cold sweat. *Get me a lawyer!*[25]'

Those are the questions that remain, even if – on the face of it – inner city problems seem less intractable than they did back in 1981. Who runs the regeneration? Who is it for? How should it be marketed? And how should it be planned, if at all?

Yet while the traditional political battles between right and left are fought out over the inner cities, new approaches and new thinking are already at work outside the government – and changing the way we think about them.

3
DARKER CORNERS

It is becoming unsafe for a man to traverse certain parts of London at night, save in company.
  The Times *10.11 1856, quoted in Geoffrey Pearson,* Hooligan, *London 1988, p 142.*

The Prince of Wales made a successful visit to Australia in the Autumn of 1985, and returned to a UK shocked at the Broadwater Farm riot and the death of PC Blakelock. His reported remarks about his fears of inheriting a 'divided kingdom' made the headlines while he was away.

During his day-long flight home, the controversy in Britain deepened further. Lord Stockton – formerly the Prime Minister Harold Macmillan – launched an extraordinary attack on the government over the miner's strike, and accused them of 'selling off the family silver'. The government was facing what looked like emerging opposition from the old establishment of gentry, church and even royalty.

Prince Charles was no stranger to controversy. A visit he had made to Hackney's community scheme in Black Road, Macclesfield, had done much to ignite his fascination with architecture and the inner cities, and his entry into the public debate in 1984 was startling.

Charles had been asked to address the Royal Institute of British Architects for their 150th anniversary dinner at Hampton Court in May 1984. It was supposed to mark the end of a period of rehabilitation for the profession, after doing penance for high rise blocks. When Charles' staff discovered that, instead of congratulating the RIBA, he was going to launch an attack on the profession in his speech they went to great lengths to dissuade him. But Charles was adamant, and the massed ranks of 700 architects heard the Prince of Wales accuse them of designing buildings 'for the approval of their fellow architects and critics – not for the tenants'. The planned Mies van der Rohe tower for Mansion House Square he dismissed as a 'glass stump', and Peter Ahrends' hard-won compromise design for the National Gallery extension as 'a vast municipal fire station.' Both buildings were refused planning permission, and Ahrends got no more work for 18 months.

Now, as the Prince flew home from Australia, he was reading a slim green paperback. This was *Utopia on Trial*, a stinging attack on the design of public housing by Professor Alice Coleman and a research team from King's College, London. By the time the plane approached Heathrow, Charles had finished the book, and had become a firm convert to the idea that the design of housing estates could have an enormous affect on the level of crime there.

Even as he read, a young black barrister was going on trial in London for causing the death of a black teenager, after organizing a group of black youths to confront some racially-motivated whites and take their revenge. In the ensuing street battle one of his group was killed.

The rising crime rate, and the fear of it, is a measure of the alienation of inner city areas, bound up with the other problems of misery and poverty in such a way that nobody is clear how much is cause and how much effect. As Professor Coleman explained in her book, it is also related to architecture and the estates that are now regarded with horror by their inhabitants and anyone who visits them.

An undercurrent of violence and fear has always been part of inner city life. We are beginning to believe in the inevitability of rising crime, especially violent crime, evidence for which is trumpeted by the media. Fewer teenagers in the next few years may mean that the crime rate will begin to fall, but still crime has multiplied seven times over in the last 30 years, and one in four males now commit a 'reasonably serious offence' before the age of 28.

In spite of this, inner city crime has rarely been high up the political agenda. This may be because of the mystery about why it happens, but there is also an old-fashioned and rather patronizing feeling that the existence of a 'criminal underclass' or sub-culture is endemic to cities, and there is little that can be done about it.

There may also be political reasons. The Right has traditionally failed to recognize inner city deprivation as a key issue, though they have always championed 'law and order', and have been afraid of disorder spilling out of inner cities. The Left on the other hand see crime merely as a symptom of social malaise. In this respect, politics has failed to serve inner city people, whose lives are far more affected by the problems of crime than anyone else's. People in inner city Liverpool, for example, have to live with a burglary rate of one in four homes every year.

Fear helps make predictions of rising crime self-fulfilling. The more people bar their doors, the less a sense of community remains to tackle the symptoms and watch over neighbours' lives and property. Instead of the community feeling of *EastEnders'*, Albert Square, inner city estates are often places of loneliness and isolation.

The fear is fed by newspapers and television who present a powerful image of inner city life, which includes daily violence to old ladies, and muggers – who are always black – terrorizing a population largely composed of scroungers and lay-abouts. Such a caricature is both dangerous and wrong.

The first myth is about the ethnic minorities. Media coverage of the riots, emphasizing the involvement of West Indians, has strengthened this impression. Home Office researchers Mary Tuck and Peter Southgate visited Manchester's Moss Side – shortly to be engulfed in rioting in 1981 – and found that the police experiences of whites and West Indians were remarkable for their similarity. The differences lay in where they lived: flat dwellers on the notorious Hulme estate were much more likely to suffer a variety of crimes ranging from break-ins to fraud. The only real difference in Hulme was between whites and West Indians who were under 25, where one third of the West Indians were critical of the police: 'Rioting by young people,' wrote the researchers, 'in a sense becomes easier to comprehend in the light of such a figure.' As they also pointed out, the Moss Side area was considered 'bad' long before immigration, and also before part of the area was demolished to build the Hulme estate.

The second myth is the one of widespread crime. Any crime represents a human misfortune, and in that sense even one is too many, but the widely held idea that simply popping your head outside the front door risks a hideous mugging is not accurate. Home office researcher Malcolm Ramsay found in 1982 that mugging was actually a rare crime, affecting only 30 out of each 100,000 people – and most of them young rather than old. This went up to 1 in 25 in Manchester, but was only 1 in 100 in London, and of those, only three per cent of victims needed more than 12 hours in hospital. He also found that the proportion of convicted black or ethnic minority muggers was only in proportion to their percentage of the local population.

Obviously there are links between unemployment and crime, especially when crime is the only way of buying Christmas presents for the family, clothing the children or sometimes, finding relief from boredom. Journalist Paul Harrison, whose *Inside the Inner City* gave a vivid picture of life in Hackney, quotes one probation officer as complaining: 'I have two experienced jewel thieves on my books, and all I can offer them is a job cleaning a store for £40 a week'. But it is another myth that as far as crime and violence is concerned, we have never had it so bad. This belief may stem partly from the kind of soft-focussed feelings about the past that every generation has, harking back to what Raymond Williams described as a 'golden age'. Sociologist Geoffrey Pearson also showed recently in his book *Hooligan* that every age shares the same belief that disorder and crime has never been so bad.[2] The attitude was summed up in the recent BBC Reith Lectures by Oxford Professor A H Halsey, who described working class places of 50 years ago as 'areas of domestic peace and neighbourly trust of a standard we do not know today.'

On the other hand, the former Metropolitan Police commissioneer Sir Robert Mark described the rumbustuous Saturday nights in Manchester when he was a young constable. 'A good time was had by all,' wrote Sir Robert, gaily describing 'quite a battle in which uniformed and plain clothes men cheerfully joined.'[3] Manchester, Leeds, Sheffield all suffered years of gang warfare in the last century. In Salford before the first world war, women did not dare to go out alone after dark. Broadly similar debates about increasing crime have been going on as long as inner cities have been a problem – since long before *Punch* magazine blamed Jack the Ripper on the neglected East End slums.

The eighteenth century novelist and magistrate Henry Fielding believed of London's alleys that: 'had they been intended for the

DARKER CORNERS

very purpose of concealment, they could scarce have been better contrived. Upon such a view, the whole appears as a vast wood or forest, in which a Thief may harbour . . . as wild beasts do in the deserts of Africa or Arabia.'[4]

The Victorians believed there was less violent crime: 'the modern thief depends on his skill', said Cornhill Magazine in 1862. But there was a wave of 'garotting', an unpleasant form of what we now know as mugging, in 1850 in Manchester and in 1862 in London. Summer disturbances in 1898 led the *Times* to talk about 'something like organized terrorism in the street', and Geoffrey Pearson found that one in four of London's policemen were assaulted *every year* at the turn of the century. The Glasgow gangs were especially notorious, staffed by the mixture of Highlanders, Irish and Ulster Protestants living in the 19th century tenements which were still occupied until the 1950s. The slumland drink, 'Jake', made up of red wine and eau de cologne or meths, fired years of gangland feuds which were ignored as far as possible by the police. The ferocity of the street battles in 1935 led to the appointment of Sir Percy Sillitoe – later Director-General of MI5 – to be appointed as chief constable, with the aim of beating the gangs of what he called 'unemployable louts' at their own game.

Football violence was not unknown in other cities between the wars, with Spurs and Arsenal fans fighting in the street with knives in the early 1920s. In October 1931, the army was called out in four cities, to face rioting demonstrators about cuts in the dole, combined with organized looting. A decade later, with the British crime rate still rising, the inspectors of Constabulary were able to claim that the statistics 'have touched the conscience of the nation and aroused the deepest concern.'[5] It could have been written today.

This is the background to the fear of crime. Historical evidence is that the fear is not necessarily related to the danger or how widespread it is. In fact, the overall crime rate is now dropping, while the rate of *violence* still shoots up – though figures for the fear and isolation that crime brings are harder to come by. Yet the victims are increasingly apparent.

In January 1989, two fires in council flats in south London that had been barricaded against burglary led to four tragic deaths. One of the couples, Victor and Audrey Johnson, were living behind a wrought-iron grill, with bars across the fire escape, in the Grantham Road estate, Stockwell, when someone poured petrol through their letter box and set it alight.

This kind of isolation without privacy – loneliness, with the risk of repeated burglaries – has become a widespread feature of inner city life. Far from being hotbeds of revolution, as inner city estates were painted by the press after the rioting, their watchword tends to be 'don't get involved'.

II

'When a loved landscape is altered out of recognition, we lose not only a place, but a part of ourselves,' said the novelist Margaret Drabble.[6] A landscape that has changed so rapidly in one generation adds to the dislocation that is now so much part of inner city life. Alienation is not confined to crime and its after-effects.

If Margaret Drabble is right, then people in the post-war inner cities must have lost great chunks of themselves as their neighbourhoods faced up to redevelopment and the bulldozer. Inner city communities have taken the full brunt of changes in the 20th century. People who spent their whole lives in one area – however dirty and unpleasant – felt dislocated if the new blocks of flats bore no relation at all to where the old homes were. It is not just the changing skylines that Prince Charles complains about, or the changing road layouts, but new forms of living, new forms of lifestyle, new forms of transport, even new forms of organized religion.

After the Blitz came the slum clearances, and whole districts of Victorian terraced homes disappeared under the bulldozer in a frenzy of modernization. Nor were slums the only things that had disappeared in the redevelopment. The social cohesion and community links had weakened as well: the links that had sustained the communities during the Blitz and had provided advice and support to those who were now entirely dependent on the state.

The impact of traffic on the inner cities was especially marked, because the urban motorways that fed the big cities tended to be planned through the poorer areas. Inner city people were more exposed to the danger, noise and dirt of the motorized city. Children could no longer play safely on the streets.

Traffic flow and its requirements were all important in the 50s and 60s, and there was talk – as there is 20 years later – of London 'seizing up'. The British motorway programme began in the 60s, a generation after the autobahns of Germany opened: Britain's

Darker Corners

leading planner Sir Colin Buchanan says that he has still not caught his breath again since the time he first saw them in operation in 1937.[7] Hitler's road planning took the new profession of highway engineers and surveyors by storm as well: their visit in 1937 marked the beginning of the idea of major roads in the UK.

It was Buchanan who began to change attitudes with his crucial 1963 report *Traffic in Towns*. He saw that pedestrians must be protected from the burgeoning traffic, but there followed a profusion of overhead walkways and pedestrian underpasses, which have made the inner city environment even less inviting. The gleaming underpasses that so impressed planners in the later 1960s are now muggers' havens.

It was not until the 1970s that a brake was put on urban road projects, mainly because of the energy crisis of 1973. The controversial London 'motorway box' proposed by the GLC was abandoned after 1975. But some of the biggest road schemes stayed on the drawing boards, and played a key role in undermining the economics of parts of the inner cities. Under the threat of eventual redevelopment, owners were unable to sell their homes or shops – or to invest in them either. It may be no coincidence that some of the worst of the 1981 riots happened at places which had been 'blighted' by major road schemes. Brixton was to have been a big junction on London's 'motorway box', and under the latest London Road Assessment Studies of 1988 Brixton may play host to a similar blighting scheme all over again.

The greatest of all the changes in inner cities has been in housing design. Redevelopment with high rise and system built flats from the 50s to the 70s provided a large number of new homes at great speed, and a great deal of work for the building industry. But after the vast expenditure, much of it still not paid off by the local authorities, we found ourselves at the International Year of Shelter for the Homeless in 1987 back where we were when we started – except poorer. 103,000 families were homeless and the housing stock was probably as bad as it had been a generation before.

The high rise and system built flats have had a disastrous impact on inner cities, because they were concentrated there and have often finished their useful lives as the lowest possible rung on the housing ladder.

The disaster approached slowly. Criticism of the ideas were already drifting over from the USA as early as 1961, when Jane

Jacobs wrote that 'low income projects are worse than the slums they replace. This is not the rebuilding of cities,' she went on. 'This is the sacking of cities'.[8]

The first high rise flats, designed by the architect Sir Frederick Gibberd, were built in Harlow new town in 1950. Gibberd also designed probably the last local authority tower block, Nettleswell Tower also in Harlow, just before he died in 1983. Subsidies were given by the government for flats of over six storeys from 1956, and from 1963 Sir Keith Joseph as housing minister was busy encouraging the use of system building. It was widely taken up when the new Labour government under Harold Wilson interpreted the 'white heat of technological revolution' as meaning a target of up to 500,000 new homes a year.

The top building year was 1968, when just over 400,000 were completed. But their failure to reach an impossible target did not dampen the enormous ambitions of both politicians and professionals. Housing minister Richard Crossman recorded a meeting with developers in his famous diary, 'I asked why it was only 750 homes they were building in Oldham,' he wrote. 'Why not rebuild the whole thing?'

Speed was all-important. Tower blocks were not cheap to build – probably 25 per cent more per flat than low rise. System built panels also ran up against problems of sound proofing, and the improved panels were much heavier and more expensive. Yet money was not allowed to stand in the way. Professionals opposed to the idea were howled down at meetings – even in 1963 a government survey found that 71 per cent of tenants wanted to live at ground level – for it was felt that people had just not had the chance to experience the alternatives to ground floor living. Brochures by proud local authorities like the London County Council spoke of the dramatic effects under the heading 'Open Space, Tall Blocks'. Both open space and tall blocks turned out to be disasters.

The tide began to turn against tower blocks early one May morning in 1968, when there was an explosion in Mrs Ivy Hodge's Flat 90 of the 22-storey Ronan Point, in Newham, south London. The flats above the 18th floor, and the whole of the south east corner collapsed like playing cards. Five people were killed. The public inquiry that followed found that 60 mph winds could have had the same effect. But Ronan Point was rebuilt and was still in use more than a decade later, when a young mother threw herself from the 21st floor in another block on the same estate. Her name was April Merrin, and her constant pleas to be allowed to move had fallen on deaf ears in the council's housing department. The tragedy led to a political upheaval in Newham Borough Council, coinciding with the take-over of other Labour inner city councils by younger radical leaders. It also led to a vociferous and powerful campaign by tower block tenants in the area.

Tenants played a vital role in the campaigns that followed, spurred on by other deaths. Another mother in April Merrin's block threw herself to her death in 1985, and several children have been killed falling from balconies and windows from high blocks. Newham, like many other councils, forbids families with children being given flats above a certain height – because of the danger to toddlers, and the stress on their families keeping them away from windows or doors: Bristol researchers in 1986 found one mother so worried about the height that she kept her child lashed to the leg of a chair.

But the pressure from increasing homelessness has made such regulations more and more difficult to follow. Families have to go somewhere, and often they find themselves being offered and accepting high rise flats. When Michael Fenton fell to his death in 1988 at the age of just 20 months, from the tenth floor of another Newham tower block, tenants presented the chief housing officer with a wreath. 'We have 7,000 families on the transfer list,' he told them in reply, 'and just 150 houses a year to let.

Young children are still housed on upper storeys of Newham tower blocks, as they are in many other cities, with little prospect of taking them out. The Newham tenants' campaign focussed not so much on the psychological problems of living in the 'cities in the sky', but on the appalling conditions that tower blocks had disintegrated into, when the council barely had the funds for basic upkeep. They held 'cockroach days' and 'heating days' to draw attention to the problems, and organized the first nationwide conference on tower block living. After the conference, Ronan Point tenants Barry and Elaine Meakings invited the campaigning architect Sam Webb to their flat to look at some cracks in their concrete walls.

By March 1984, Newham Borough Council's housing officials had Webb's dossier on Ronan Point on their desks. The evidence of structural decay spoke for itself, and within two months councillors had agreed to empty the building and rehouse all the tenants.

Tenants crowding into the council chamber cheered the decision, and some were close to tears.

It was only when the block was empty that the council could carry out the ultimate experiment on Ronan Point. They wanted to test it to the point where it fell down, the only way of providing useful enough data on the Larsen-Neilsen system of construction which was used so widely in the 60s and 70s. The experimental fire they started had to be ended suddenly after just 12 minutes to stop it getting out of control. Movement between the wall and the floor was already twice the safety limit, and the press photographers fled as their safety glass shattered in the speed of the fire.

But Webb's report was even more worrying. He had found a weakness in some joints known as 'H2' that may have contributed to the 1968 collapse. Instead of being packed with mortar and fibre glass, as they should have been, Ronan Point's joints were supported with soft cardboard and a mixture of rubbish and cigarette ends, and it was this concoction that was keeping it up. 'When the collapsed part of Ronan Point was rebuilt, why were the defects in the H2 joints not discovered?' Webb asked the *Times* in October.

Ronan Point finally bit the dust in 1987, and the rubble was used for building the Barking relief road. Seven other tower blocks are due for demolition in Newham in 1989, but others may also be safety risks. The 23-storey James Sinclair Point, which Michael Heseltine visited in 1986, was already considered a 'fire hazard' and over 80 per cent of the tenants wanted to leave it. A year after Heseltine's visit, a panel wall blew in on the 15th floor in the great hurricane of October 1987. Six months later it was still being propped up by two temporary strips of timber.

Sam Webb's campaign about tower block safety continues. Tenants from the Royston Hill block in Glasgow took the council to court to force them to release the committee minutes from 1968–70 – which was when they decided that strengthening the block would cost too much. In January 1987, a group of Royston Hill tenants were told by a housing official that they had no need to worry about their flats because 'there's never been another explosion in a high rise block since Ronan Point.'[9]

The following morning an explosion ripped through the eighth floor of Wingate Towers in Liverpool, demolishing the internal walls and fire doors and putting six people in hospital. When the Glasgow tenants tried to phone their official to ask what he thought, he was permanently engaged. Like other housing officers, no doubt, he was pondering the implications of bad design combined with an appalling maintenance record and rising vandalism.

Nor have the low rise monster estates been any more successful. Many of the systems were warranted by the government's National Building Agency to last for 60 years, but the agency which by now would be facing angry councillors has long since disappeared.

The most extreme example of a failed system built estate is the notorious Divis Flats in West Belfast, built in the late 60s, where 2,500 people live in 12 decaying blocks: where tenants have to put up with backsurge from the drains into the baths, piles of rotting rubbish, rubble and asbestos. 'What we have here is men, women and children, thrown together and expected to live in conditions not fit for animals,' said Dr Hendron, the local GP and SDLP candidate. Problems at Divis reached a head in 1981 when the Divis 'Demolition Committee' began to wreck each flat that became vacant, so that they could not be re-let. Their offices were raided by the police and organizers charged with criminal damage, but Judge Doyle gave them only a nominal fine. 'Something must be done about Divis – and soon,' he told the court.

Divis is a Republican stronghold, and the problems are compounded by having an army helicopter pad on top of one of the blocks above the estate, and frequent military patrols. An exhibition called 'Demolish Divis' was held in London by the TCPA in 1985, opened by actor Stephen Rea. At the time of the exhibition it was estimated that 22 people had been shot there since the tenants first moved in. It is a frightening example of the extremes of urban decay.

The problems of cities in Northern Ireland are beyond the scope of this book; but even a brief look at the divisions of Belfast can give an idea of what could happen in extreme circumstances on the mainland. Like other British cities, Belfast lost its heavy industrial base long ago and has suffered years of neglect and growing inner city tensions. Now it finds its local government emasculated by direct rule, far beyond what has happened on the mainland, and responsibility for housing has been given to the Northern Ireland Housing Executive in an attempt to defuse discrimination. Without responsibilities, elected politicians have little to do but posture, playing into the hands of terrorists who have their roots deep in urban despair. It is terrifying to speculate that Belfast could be a vision of the future for other cities facing enormous economic problems without the powers to tackle them.

The religious divisions that fuel Ulster's violence are mirrored in many mainland inner cities by racial divisions that could be every bit as explosive, and which provide a whole new dimension to add to crime and deprivation. There are now around 1,000 racial attacks every year in London alone. Such attacks are on the increase, ranging from the destruction of temples, as in Coventry in 1981, to the murder by firebomb of a whole family in Ilford in 1985.[10] Black or ethnic minority tenants are often in the very worst housing because of their late arrival. They are statistically the most likely to suffer break-ins in councils flats. Indeed, Home Office figures show that Asians are 50 times more likely to be attacked than whites, and Africans or Caribbeans 36 times. Estates suffer from a series of problems, ranging from racist graffiti to arson attacks, muggings and murder.

Tenants associations are sometimes reluctant to tackle the problems of racial attacks. Local authorities' rules for evicting racial abusers are difficult to enforce, and when Newham Council actually did evict one family in Canning Town, for harassing a black neighbour in 1984, it can lead to a dangerous backlash of support for the abuser.

Race completes the vicious circle of crime and bad housing. The three are inextricably bound together, and in inner city 'sink' estates they are mixed in with every other conceivable social problem as well. The estates themselves are part of that circle. As one tenant from the Hulme estate in Manchester told a 1985 conference: 'It is these new slums, combined with high unemployment, that generate vandalism, destruction, illness and depression. These factors . . . breed an attitude that poverty itself is a crime and therefore we are all criminals, and Hulme is our punishment'.[11]

III

The cameras whirred, and environment secretary Kenneth Baker looked on proudly as contractors moved into the notorious Mozart Estate in Paddington — just 12 years after it had been completed. Their object was to remove four of the estate's concrete overhead walkways. As the walkways hung above on cranes, with the metal tubes hanging out of the end like veins, the other object of attention for the TV cameras was the diminuative figure of Professor Alice Coleman.

Dr Coleman of King's College London, a former schoolteacher and for 30 years a geographer and statistician, had plunged herself into controversy the year before with her trenchant assertion of the link between crime and overhead walkways – together with 15 other design features in many of the worst housing estates in inner city Britain. Her enthusiastic book *Utopia on Trial* was published in 1985, and won the interest and approval of both Prince Charles and, later, the Prime Minister. Dr Coleman's work turned her into one of the most controversial figures in housing through her argument that bringing children up in flats where they never learn to respect other people and their property can turn them towards crime. The simplicity of this viewpoint infuriates other housing pundits, especially on the Left, and has brought down a torrent of abuse: one academic even referred to her as a 'bitch'.

In Dr Coleman's tiny room in King's College is a graph mapping out the rise of crime since 1900. Looking at the graph she can point to the years where flats began to be built again in the 1930s as a reaction against all those suburban semis. She can point again to when they began to be built so assiduously under Harold Macmillan in the 1950s. The crime rate was also high in the time of Dickens, when the poor lived in rotting tenements. But as the tenements gave way to late Victorian terraced houses, there was a 50-year lull in crime. Dr Coleman argues this was because terraced homes, preferably with front gardens, are a far more successful way of 'socializing' children.

Adding front gardens to ground floor flats can turn menacing gangs of youngsters into polite kids, she believes. The reason is that instead of just banging on their friends' front doors and waiting for them to emerge, they must go through the garden and will tend to meet the parents, who can then greet them later on the estate: new relationships are thus built up between the generations.

'Traditional front gardens also teach respect for people as well as property,' she told the *London Evening Standard*. 'The child knows Mrs Jones as the lady with the yellow door and red roses, who talks to him and his parents. The more anonymous the estate, the more children see tenants as depersonalized units, and the less they refrain from violence.'

Building Futures

Alice Coleman's ideas coincided with a renewed public interest in crime after the 1981 and 1985 riots. 'Designing-out' crime became part of a wider debate that included a series of other ideas. Among these was the idea of 'community policing', a way of re-establishing personal links between people in the neighbourhood and the policemen on the beat. The idea that these links should be reforged has become increasingly accepted since it was put forward in the early 80s by the Chief Constable of Devon and Cornwall and former Metropolitan Police officer John Alderson. 'The police have to lead,' Alderson said, explaining the concept, 'to encourage self help and encourage the feeling of security through growth of care and the lowering of neighbourhood tensions, and to capitalize on existing social organizations to achieve these aims'.[12]

Also by 1983, many initiatives to combat crime in estates involved security measures by the developers. Bellway Homes, for example, provided extra locks, and because the houses took rather longer to escape from in a fire, smoke detectors as well.

There was also what became known as 'Management Improvement', pioneered by the Department of the Environment's Priority Estates Project (PEP), which began work on three estates in 1979. Management improvement meant asking the tenants what they wanted, and providing it: cleaning up graffiti as soon as possible, and cutting out the wait for housing repairs. Above all it meant involving tenants in the management and decisions affecting their own estate. One of the pioneers was Anne Power of the North Islington Housing Rights Project.

The PEP claims to be able to reduce crime and cut the number of empty flats, by concentrating resources, improving management and involving people. Within a year of PEP moving onto an estate, there is usually less vandalism and lower rent arrears. For example, when Anne Power set to work at the GLC's Tulse Hill estate, 90 of the flats were empty. Tenants were interviewed about what they wanted changed in the way the estate was run. A housing office was opened there and extra police patrols were diverted via the estate; eventually they also got their own repair team. As a result there was a near-miraculous 80 per cent drop in break-ins.

The local repairs also save money. 'Almost any estate with 20 or more empty units and a vandalism problem cannot but benefit from localized housing management and pay for itself,' wrote Anne Power. The Department of the Environment was impressed.

Darker Corners

But, Power warned, that – once started – the efforts must never let up.

Dr Coleman was less impressed with Management Improvement because she said it was not enough to cut down the crime statistics. PEP's newsletter of March 1985 carried the headline 'Hard work transforms a nightmare estate', with housing minister Ian Gow praising their work on one north London estate. Seven months later the transformation was less easy to perceive because this was Broadwater Farm before the riot which made it famous. By this time Coleman and her team at King's College had finished *Utopia on Trial*, and were feeling justified in their scepticism.

They were following the pioneering work of the American geographer Oscar Newman, the man who coined the term 'defensible space' – the space for which people felt responsible between their front doors and the garden gate. He found precious little of it in the council estates of New York. It was the American critic Jane Jacobs who first explained how residents must overlook space on the estate in order to prevent vandalism. But Newman's work in the early 70s had taken him to all 169 public estates in the city, looking at levels of crime and vandalism – which in one area had made necessary two armed guards on permanent duty at the local library.

Newman found four design points which seemed to attract crime. They included the parts of the estate which were not open to surveillance from anywhere, and the existence of alternative escape routes for the criminals – like the Mozart estate's overhead walkways, which could lead a mugger directly out of the estate after committing a crime. Also, people did not feel that they had any personal responsibility for the acres of shared grass around the estates, which soon became littered and vandalized. Visiting the notorious Aylesbury estate in south London, Newman recorded: 'It's almost as if creatures from another world have come down and built their own environment – it's that foreign'.

The Home Office commissioned a report to refute Newman's findings. As with the high rise blocks and tenements, the prevailing expert opinion was that 'American experience does not apply to Britain'. But to the surprise of Home Office officials, their studies of 52 London estates began to confirm Newman's findings. What's more they found that the higher the proportion of children on estates, the higher the crime rate tended to be – which was one of the factors behind the removal of children from big estates.

Building Futures

Alice Coleman was already known for her major survey of Britain, the Second Land Utilization Survey, and her work on wasteland and land for housing. She became increasingly interested in housing estates and Newman's work. When she decided to follow it up, she flew to New York to see him, but: 'he wasn't very keen to see me at first,' she said. Newman had been battered by angry attacks since he published his work – a phenomenon she was to discover for herself.

Her team's study of 4,099 estates in London and Oxford looked at evidence of anti-social behaviour which included litter within three metres of entrances, excrement, vandal damage or the proportion of children from the estate in care. From there they uncovered 15 design variables – and later a 16th – which seemed to have a relationship to crime. These included hidden entrances, walkways, internal corridors, and others which undermined a sense of identity and privacy. Each block was given a 'disadvantagement score' according to how many of the 16 design faults could be found there. The average of all 4,099 was 8.1 – private blocks on average were 4.0 and council blocks 9.1. Even within the blocks there was a difference: there were 10 crimes per 100 people on average in flats with landings, and as many as 17 on flats with internal corridors. The solution, she suggested, was to partition corridors so that people in each section began to know each other as a community, without the distraction of the rest of the neighbourhood walking through.

So what else should be done? Coleman suggested front doors that looked directly onto the street. Walkways could also be taken down, and each block separated from the others with their own piece of ground. The area nearest the flats could also be split up into front gardens for the ground floor tenants, each one with its own garden gate. Children especially should not be brought up in flats.

Utopia on Trial was a powerful attack, not just on the practice of local authority housing, but on the years of bad design that left out people's real needs. It had led to the situation where 'many people feel hopelessly trapped in barbarous barracks, unable to afford the price of escape into scarce private housing and dependent upon local authorities who have nothing better to offer.' Meanwhile, the 'DoE's Housing Development Directorate continues to act as a fountainhead of design wisdom and shrugs off all criticism.'[13] The government should, Coleman said later, 'phase the Department of the Environment Housing Development Division quietly out of existence and return housing initiative to the free market'. She pointed out that where the DoE had done its own design improvement at Clover Hall in Rochdale, they simply added to the social problems by removing all the party fences.

The DoE wheeled out their expert Anne Power from the Priority Estate Project to counter Dr Coleman as the champion of the Home Office. A gladiatorial battle was emerging. The Home Office was especially interested because of the chord Dr Coleman had struck with the police, some of whom felt she had given intellectual respectability to things they had always known in their hearts. Metropolitan Police commissioner Sir Kenneth Newman told her, 'In a way we already know all this from our own experience on the beat, but you have crystallized it scientifically'.

Coleman also found herself invited up to Liverpool by the Militant-backed leaders of the city council to give her approval of their massive housing programme – which had turned its back on flats and gone for semi-detached homes with gardens. Alice Coleman obliged: 'Liverpool has got it right,' she told the local paper. What she liked was the return to two-storey semi-detached homes in streets, avoiding the hated cul-de-sacs,. With their bay windows, bricks and front gardens, the Liverpool homes were an extraordinary turnabout by a city castigated, at the time, for its revolutionary zeal.

At the same time, design improvement had come to the attention of Sir Keith Joseph – himself responsible for some of the 60s housing developments during his term as minister. From Sir Keith, the ideas eventually reached Mrs Thatcher herself, who in 1988, decided on a major expansion of the experiments to test out the *Utopia on Trial* point of view. Three full-scale trials, costing £10 million and lasting for five years, have been commissioned from King's College by environment minister Nicholas Ridley – marking an acceptance from the DoE that Coleman's views need looking at. The projects 'will help us understand the complex relationships between design, environment and behaviour patterns,' said Ridley.[14] On these experiments may depend the future of mass housing.

IV

Does design improvement work? One of the problems in deciding this is that it has been tested on some of the worst estates where countless other 'miracle cures' have been tried – sometimes at the same time and backed by rival ministries. All of them could claim the improvements in vandalism as down to them.

Longbenton estate on Tyneside, for example, was part of the two year North Tyneside Crime Prevention Project set up in 1986. The Home Office paid for a committee of different agencies to run the project, which included a concerted campaign by the police to persuade tenants that crime was still only a very small risk, together with local housing management and some design improvements. By the end of the project, crime levels were much reduced. But who could claim the credit? Opponents of Alice Coleman's ideas argued that some particularly active local villains had been sent to jail just as the project started. The notorious Killingworth Towers – where burglary was so rife that burglars were said to find their own stolen furniture gracing the flat they had just broken into – had also been recently demolished.

At the Mozart Estate in Paddington, home for 3,500 people, the results were more clear cut. Coleman had awarded it a design disadvantagement score of 12.8 out of 16, and efforts to improve the estate's security had failed before Alice Coleman, Kenneth Baker and the cranes removed the four overhead walkways. At first the DoE had refused to fund the Coleman plan, which included getting rid of the children's play areas – 'schools for vandalism', Coleman called them, but then money became available to remove just four walkways and see what happened. Each weighed 100 tons, and had to be burnt loose at a cost of £96,000.

The beat policemen were asked to monitor any changes. Sure enough, in the same week that the walkways came down – splitting the estate into separate blocks – the burglary rate dropped by 55 per cent, settling down to about a quarter of what it had been. Further experiments were delayed, partly because of battles among rival tenants' associations, and the long-term impact on the crime rate remains disputed.

Results aside, Dr Coleman has found herself the subject of heavy abuse from critics. 'She is not interested in the possibility of multiple centres', said the planning critic Alison Ravetz. The radical architect Brian Anson called Dr Coleman's supporters 'determinists' who believed that tenants simply could not help themselves. 'Their answer to the petrol bomb-throwing kid is "Take away his walkway!" Is this the way to solve the social malaise?'[15] Many believe that living in flats and having front gardens has only a minimal effect on the crime rate compared to the massive influences of unemployment, poverty, the consumer society, television and the collapse of values? Even after the gardens are in place and the walkways are gone, there will still be enormous poverty.

The vision of family life conjured by Alice Coleman's garden fences is reminiscent of Mrs Thatcher's 'Victorian values' – where people respect each other's property, and tend to own the homes they live in as well. People brought up in flats, said Coleman, have 'no inbuilt sense of a socially stable environment. They accept lower standards as normal.' Language like that leads to anger from people who are irritated by what they see as 'bourgeois values'.

Dr Coleman never set out to cure the basic ills of society. 'There will always be some crime,' she says. As an attack on the inhumanity of mass housing design since the 30s, *Utopia on Trial* is powerful and unanswerable, but the book's ideas are not the only answer to crime.

The problem is that, as an analysis of the cause of crime, she leaves poverty out of the picture completely. The statistics by themselves do not make it clear what is cause and what is effect.

When the DoE did their own research in the 70s, they found that there were more complicated forces at work. Why otherwise could they find some tower blocks with little vandalism or crime.

It was this that made them focus on management as the key issue, and led them to back Anne Power of the Priority Estates Project, which is now undergoing a two-year review to see if their results are as successful as they claim. At the same time PEP is moving on to its next stage, setting up 'Estate Management Boards', with a majority of tenants, as legally responsible for running their estates in six different cities.

The debate on crime and housing continues. Among the most interesting changes are the shifts in opinion on the way places and houses ought to be designed. How can professionals breathe life into the places they create? More difficult, how can they breathe life into the concrete anonymous places that have been created in the previous generation, the street levels without doors or windows, and expanses of paved pedestrian areas.

The movement to bring more vitality and diversity to inner city streets, pioneered by Jane Jacobs in America, finally came home officially when the architect-planner Francis Tibbalds was elected president of the Royal Town Planning Institute in 1988. Tibbalds launched his presidency with a speech in support of Prince Charles, calling for colourful, designs on a human scale. Housing estates should be 'good, interesting, decorative new buildings, sensitively integrated' – for the sort of town plan 'in which one's mother doesn't become confused and lost,' said Tibbalds. 'No more will people say "planners do it with their eye's shut".' The message was not a new one, but it came from the top of the profession. It was no coincidence that the design of the controversial Canary Wharf mega-development in the Isle of Dogs, announced the same year, was very different from the kind of development that left drawing boards even five years before. The artists' impressions included more intricate streets, with stone buildings, and statues and sculptures in post-modernist style.

But the fact remains that there is very little public housing being built, and very little private sector housing that can possibly be described as 'affordable'. Many people in inner cities are unaffected by changes in design fashions, still living in the mistakes of the past, without any prospect of finding anywhere else. Can the old estates be radically improved?

One of the great success stories for the re-design approach has been Lea View House in Hackney. Lea View was a 'sink' estate, dirty and hard to let, with 90 per cent of its council tenants wanting to move out. Theft and muggings were common – until it became the scene of the first refurbishment scheme to fully involve the people who lived there.

Hackney Council appointed the architecture firm Hunt Thompson Associates, which was to rise to prominence as one of the foremost firms of community architects. Hunt Thompson set up an office in Flat 3 of the estate, with four staff, and started organizing visits for the tenants to similar refurbishment schemes so that they could see what they wanted. The plans were drawn up by both sides.

The council's direct labour organization arrived on site to start work one morning in 1982 to find an estate that had in some ways been transformed already. They were greeted by a banner with the words 'HELLO DLO' and an invitation to a breakfast party. By Christmas the two sides of 'Them' and 'Us' were getting on so well that there were joint parties between the workforce and the tenants.

The tenants involved were pleased with the final results: 'I just walk around my flat. I'm so chuffed with it. It's been worth every meeting,' said tenant Dolly Pritchard.[16] But there was another change after the work was over: crime and vandalism had been almost wiped out. By 1987 there had still been no break-ins at all.

Wigan House, a block on the same estate, was refurbished at the same time under the same government guidelines — but without involving the tenants — and reverted to being a slum within six months. They were soon boarding up the ground floor flats again. 'At Wigan it is difficult to believe that there was an identical tenant population living there as at Lea View,' wrote John Thompson in the *Urban Design Quarterly*. 'Basically, bad environments destroy people.'[17]

So what is going on? Behind both Alice Coleman's ideas and the work of the Priority Estates Project there is a 'hidden agenda' of tenant control and community architecture. From all of them there is evidence that *what people feel they have created, they then protect*.

In other words, tenants used to feel it was nothing to do with them if they found kids spraying the walls — but the process of participation makes them more likely to intervene confidently. Even at Broadwater Farm, where tenants have taken many of the decisions about spending there since the riots, vandalism has been cut and it now has the second lowest crime rate in Haringey borough. Among their projects has been building a memorial garden for both the people who died during riots of 1985. Their design works have helped create 150 jobs.[18]

Defensible space encourages people to feel responsible for the land between their front window and their hedge — or so the theory goes. The question is how to make people feel responsible for the whole estate? Getting involved in running or improving estates has to be a collective process, which means that people get to know and trust each other more. It means that they can identify strangers and challenge them, or at the very least watch over their neighbours. Getting together provides a way of breaking out of the siege mentality in many big estates, where people feel increasingly barricaded in. But it also means that tenants must understand the process they are taking part in.

Professions have tended to feel that groups of amateurs would not be able to understand plans and projects — let alone reach agreement about complicated planning or architectural concepts. But techniques for helping them are being developed. Dr Tony

Building Futures

Gibson of Nottingham University's Education for Neighbourhood Change group has been one of the most influential, producing a series of cardboard 'games' which can help neighbourhoods take decisions about their environment. It was Gibson who first coined the phrase, borrowed later by Prince Charles, that professionals should be 'on tap, not on top'.

Dr Gibson produced the action kits as a way of finding an answer to his own question – 'why do the talkers always win?'. Taking control of the environment 'cannot be done merely by talking', he told a conference of community architects in 1986. 'These [talkers] will be mainly professionals, leaving the rest of the community alienated, or unable or unwilling to contribute their own special knowledge, experience and judgement'. His widely-used kit 'Planning for Real' uses cardboard cut-outs to build large three-dimensional maps of a neighbourhood. These can then be altered by groups of local people, moving cardboard schools, playing fields, car parks or bus stops, as they work out how they want their area changed.

Planning for Real was developed in the early 1970s, with over four years of tests with children in classrooms. Teachers found that it kept the bright pupils interested, but also motivated those who were usually silent. The experiments eventually came to the ears of the Department of the Environment, which suggested trying it with adults. The game became known in DoE-speak as 'Manipulative Display' – Mandy for short.

The first full trial took place in 1977 in the Dalmarnock area of east Glasgow, and it has since been used over and over again – especially when tenants want to come up with plans of their own for wasteground. Planning for Real has been used in King's Cross, Nottingham, and even after an earthquake in Italy, but most notably in Birkenhead, where local people were able to cluster round, moving the cut-outs to represent zebra-crossings, or gardens, or whatever they felt they needed, on a massive 25ft by 5ft model of the neighbourhood. It was taken round in sections to bingo halls, clubs and schools, and the whole process resulted in a draft plan for the area and a changed relationship between locals and officials. 'You think of them as government officials and they are up there and you are below,' said one resident. 'But since we have got more involved in the model and the housing estate, you are getting to know more of them and what they do, and they are getting to know more of what we do and you are getting closer...

They turn out to be the same as you!'[19] As a result, local people took over the empty Laird School of Art as an 'enterprise centre' in an area of high unemployment. The Laird eventually won a Times/RIBA Community Enterprise Award, presented by Prince Charles in 1986.

Decision-making techniques became more complicated when they were needed to plan the housing co-operatives in Liverpool, where architect Bill Halsall found himself taking groups on bus tours around similar developments so that they could imagine the choices before them a little more clearly. When it came to deciding who will have which home, Halsall used large maps of the site. Co-op members then milled round using markers to show which house they wanted, shifting round to be next to the people they wanted to have as neighbours, until a compromise was reached. It put the lie to the much-quoted opinion that ordinary people are not able to make decisions like that, and that they must be made instead – and often made badly – by distant officials.

There are other projects which have involved people in tackling crime more directly. Neighbourhood Watch schemes are well-known, and some estates such as Barrowfield, next to Glasgow's Celtic football ground, have set up their own community security patrols. Inner city estates have enormous problems of crime and alienation, and even when energetic local groups of people get together to tackle these problems in their own spare time, they are often undermined by lack of funds or by patronizing bureaucracy. Yet the evidence is that giving opportunities to these kind of groups can make a real difference. Whether closer relationships between professional 'enablers' and tenants really can have long-term effects remains to be seen, but involving people may at least be a good starting point to look for answers to the problem.

Crime, alienation and now drugs are among the worst problems facing society, and they are suffered in inner cities in an intense form. And in many ways crime and alienation are different sides of the same coin. Community pioneer Paddy Doherty of the Derry Inner City Project said as he received the first Times/RIBA Community Enterprise Award from Prince Charles, that 'apathy is frozen violence'.

They may be a danger in melting that apathy, of turning it into violence. It may also be that governments prefer having drug-ridden, sullen but hopeless inner cities to coping with them as riot areas. But the point is that apathy is not far removed from

Building Futures

violence, and we need to find ways out of the vicious circles that breed both.

Institutionalizing the inner cities since the war seems to have deepened the spirals. We need instead a series of partnerships between people and professionals to confront the problems. Neither side can manage alone.

4

FROM GARDEN CITY TO CITY GARDEN

Some people have probably wondered about the relevance of organizing a garden festival in a derelict area of Liverpool. I think it is most appropriate.

HM the Queen, 2.5.84

The colour that most people associate with inner cities is grey. It is the colour of drab housing estates and abandoned factories. Although there are brighter colours in the litter and peeling advertizing hoardings, grey is the dominant shade of the old decaying centres of cities. The movement to transform that colour to green is one of the most exciting processes of regeneration.

Until recently, the flowers and plants growing on derelict parts of cities were despised as weeds. An overgrown, derelict site was considered a sign of decay, and replaced with easy-to-maintain concrete wherever possible. It was not surprising that the counter-attraction of healthy, natural living led people to leave the inner cities if they could possibly afford to. The Germans have dubbed this 20th century phenomenon *Die Flucht ins Grune* – 'the flight to the green'.

Greening the inner cities is an attempt to reverse this, and it starts with a series of questions. Why should the flight to the green necessarily be *out* of the cities? Do cities *have* to be grey and smoky, and can our vision of cities begin to change?

BUILDING FUTURES

Challenging the traditional concept of what inner cities mean has resulted in wildlife sanctuaries and farms flourishing where lorry parks used to be, vegetables growing next to shopping centres, and downtown rivers smelling better. The derelict remains of Britain's first industrial revolution are giving way to nature, under both official and unofficial pressure.

In 1971, at the height of the property boom, London's first inner city farm appeared in a run-down part of Kentish Town – providing a strange contrast between city and country, cow dung and concrete. The originator of this unlikely project was Ed Berman, an American street theatre organizer, who thought up the idea one afternoon when he was working in a disused timber yard above a north London railway embankment. Berman was a Rhodes scholar who had trained as a Biblical archaeologist. Since arriving in Britain at the end of the 1960s, his group Inter-Action had been organizing 500 street theatre performances every year in the most deprived inner city areas of Britain. The Kentish Town timber yard and derelict buildings had been lent to Inter-Action as a headquarters at a peppercorn rent by Camden Borough Council.

As he walked round this forgotten corner of London, Berman noticed that the patch of soil where the timber sleepers used to be stacked had not been touched for a generation at least. Nor had the land with the wildflowers beside the railway line, next door to his timber yard. And he remembered how in city after city, he and his colleagues had found the same thing: newly-built housing estates with piece of tarmac set aside for the children – while over the wall or through the fence would be a stretch of abandoned wasteland, usually owned by British Rail or the local authority. This would be covered with flowers and undergrowth, and filled with the kind of mysterious rubble and holes which are so irresistible to children.

The Kentish Town site also included derelict stables, which had once housed railway shunting ponies. This gave Berman the idea of turning the stables into farm buildings, so that they could keep animals and grow vegetables. They could even set up a riding school, which was to be the only one in the capital not owned by the Queen.

City Farm 1 opened the following year, spilling over onto the British Rail land next door. A British Rail property board official arrived at the site in a chauffeur-driven car to witness for himself the chickens, ducks, geese and goats. Berman had been able to beg and borrow a great deal of what they needed to equip the farm – the staircase in the stables came from a West End production of *No No Nanette* – and the whole enterprize had cost just £6,000 to create.

Some of the people who lived nearby became involved. There was an old people's gardening club, and the local toughs helped organize riding for the mentally handicapped – the same people that had thrown stones at them in the street before. As the word spread and the farm grew, up to 50,000 children from schools all over London were being sent on visits every year, and many more were brought by their parents or friends.

Almost 20 years later, City Farm 1 still thrives in Kentish Town, and more than 60 others like it have been set up around the country – many in the most depressed inner city areas. They are symptoms of a change in the way people think about cities, a realization that the green of the countryside can also be part of city-living. In fact, unless those inner cities are treated with the care usually given to country environments, the forces for regeneration are unlikely to work for long.

II

In the early 1980s, it was still possible to hear local councillors arguing about whether to choose the merits of jobs and housing *or* the environment for inner city people: about whether the quality of housing, and the landscaping around it, should be sacrificed to increase the numbers of homes. A similar battle was taking place between academics and planners: between those who believed that the drift of people from cities to the suburbs or countryside should be stemmed – and those who thought that people should be helped to leave. Today the green cities movement has come to represent an alliance between these two opposing intellectual forces which have dominated thinking for the past century.

For the British, cities have traditionally been unpleasant, corrupt and unhealthy. It was not until 1833 that the government got around to looking at 'the best means of securing open spaces in the vicinity of populous towns'. The first public park was built by Joseph Paxton – the man who later designed the Crystal Palace – in Toxteth, which was the inspiration for Central Park in New York.

The traditional city, surrounded by a declining and poverty-stricken countryside, was turned on its head in 1899 by Ebenezer Howard, the House of Commons shorthand writer who invented and built two garden cities. His book *Tomorrow: A Peaceful Path to Real Reform* still reads with extraordinary clarity and force, and includes the famous diagram of three magnets pulling people in three different directions. One of the magnets was called *Town*, and is described by Howard with words like 'slums', 'gin palaces', 'foul air', and 'unemployment'. Then there is *Country*, which has 'land lying idle', 'hands out of work' and – interestingly, because we don't perceive this as a particularly rural problem today – 'no public spirit'. The third magnet includes the best of both worlds, and is labelled *Town-Country:* it has 'bright homes and gardens' and 'no smoke, no slums'.[1]

This is Howard's proposed garden city, where people could live in a pleasant, healthy environment, and have a stake in the land. The idea was that the prototype Garden City would benefit both town and country. It would give opportunities outside the city, and would channel work and money back to the declining rural areas. But Howard's 'marriage of town and country' was also meant to have an effect on London, so that it would stop being what the Prime Minister Lord Rosebery called a 'tumour, an elephantiasis sucking into its gorged districts half the life and the blood and the bone of the rural districts.'[2] Garden cities would end over-crowding and improve the health and life of the city people left behind.

Howard wanted London to be cut to a fifth of its population, which meant that garden cities would have to be popular enough to attract a very large number of people. 'These wretched slums will be pulled down, and their sites occupied by parks, recreation grounds and allotment gardens', wrote Howard optimistically. Little did he know that within two generations, the extra space would be taken up by towering modern slums, vandalized wasteland and municipal grass which nobody walks on.

Howard and the garden city evangelicals set to work. In three months in 1908 he gave 38 lectures in draughty halls around the country.[3] While the eminent men recruited to the cause were pamphleteering and lecturing, Howard pottered around Hertfordshire on his bicycle and bought the site for Letchworth, the first garden city.

Critics have accused Howard and his successors of being 'anti-city', of sucking investment away from the inner areas into new towns. The Left were also suspicious of Howard's blueprints. They wanted the state to be responsible for helping the poor, rather than relying on people moving out of the cities voluntarily, and they doubted whether it would be the urban poor who would benefit from the first garden cities. Their suspicions might have been confirmed by George Orwell, who after a visit to Welwyn in the 1930s wrote: 'If only the sandals and the pistachio-coloured shirts could be put into a pile and burnt, and every vegetarian, teetotaller and creeping Jesus sent home to Welwyn Garden City to do his yoga exercises quietly!'[4]

In fact, inner London was changing, even as Howard wrote. The city's population began to drop in 1911, and at one stage Londoners were moving out to country towns at a rate of 50,000 a year. Yet the great opportunity to improve the inner city environment with parks and open spaces has never been taken in a systematic way. The National Playing Fields Association's goal of ten acres of public space for every 1,000 people, formulated in 1925, has never been achieved – even though there has been land lying idle because of the drift of industry and people away from cities. According to the Civic Trust, an area twice the size of Leeds is now derelict in British cities. A decade ago, a Department of the Environment consultant found that as much as 11 per cent of Liverpool – three quarters of it owned by Liverpool City Council – was wasted.[6]

New towns alone have clearly failed to live up to their promise of improving the old cities. Environment ministers who were also inner city MPs – like Labour's Bob Mellish from Bermondsey – asked themselves why they had been so busy encouraging industry to move out to the new towns, when their own constituents needed the jobs so much. Increasingly, experts came to believe that the best way to help the city environment was not starting afresh somewhere else. A new 'pro-city' consensus emerged, condemning the thinking that had encouraged people and factories to leave the big cities, believing that some of the greenery of the countryside could be provided in urban areas as well.

The green city movement is often described as opposing the 'anti-city' lobby of new towns and garden cities. In fact it seems to be one place in the debate which unites all sides in a combination of both traditions. The garden city idealists no longer accuse their opposition of squeezing people into cities, of 'town cramming'. Equally, few practitioners would agree with the American architectural writer Jane Jacobs, when she wrote that planning in the Howard tradition was just about creating grass for 'Christopher Robin to go hoppety hop'.[8]

Instead the enthusiasm for bringing the countryside into town has combined with sheer anger about the neglect of inner cities. The two together means that the wasted space can be used to achieve some of Howard's ideals *in the cities*. Howard's own campaign for garden cities shows how this alliance has developed. The Town and Country Planning Association (TCPA), which he set up in 1899, remains an enthusiastic supporter of the theory of new towns, but has also been at the forefront of campaigns to tackle inner city problems by improving the environment, and setting up a centre to help people to organize their own greening projects in Manchester. The TCPA also played a major role in an Anglo-American conference to pool ideas, the Green Towns and Cities Congress of 1984, which attracted 350 park managers, planners and landscapers to Liverpool. The permanent campaign 'think green' was the result.

The movement as a whole has become a varied and powerful lobby, towards encouraging wild spaces and luxuriant greenery for the inner cities.

III

Attitudes to wildlife in the city vary considerably. Some see it as a nuisance, or a symptom of inner city decay. But there are others who realize it can be valuable in itself and for others. A succession of naturalists began to see it in a more positive light, until landscape architect Chris Baines popularized the idea of city wildlife by trudging through it in his gumboots on BBC television's *The Wild Side of Town*.[9]

After the series, nature in inner cities began to be recognized as an untapped resource. Up to 200 remnants of ancient woodland which once covered the whole of Greater London can still be found. London's River Lea or the New River – the 400-year-old canal which used to bring drinking water 38 miles into London – has become a haven of unexpected flora and fauna. In some Victorian cemeteries the monstrous tombs and graves have all but disappeared in the undergrowth of grass, blackberries and thistles: walking past Karl Marx's tomb, through the overgrown Highgate cemetery in London, is one way of experiencing the triumph of nature over man.[10]

Bomb sites left untouched since the Second World War were also providing nature for the cities. Shakespeare Road, in the heart of Brixton, is next to the railway line to Victoria, where the seeds of rare varieties of birch and sallow coppices originally came there on trains from Kent.[11] A strong local campaign was fought to save the site in its overgrown and cluttered state when it was bought by a housing developer in 1986. Unfortunately, when the developer lost the public inquiry because the inspector decided that the site's natural history was too valuable to lose, he sent the bulldozers in leaving only the few trees protected by Tree Preservation Orders.

Despite setbacks like these, progress was being made. In 1977 the naturalist Bunny Teagle spilled a pint of beer over George Barker of the Nature Conservancy Council (NCC) in a Manchester pub. As a result of their introduction Teagle was commissioned to survey wildlife sites in the West Midlands, and the report *An Endless Village* was published at breakneck speed by the NCC – fascinating the media with the stories of rare spiders and voles nesting under Spaghetti Junction.[13]

The intellectual basis for interest in urban wildlife came from the landscape architect Nan Fairbrother – whose name was used for the amalgam of British urban wildlife groups formed in 1985. Her book *New Lives, New Landscapes* was published in 1970, just before she died, and questioned why the little greenery surviving in cities always had to be tidy, clipped and soulless. 'The choice is not between old and new but between good and bad,' she wrote. 'The true tragedy is not that the old must go but that the new should be bad.' Good meant variety, and for Fairbrother and many of the others who have led the way in the revival of cities, variety makes places that are more exciting, more lively – and above all, more human.

The campaigner for urban wildlife, Chris Baines, discovered his enthusiasm as a result of a serious motor accident. When he came round in a Sussex hospital, he began to feel that the conventional landscape architecture he had been doing was wrong. Why, he asked later, should an estimated £1,000 million spent every year in Britain just to mow municipal grass not be spent on something more exuberant and heart-warming – on *real* greening. By then it was clear that creating 'abandoned' wild landscapes cost between a tenth and a quarter of conventional landscape design. Baines saw how conventional city landscaping had led to innumerable versions of the flat soulless turf of Burgess Park, built on a bomb site in south London, empty of people and surrounded by a wire fence. This was better than rubble – but not much better.

Using nature as part of urban design began to be practised

throughout Europe in the 1970s. Similar projects were also appearing in British towns, often inspired by the former Nature Conservancy Council director Max Nicholson. His firm Land Use Consultants was transforming slag heaps in Stoke-on-Trent into a forest park, and designing a wooded housing estate on the derelict Catterick Garrison in Yorkshire. It was also Land Use Consultants which built London's first ecological park, opening after enormous volunteer efforts for the Queen's Silver Jubilee in May 1977 on a rubble-strewn lorry park next to Tower Bridge. It cost just £2,000. The three-acre park was part of the Jubilee walkway, the route the Queen took at the height of the celebrations, and included mature trees and shrubs, freshwater pools and rock plants – a man-made ecosystem with frogs, newts and slow-worms. The William Curtis Ecological Park lasted seven years, closing in 1985 when it had been agreed to hand it over to developers. By this time the park had played host to 25,000 schoolchildren, and to a long procession of politicians, planners and landscape architects.

By the time the William Curtis had disappeared under concrete, other reserves had opened – and there are now over 300 in British cities. One of them is the Gunnersbury Triangle in North London, which is made up of allotments cut off from the outside world by three railway lines, and now turned into woodlands. Gunnersbury was at the centre of one of a number of public planning inquiries in the mid-1980s where planning inspectors became keen to protect city wildspaces. Conservationists managed to defeat development plans for wildlife sites at six of the nine public inquiries between 1983 and 1987. In his report on the Crayford Marshes in Bexley, the inspector was inspired to write : 'To see a heron land or take off, hear the flight call of a redshank or spot other birds among the network of water-filled ditches (intriguing to the ecologist, amateur or professional), is to appreciate the intrinsic value of the area'.[14]

Officialdom was becoming intrigued by green ideas. Manchester was among the cities that led the way, developing green 'fingers' of parkland along the river valleys and deep into the city, providing people who lived there with easy access to woods and lakes. As early as 1975, Greater Manchester county councillors had agreed a programme of restoration, and since then they have been active cleaning valleys and setting up country parks on the edges of the city. In the eight years before 1982 over 4,000 acres were restored and nine million new trees planted.

Despite this enthusiasm, some officials still found it hard to understand the new green ideas. In 1978, the GLC preferred to spend nearly £150,000 building a car park on a derelict site on the Hackney Marshes, rather than giving the go-ahead for a city farm which would have cost them nothing. When the Weller Street housing co-operative in Liverpool was putting the finishing touches to their homes they were advised by city council experts against the shrubbery or plants they wanted for the landscape scheme. 'Nice-coloured tarmac' was much easier to maintain, they were told. 'You can have red or green.'[15]

Housing co-operatives like Weller Street are important in the greening process. They are among the many small groups involved in partnerships with officials or large organizations to get the resources to where they are needed. One such partnership is UK 2000, formed under the chairmanship of Richard Branson, providing 5,000 temporary jobs in the environment. UK 2000 is a grouping of seven green organizations, from Friends of the Earth to the Tidy Britain Campaign, which co-ordinates the work and resources. It was said to have originated with Mrs Thatcher's horror at all the litter she saw during a drive between Heathrow and Number 10, but in fact its origins lie in a report by the Dartington Institute, which noted that public parks were deteriorating, and recommended an Urban Environment Commission to set up.

Other idead were also at work. 'We looked at the beautiful things in the country and wondered why they could not be recreated in the city,' said one young Liverpool geography graduate, Grant Luscombe, in 1975, who promptly set up the Rural Preservation Association to support small groups which were working to green the inner cities. It operated – in spite of the name – in some of the city's most deprived urban areas. In1979 they launched the Greensight Project, an 'ecological' approach to urban regeneration, with Liverpool City Council,the MSC and other local organizations. The idea was to plant shrubs, trees and grass and build gardens and meadows on 26 derelict sites in Toxteth. The project began on sites where homes had been demolished and never redeveloped, and went on to fill some of the gaps in the streets. When the riots erupted less than three years later, the gardens survived, even though many other buildings were destroyed.

The idea of giving away plants as a way of enriching people's

BUILDING FUTURES

lives has been taken even further in the small American town of North Bergen, New Jersey, where 72-year-old major Leo Gattoni organized 40,000 vegetable plants to be given away free, paying for some of them out of his own pocket. The idea was been a runaway success. Vegetable plants appeared all over the town, from fire escapes to doorsteps or street corners, and Mayor Gattoni is planning to extend the scheme.

Cabbage plants all over town are not very neat. But the urban green movement is actually aiming for inner cities which are *less* tidy than the conventional planners' ideal of homes, factories and roads all neatly separated from each other. There is also an administrative untidiness in that there are now far more organizations involved in improving the environment: voluntary groups, residents' and tenants' associations and civic societies are all making themselves responsible for small corners of neighbourhoods. Comprehensive redevelopment is giving way to a voluntary local approach that works from site to site.

With volunteers providing the main source of energy, there is inevitably a problem in the most run-down areas where fewer people are prepared to take on the work that needs doing. Problems also became apparent in the aftermath of the environment schemes which were part of Michael Heseltine's armoury when he was given special responsibility for Merseyside. Money for small green improvement schemes was suddenly available, but few considered how these improvements were to be maintained after the builders had gone – or if they did, their conclusions were not passed on to most of the communities involved. There are now derelict sites all over Merseyside, improved just a few years ago, which are once again full of rubbish.

Heseltine's first garden festival scheme in Liverpool in 1984 inspired thousands of Merseysiders to send in their spare bluebells, in response to an urgent SOS. It was hailed as a great success, the biggest land reclamation scheme in Europe. It used £10 million in derelict land grant and planted as many as 6,000 oaks, and was followed by garden festivals in Stoke-on-Trent in 1986 and Glasgow in1988, with one planned for Gateshead in1990. But Stoke lost over £5 million and ended in recriminations.

Today much of the 250-acre Liverpool site is fenced off and closed to the public, awaiting redevelopment. Glasgow's site has been taken over by developers Laings, who already owned it. The government has decided not to back any more garden festivals after Ebbw Vale in 1992.

Yet there have been enormous spin-off benefits from all the festivals. One reason why Liverpool festival's success was not permanent may be that the whole project had little to do with local people. Rod Hackney, the president of the Royal Institute of British Architects and Prince Charles' unofficial architectural 'adviser', put it like this: 'Unemployed bricklayers in Toxteth and Stoke-on-Trent watched bemused as large organizations with their outside workforces set about erecting the International Garden Festival . . . Perhaps the large losses made by these festival schemes would not have happened had the organizations used the local human resources available to them.'

Simply moving into the inner city areas with a chequebook, measuring tape and a team of workmen is not enough. At best the sites simply revert back to their original state. At worst, the work tends alienate any local organizations that — against the odds — have managed to find a role.

So two problems have emerged. How can public money reach the communities that need it most to improve their own environment? And second, how can local people be brought into the greening process — or for that matter, the development process — so that they can feel a pride in their own achievements and make them last?

IV

'The inner cities are not a human desert,' wrote Lord Scarman after the 1981 Brixton riots. The 'wasted people' who live there can be — and *must* be — involved in the process of improving their own neighbourhoods.

But involving them was easier said than done. Officials had been toying with 'participation' in planning for years. But could local people actually *initiate* plans themselves? Those that wanted to were caught by Catch-22: they had no professional plans, and without them they could not persuade anybody to put up the money. Yet without money, there was little chance of getting plans drawn up.

Community technical aid centres grew up in the inner cities in response to this problem. Neighbourhood groups can go there for assistance from a series of professionals — landscape architects, planners, fund-raisers, solicitors, surveyors — all under one roof, taking on projects ranging from £150,000 leisure centres to cleaning up small patches of wasteland. They can have applications for grants drawn up in a way most likely to appeal to funding bodies, or plans prepared so that they are cost-effective. This 'enabling' process has become part of the 'hidden agenda' of greening the cities.

The first statutory planning participation was enshrined in the 1968 Town and Country Planning Act. The notices in the press which the act made compulsory read like archaic legal English – but they were a first step towards informing people. Then came the 1969 Skeffington Report on *People in Planning*, which called for a better system to publicize planning applications. There was also a suggestion that a national network of centres should be set up where people could go for advice about planning problems. The Town and Country Planning Association made a start in 1972 with their National Planning Aid Unit, referring community groups to a nationwide network of volunteer advisers. But the unit lost its government grant in 1986 after they campaigned to pull down the notorious Divis Flats in West Belfast. Skeffington's ideas were never implemented properly.

Resources began to be available to the inner cities after the expansion of the Urban Programme. Community groups were able to turn protest into something more positive, but they needed professional skills. They also had to battle against experts who believed it was impossible for neighbourhoods to agree on issues like where the public benches should be, or how their new homes should be designed. Most important, they needed a new kind of professional – someone who was answerable to them, not to the council; someone who could match expertize with their own detailed knowledge about the needs and possibilities of their own neighbourhood.

The answer has been the spread of community technical aid centres in inner cities. The voluntary arts group Free Form first discovered the need when they were painting murals on the walls of derelict sites in the East End of London. The Rural Preservation Association – now Landlife – discovered the same need as they distributed pot plants in Liverpool. City Farm 1 in Kentish Town gave birth to its own technical aid team to help people set up more farms like theirs.

Within a short time there were organizations set up specifically to provide technical aid. COMTECHSA (Community Technical Services Agency) was set up in Liverpool in 1979, and CTAC

(Community Technical Aid Centre), was launched in Manchester by the TCPA at the same time There are now nearly 80 similar organizations. Most of the success stories – and there are many of them – are on a small scale, organized over long periods of time by indefatigable community groups. Groups of people decide they need a community centre, garden or church and know of wasted or derelict space. They then go to a centre and together draw up detailed plans, translating their ideas into professional designs. Hence the successful completion of a Sikh temple in Cheetham Hill, Manchester in 1987, a Krishna temple in Bolton and a Bengali Centre in London's East End – all joint projects between technical aid centres and local religious communities.

These new techical aid professionals see themselves as outside the conventional divide between private sector developers and public sector experts. They aim to be 'on tap but not on top' – the phrase borrowed from the movement by Prince Charles – 'barefoot' planners, living and working among community groups to spread expertize and, with it, power. Inevitably they had an uneasy relationship with the old-style architects, and some enthusiasts felt that the official body, the Royal Institute of British Architects (RIBA), was trying to keep these community schemes within the old framework of professional and client. It was an argument that recurred repeatedly as the new professionals grew in influence.

In October 1982, 29 people met in Liverpool to exchange information about different technical aid services and methods, and the result was the Association of Community Technical Aid Centres (ACTAC) – launched a year later by the then environment minister Sir George Young. ACTAC has been hampered since then by funding difficulties, but they have been instrumental in setting up the National Community Partnership (NCP) to present a joint front for the voluntary sector at national level. The Department of the Environment has funded technical aid since 1982 on a 50-50 basis, and they have achieved at least £14 million worth of schemes since then.[16] By 1986, CTAC Manchester estimated they were working on £3 million worth of projects at any one time.

Technical aid has grown up alongside the better-documented community architecture movement. Community architects draw their inspiration from architects like Ralph Erskine, who opened a local office in a disused undertakers when he was working on the Byker estate in Newcastle in 1969, and Walter Segal, who helped families build their own timber-framed homes in Lewisham in the late 1970s.

Prince Charles was fascinated by the achievements of the people of Weller Street in Liverpool and Black Road, Macclesfield. Both were creating better homes for themselves in areas which had been blighted and semi-derelict for years. 'I was electrified by the atmosphere I encountered,' he told the Institute of Directors in 1986.[17]

Rod Hackney was the architect involved at Black Road, after moving in there himself. He began the process of helping the inhabitants, who were living in condemned terraced houses declared by the council to be 'substandard', to rebuild their own homes. They formed themselves into a trust and organized a self-help programme to restore the houses. Outside contractors even let them use their equipment over the weekends. Hackney set up his office in the street, two doors away from his own home.

It was when he was writing about the success of the Black Road project in the *Times* in 1975 that architecture correspondent Charles Knevitt – later to be first director of Prince Charles' Inner City Trust – coined the phrase 'community architecture'.

Prince Charles entered the debate in 1984, hailing architects like Hackney at the RIBA's 150th anniversary dinner in his 'monstrous carbuncle' speech. But the media attention the community architects achieved irritated some of the people involved in providing technical aid. They felt they had been doing exactly the same for years without any attention from the media, let alone royalty.

Tom Woolley, head of the Hull School of Architecture, became an unofficial mouthpiece of technical aid. He tells how, in his student days, he asked his professor why training did not include anything about peoples' needs. 'If you are interested in people, you should become a sociologist,' was the reply. Woolley became the focus of resistance against community architecture. 'Quite a lot of architects jumped on the community architecture bandwagon and have made a name for themselves as a result,' he claimed.[18]

The tension came to a head in 1985 with the first so-called Community Urban Design Assistance Team (CUDAT). This was an American idea, whereby professionals study a run-down area, and then spend a weekend there brainstorming with locals and officials, and finally come up with a plan for revitalizing it. The RIBA's community architects were invited, as the first British CUDAT, into the St Mary's area of Southampton in 1985, but it was not a resounding success. Five months preparation ended in an intense weekend with the slogan 'Put the Heart back into St Mary's', together with a special message of encouragement from the Prince of Wales.

Locals felt that the final report enabled them to speak to the council on equal terms. But there were frustrations too. 'Local groups can't go along and change a road,' local vicar Charlie Hall said later. 'They have actually got to wait for the city to do it. After two and a half years, that is still to happen and we are still annoyed and frustrated'. Technical aid people later accused the organizers of raising hopes without providing the continuing back-up that the community needed after they had left.

But CUDATs are far from over. An Anglo-American group of architects tried again in a run-down steel mill district of Pittsburgh. The project coincided with the American conference on community architecture presided over by Prince Charles. Participants were so entranced by the experience that they are to try again in Newcastle in September 1989.

The First International Conference on Community Architecture, *Building Communities*, was planned in 1986 with the various different groups looking on suspiciously. Knevitt and the journalist Nick Wates, whose book *Community Architecture* appeared the following year, met a series of difficulties: the National Community Partnership was concerned that the fees were too high for the community groups who were being discussed to be there. Some participants were worried about working with the sponsor, Regalian Properties, which was involved in buying up blocks of council flats and refurbishing them for sale. But special rates for community groups were agreed, and the conference went ahead with demonstrators outside from CASE, the Campaign Against the Sale of Estates. Hackney introduced Prince Charles to the assembled delegates as 'our patron and our friend' and took the wind out of the opposition by inviting demonstrator Brian Barnes to address the conference from the rostrum.

That same month Dr Hackney had been elected president of the RIBA, after one of the most bitter elections in its 150 year history, taking on the official candidate and winning. Hackney ran an aggressive campaign, describing the Institute as 'a lot of old people continuing an exclusive club'. He won an unprecedented majority of 1,500 votes.

The conference was a tremendous success, putting community

architecture firmly on the map, spoken in a language that everybody – including the media – could understand. But the divisions remained. Two separate initiatives for funding inner city improvements were launched at the conference. One, by the National Community Partnership, had been planned for months by ACTAC and others. The other, which attracted all the media attention, was Prince Charles' Band Aid-style Inner City Aid, with Charles Knevitt as director, which aimed to raise separate cash for community architecture projects. Neither found the fund-raising easy and Inner City Aid ran into difficult relationships with some of the other Prince's trusts, and a year later was reported to have raised less than £30,000.

In fact, despite an increasing demand for the services provided by most technical aid centres, funding for projects was becoming increasingly difficult for everyone. Government grants also mean central government control, and most centres have had to fall back on earning consultancy fees. But only a small amount of money can be raised in that way to help them towards the self-sufficiency which gives them independence. Community architecture work is also expensive. But extra fund-raising time, public meetings and evening work make adequate payment very difficult. ACTAC believes that the RIBA recommended fee was only about half what it should be.

The problem of how to pay for technical aid and community architecture remains. But the importance of these new methods of restoring the most run-down neighbourhoods is being recognised. A new kind of professional has emerged, as Ivan Illich predicted in his influential book *Disabling Professions:*, one who is able to work *with* the consumer.

If the new methods work, the long-term effects may be much more radical. 'We must *empower* people so that they are working, not only to mitigate immediate circumstances, but so they can change the whole way their environment is developed,' said Tom Woolley. 'If there is an upturn in public spending it must be under local control and not simply managed by professionals and bureaucrats as before, however sympathetic they may be.'

The greening of the inner cities has meant more than simply using nature in planning. It has also meant rebuilding to a human scale and in a human way, communicating, taking advice, and discussing – which is why the alternative economist Paul Ekins told the Building Communities conference that they had been 'witnessing the greening of architecture'.[19] Whether this greening of architecture lasts depends on the commitment of politicians and the understanding of the professionals. There is still some way to go.

V

Community architecture schemes are still a drop in the ocean of inner city deprivation, but what about the better environment that is slowly emerging? Is greening really useful, or is it no more than a camouflage – a sop to placate people while the real problems of poverty and powerlessness remain unchanged?

There is often the hint of a placebo in large greening projects. But there is psychological evidence that greenery is helpful. The Netherlands Institute of Preventative Medicine made a study of the 260 foot Bijlmermeer in Amsterdam, an estate ridden with social problems, which was provided with a ring of woodland. They found that the woods and new green environment were making the people there healthier and calmer.

More recently, the Nature Conservancy Council has commissioned a series of studies in Birmingham which are beginning to show how much people – no matter what culture they belong to – value wild areas in towns, and use them as places to escape to. They also find that wildlife areas play an important role as places where people are brought together. 'Natural areas [in cities] are peaceful and quiet,' said a Nature Conservancy Council document, prepared jointly with the Countryside Commission, which has become one of the most fervent exponents of nature in cities. 'They allow people to identify with nature, notice the seasons and feel a sense of freedom.'[20] Green spaces and wildlife spots are important to city living in the same way that Ebenezer Howard's green belts were intended to be – as places for recreation, and a relief from unrelenting concrete.

Second, greening a neighbourhood can bring in money. Creating an environment which is pleasant to live in means that companies find it easier to attract staff and to expand and create new jobs. Studies of the new towns – which were laid out with this in mind – show that firms there tend to have lower staff turnovers, and less absenteeism than firms elsewhere.[21] Whether this is because of the better environments there, or simply because the kind of people who move to new towns have more 'get up and go', the incentive for firms to move there is increased, and towns like Milton Keynes can create up to 4,000 new jobs a year. 'Industry and nature *should* exist side by side,' declared the chairman of the CBI's public profile group at a seminar on 'Greening the West Midlands.'

The third advantage is that if local people can improve their environments – even in small ways like creating gardens – they can improve their confidence, their pride in their own area and their staying power. They are then more likely to attract the help from outside that they need. Improving the environment can begin to break the vicious circles that have been working against them, encouraging the more enterprizing to stay and work.

And money can be made in smaller ways. It has been calculated that if all the available wasteland in Birmingham was turned into allotments for families, 3,200 people would benefit from free vegetables.[22] Ashram Acres is in Sparkbrook, Birmingham, which has a large Pakistani and West Indian community, and it has been setting up community businesses on this basis. In an area where 60 per cent are unemployed, they have been selling vegetables grown on derelict sites. Ashram Acres began in 1982 when Gill Cressey and Ute Jaekel moved into an area of large Victorian houses with gardens. The council has provided them with ten more, and the vegetables grown there go to old people's homes and hospitals. The organization operates without grants in a bid to stay independent, though over 100 people are now employed under the Community Programme clearing the sites and growing the vegetables.[23] 'We looked not just at the problems but to the assets of the neighbourhood – its land and people,' said Gill Cressey.[24]

This idea has been even more successful in American inner cities. The IBM executive Gary Waldron was sent on secondment in 1979 to help local organizations set up farms on derelict sites in New York. He never went back to IBM, and now his GLIE Farms employs 140 local people and sells $2.5 million worth of herbs a year.

Also in New York, former policeman Jack Flanagan and his grass-roots Bronx Frontier Development Corporation have set up a series of horticultural schemes, creating the Barretto Street Community Garden on a former oil company site. The enthusiasm generated locally led to local people buying a nearby block of flats, which they renovated and now manage. Flanagan persuaded the local zoo to provide him with manure for the farms, which is now marketed by the community gardens as 'Zoo Doo'. (Back in London, City Farm 1 is also selling the manure from its six cows, eight horses and two sows.) 'Productive greening can improve property values, stimulate investment and have a positive effect on people's lives,' said Flanagan. 'If it can happen in the Bronx, it can happen anywhere.' By 1985, local groups in New York had created 448 community gardens on vacant land.

Increased economic activity was added to the list of the benefits of environmental improvement in an Association of Metropolitan Authorities' report in 1985. The others were 'enrichment of life' and 'mental health and well-being'. At the same time another report was estimating that 200,000 new jobs could be created in environment improvement around Britain.

Productive greening schemes are just another drop in the inner city ocean. But where these local solutions work, the results are worth it – and the benefits are not spread so thinly that they disappear altogether, as they tend to do with conventional public spending. The achievements of the housing co-operatives in Liverpool or Glasgow, the city farmers and the wildlife parks, have brought real benefits to the people involved: life attracts life, and the vicious circles can begin to be broken.

Ed Berman of Inter-Action, the man behind City Farm 1, puts it like this: 'I don't think anybody thinks that greening the city is as important as jobs, crime prevention, good race relations or housing . . . But it is a critical factor in the inner city formula.,'

The green cities movement is all the more vigorous because it draws on people who like cities and people who don't. It also brings together the people who believe in planning as a solution – the ones who want to set objectives – and those who don't.

A generation ago, greening the city simply meant letting variety break through the tidy maps in the planning departments, and glorying in cities growing wild. Louis Le Roy's exciting Kennedylan scheme in the Netherlands in1966 – when he filled a 15 km strip with over 1,000 kinds of plants and shrubs – was praised at the time as an 'un-plan'. But there is now a feeling that for people to keep their neighbourhoods changing for the better, they need a lever on system. They need *some* sort of planning to reach their goals.

Twenty years ago, Jane Jacobs called for diversity in the neighbourhood. Big parks depress an area – small parks bring variety and life, she said. It has taken a long time for planners and architects to lose their horror of clutter, or 'town muddling' and 'hopeless confusion', as one planning exhibition in the 50s put in. When Jane Jacobs asked what was wrong with clutter, it took a good generation before professionals began to agree that perhaps nothing was. Now, when neighbourhoods are allowed to draw up their own plans, their schemes tend to be for housing *as well as* shops, sports facilities, community halls, gardens, doctor's surgeries. Neighbourhoods have a variety of needs, and one of those needs is for nature, greenery and space. So tackling derelict land, as the Civic Trust argued in 1988, does not mean building on all of it. A sizeable proportion of it must go green if city living is to be made more balanced and liveable.

This kind of balance is important if progress is to be continued. As big developers get more interested in inner city areas the danger is that the green 'lungs' that have grown up will be sacrificed all over again – as the Camley Street wildlife park may be now that it is in the way of the King's Cross development. Ironically green projects may be victims of their own success as developers showed no interest in many of these places before they were greened. But if it is understood that green cities are here to stay, then we will start seeing more radical ideas being tested – like the city forests proposed by the Countryside Commission, or major extensions of allotments, or using empty tower blocks as greenhouses. Prince Charles even pointed out on his BBC programme that crushed tower blocks made a very good base for growing vegetables.

There has to be a compromise if the most deprived areas of cities are to find a greener prosperity. We need enough planning to achieve what people want, but not so much that all the vitality disappears.

5
FROM YOBS TO YOKELS

They spend their time mostly looking forward to the past.
John Osborne, Look Back in Anger

A frightful vision haunts the minds of some of the most trenchant critics of British society.

It is the figure of the sturdy but unemployed Briton – dressed in an agricultural smock, paid to provide a rosy view of 'English heritage' for hordes of American and Japanese tourists. It is a disturbing picture of the UK as a vast historic theme park, full of yokels, knights and jolly Mr Pickwicks – as Bernard Levin put it, 'A gigantic Old Curiosity Shop.'

This is Britain finally sidestepped by the world, with any vestige of greatness long gone, a country with no clear role left for those cities that were once the workshops of the world. At the end of the 1970s, when British cities seemed to have lost their *raison d'etre,* a giant 'Theme Park UK' seemed like a solution.

The population of inner cities had reached a new low, and experts were convinced that the trend would continue. Then, as the figures began to be collated in the mid-1980s, there was a blip on the screen. The population of London was beginning to rise – just by 1,500 in 1984, but ten times that in 1985. 'Far from being doom-laden, 1984 appears to have heralded a momentous event in London's history,' said Newcastle University's population expert

Tony Champion. The same pattern was being repeated across the country, with nearly every city at least seeing their rate of decline slow to a trickle.

Geographers are still convinced that the trend for Britain's big city populations remains down. Yet something strange was happening in the mid-80s, and the experts wrestled with what it could be. Was it that people suddenly could not afford to leave the inner cities – or was it really a revival in urban areas? Had the cities begun to find a new role that was catching on?

One new role was leisure. The affluent urban-dwellers of the mid-80s were finding they *enjoyed* living in the city, eating out in the restaurants, windsurfing on the disused docks. Even the families who had left for the suburbs and country towns still had an interest in the city centres. One of the magnets that began to draw people back in, and to open their pockets when they arrived, has become known as 'heritage'. If cities had become monuments to a bygone industrial age, they could at least draw some benefits from it.

The economic power of museums, historic sites, castles, homes has become an important factor in the revival of inner cities. The sheer neglect of many inner city areas, especially docks and wharfs, has meant that historic features have often survived. Backed by an increasingly powerful conservation lobby, places which have been bywords for poverty – from collieries in decayed mining towns to empty storage vaults beneath cities – are now being turned into tourist attractions or leisure 'experiences' for all the family. They make a healthy profit for the new leisure entrepreneurs, but they can also give inner cities the economic clout which they lacked so badly before.

Boston was among the first cities to invest in this way. The Faneuil Hall market was re-opened in 1976 on the site of the abandoned Quincy Market in downtown Boston. In the first year, the authentic-looking market pushcart stalls managed to turn over $500 per square foot. Faneuil Hall was an influential forerunner for the Covent Garden scheme, which opened in London four years later.

The British enthusiasm for heritage has its roots deep in the English character, and has been all the more easy to enflame since events like the televised Coronation in 1953 made everybody proud that the British could organize such pageantry so well. Now we have a national nostalgia that is bringing us a confusion of historic architectural styles on our newest buildings – which the eminent architect Berthold Lubetkin condemned as 'transvestite architecture'.

The rise of heritage in the 1980s has a great deal to do with the failure of 'modern' experts to succeed in changing society in the 50s and 60s. The British public reacted by electing a Prime Minister who would make them feel 'great', and British marketing began to sell products by referring to things English. They were confirmed in this through the 70s by the increasingly confident activities of the conservation lobby, and by a stream of nostalgic plays and articles from British writers. Was there not something vital we have lost in the modern world, asked Alan Bennett's play *Forty Years On*? And *Daily Mirror* readers were battered week by week by Keith Waterhouse's campaign to bring back the tram to the northern towns.

Waterhouse was high on the list of nostalgic writers, calling for a new 'gentrification' that would 'unblock the walled up fireplaces, strip the plywood veneer off the old mahogany doors and pull down the fake lowered ceilings.' Otherwise, he wrote, England might be 'turned into a complex of "facilities" serving the Channel tunnel.'[2]

Are we embarrased about the past? he asked in the same article. Far from it. A glitzy fast-moving promotion of all that is English has long been under way as part of the battle for American tourists. For it was heritage, stretching from Harold's arrow to Winston Churchill's underground headquarters, that Americans felt Britain was all about. So when a TWA airliner was hijacked from Athens Airport, and the number of US visitors to Europe slumped by 25 per cent, the burgeoning tourist industry had to find new ways of attracting them. Film star Sylvester Stallone announced that he was not going to Europe, and American Express even persuaded some operators to take their advertizing stickers off their coaches in Europe for fear of attack.

One of Britain's responses to the slump was the 'Treasure House of Britain' exhibition, opened by the Prince and Princess of Wales with sponsors including Ford and the National Trust. NATO should be 'remined occasionally of the civilization more directly at risk to Russian SS20s,' said the *Economist* at the time. Travel inside the country was also exploited, as it became clear that people were going to more diverse places, over the whole year.

To attract some of these travellers, and to use their money in run-down areas, cities have been involved in three broad approaches. First they can try to promote their city for tourists by opening new museums and developing old attractions. Second, they can redevelop their historic areas, turning them into attractive places to visit or to work in. Finally they can develop new 'heritage attractions' on derelict sites.

It all depends what you can find to sell. Bradford, the northern woollen town, believed they had the lot.

II

The launch of Bradford onto the tourist market in 1980 was a popular joke in the travel trade.

This was deliberate: Bradford's councillors were counting on the funny side of the idea to get people talking. On the face of it, Bradford seemed to have little to attract anybody – why should tourists visit what was in the popular imagination a desolate wasteland of chimneys and huddled poor?

Yet the city's new economic development unit had devoted £100,000 to developing the idea. They found that Bradford's hotels were full of business travellers from Monday to Thursday each week, and empty over the weekend. They also uncovered some 'marketable' features of the area, like 'Bronte Country' within easy reach of the city, the Yorkshire Dales, and industrial heritage sites, and they aimed to promote these attractions – mainly to the over-40s.

The hilarity of the media was Bradford's greatest weapon, providing them with press and television coverage worth an estimated £250,000. Bradford added to it by inviting the first holiday-maker on a free preview of the city, together with a red carpet reception at the railway station, greeted by the Lord Mayor and a brass band.

In the first year, holidays in Bradford attracted 2,000 people, growing to 28,000 by 1985, when £4.5m was brought into the struggling local economy. They now attract over 3m visitors a year.

Bradford, and other declining industrial cities, were drawing inspiration from the run-down port of Lowell, Massachussets, which had been transformed by imaginative planning into a thriving 'heritage' area.

Lowell is an industrial town with high unemployment, similar to many northern British towns. In the middle of the last century it was the biggest producer of cotton textiles in the world, but by the

From Yobs to Yokels

mid-70s only two of the old mills were left working. The roots of revival lay in the work of Boston architects Michael and Susan Southworth, who set up the Lowell Discovery Network in 1966, when they found that the decayed industrialism was actually interesting to people. Now the massive granite Victorian warehouses are fully occupied again.

It was a local educationalist, Dr Patrick Mogan, who suggested using this industrial heritage as a way of transforming Lowell's economy, bringing a different kind of work back in by turning 'liabilities into assets'. In the 1970s local industrialists had the idea of creating a new kind of national park to cover the centre of the city. It was to take in almost 100 buildings including the old housing for mill girls, and cost well over $300m. Fortunately the city already owned most of the warehouses, because they had been sequestrated over the years for non-payment of taxes.

By 1980, Lowell had managed to convince Congress to turn the centre of the city into a national park. The city's unemployment is now below national rates for the first time in 50 years. Over 500,000 people a year visit the town to see the restored mills and canals or to ride the trams, or walk past the coloured banners and flags to visit the 'Brush with History' gallery, an artists' co-operative in the restored Market Mills building.

In a smaller way, a similar idea is being put into effect in Bradford, which adopted the slogan 'Bradford's Bouncing Back'. The local business community pledged £60,000 in one night to continue the rehabilitation and promotion process. They used the Lowell principles when they set about restoring 39 Victorian and Edwardian warehouses in the 'Little Germany' quarter of the city, aiming to turn it into an artistic district. By 1983 they had set up a Bradford Science Museum, and were organizing a National Museum of Photography, Film and Television, together with a week-long festival for the composer Frederick Delius, who was born in the city.

Other cities with imagination threw resources into developing their historical assets. Gloucester built itself a museum of packaging and a waterways museum, Manchester a Museum of Science and Engineering and an Air and Space Museum – and an exhibition centre in the old G-MEX station, closed by British Rail's Dr Beeching in the 60s. New museums were able to boost existing tourism. York doubled the number of visitors it attracted to 3m people a year, opening its first new museum in 1975 by revitaliz-

BUILDING FUTURES

ing an old one. A National Railway Museum opened on one site, bringing together exhibits from Swindon and Clapham. Next an archaeological discovery beside the shopping centre led to the unveiling of the Jorvik Viking Centre in 1984, which takes visitors on a mini-rail trip through a reconstructed Viking village, complete with smells. The trip takes only 12 and a half minutes – the operators want to move people through – but it attracts a million people a year. The managers, Heritage Projects, have opened another heritage 'experience' in an old warehouse in Oxford and are working on other schemes in Exeter and Canterbury.

The Friargate Wax Museum also opened in York in 1984, allowing their owners to fund a 'Domesday Experience' in Hastings. And perhaps the biggest of them all – attracting some ridicule – opened near London's East End in the Barbican in 1988. This was 'Royal Britain', or, as the sponsors put it, the 'immortal unending chronicle of royal heritage; featuring a cavalcade from Julius Ceasar to Princess Diana, via the beheading of Mary Queen of Scots'.

Some of the poorest cities in Britain have been involved in this development of heritage, seeing that the new battle to attract tourists might be one in which they can take part. Glasgow formed its own tourist board in 1983, and a study of their opportunities suggested that they should refurbish the old fish market, and redevelop a local historical museum. The report also decided that they needed an aquarium, a science centre and folk heritage museum – the three of them at a cost of £47 million.

Belfast raised funds for their study from the EEC. They were told they needed a £27 million 'Gateway Centre' on the banks of the River Lagan, providing an 'experience' of the sights, sounds and culture of the province which could attract 10 million people every year. Merseyside has had a maritime museum since 1984 in the restored Albert Dock – which had fought off demolition for 20 years. Bristol is planning a museum of empire.

The promotion of these places – some of which have never been on any tourist map – often involves resurrecting some local character from the past. For Islington it was the diarist Samuel Pepys, who was featured on their tourism video commissioned in 1987. For Nottingham, one of Britain's poorest cities, it was inevitably Robin Hood, in spite of the legendary hero's persecution by their sheriff all those year ago. This is 'the city of Legend, Lace, Literature and Life', one of their publicity brochures

From Yobs to Yokels

declares.

Northern cities are finding they have special qualities when it comes to the battle for tourism. This is partly because they have been relatively unvisited until now, and motor travel in the south is a frustrating bumper-to-bumper experience. Romanticized versions of the old way of life can be woven together to create the kind of aura familiar to Hovis TV advertisements. An entire city street from Gateshead, together with pubs and trams has been rebuilt at the enormously successful Beamish Open Air Museum near Newcastle, opened in 1970 on a former coal tip, which recently became European Museum of the Year.

In Gateshead itself, developer John Hall is busy trying to disprove J. B. Priestley's maxim that 'if anybody ever made money in Gateshead, they must have taken great care not to spend any of it on the town'.[3] It was he that managed to build the MetroCentre, at 2.2m sq ft Europe's biggest shopping centre, on waste ground and in high 'heritage' style. Visited by 300,000 people a week, it includes a 'Garden Village' and a town square, and 'Antique Village', complete with cottages and a village pond, plus a Roman forum. The MetroCentre is ambitious and successful, subsidized by the government as an Enterprize Zone, and has also created around 6,000 jobs. On the other hand, it is one of the foremost examples of heritage clichés in urban renewal, bearing little relationship to the area's actual past.

A variation on the heritage theme is the re-opening of derelict Victorian mills, not for visitors, but for small businesses or workshops. Brookfield Mill, for example, in Belfast was closed by the troubles until 1979, when the Flax Trust – working for social reconciliation – bought it and refurbished it as an 'incubator unit', starting 12 small businesses a year. It now employs 400 people, both Catholic and Protestant.

Most well-known is Dean Clough in Halifax, the successful dreamchild of the millionaire Ernest Hall. Dean Clough is a massive Victorian mill and once the home of Crossley Carpets until it closed in 1982, when it was the largest carpet factory in the world. In its heyday it employed 5,000 people. Now it houses 1,700 people in 200 new businesses. It has an artist-in-residence, and the Slade School of Art opened an extension there in 1988.

By the end of 1988 Hall had spent £20 million on Dean Clough, turning the huge empty building into a mixture of the commercial with the non-commercial. When the new companies needed to expand they would move out, creating a healthy turnover of 'seedbed' companies. But it was not just a social success. By 1988, the rent return was around £5 million a year, and the local authority was also raising £200,000 a year from Dean Clough in rates.

Halifax has probably exploited its heritage more than any other town in Britain. It is close to the Pennines, cluttered with Victorian buildings and steeped in industrial, textile and engineering history – or so the Civic Trust told them in two reports about the 'heritage assets' of the area which could be used. 'Child labour' is among the important features of Halifax's past listed with breathless pride in the reports. In business terms, the poor of a century ago seem a good deal more bankable than the poor of the 80s.

It is this aspect of heritage which is generating controvery. The Calderdale Inheritance Project was launched to revitalize the Halifax area with the support of the Civic Trust – but was forced to change its title in 1988 when Labour took control of the council and decided that the project was not addressing the problems of the worse-off sections of society. They called it 'Fair Shares'.

III

Wigan is almost a byword for poverty. The town's reputation is largely thanks to George Orwell, whose book *The Road to Wigan Pier* was a searing account of its desperate poverty in the 1930s. Now it is a little different. Where Wigan Pier once was, now 'we can buy Mr Huntley's range of Victorian perfumes, soaps and medicines, Country Way Kiwi fruit and lemon preserve, model miner's lamps . . .'[4] and so the list goes on.

At the end of the 1970s, a group of students from Wigan College of Technology put back the metal rails that used to be at the side of the canal, and which formed the basis for Wigan Pier. Tourism consultants told the council that 'Wigan Pier' was a highly marketable name, and Wigan Pier became the Wigan Pier Heritage Centre. It had an exhibition with the title 'The Way we Were', demonstrating an Edwardian working class way of life, and employed seven actors to play the part of mill workers. In the first year after it opened in 1982, the centre attracted 30,000 people.

'They don't wear clogs any more at the Wigan Heritage Centre,' said arts journalist Robert Hewison, who sent up the whole idea of our increasing obsession with heritage in his book *The Heritage Industry*. Hewison argued that this comforting vision of a largely

From Yobs to Yokels

mythical past is 'imaginative death,' and predicted with horror a 'Great British Museum' stretching from Land's End to John O'-Groats. He began writing the book when he discovered that a new museum opens in Britain nearly every week.

The argument against heritage has become familiar, especially from the political Left. There is a fear that pageantry and history, mixed together as they never were, are used by the ruling classes to control the rest of us – in the belief that we are only happy when we can be out waving flags at the royal family. This ersatz heritage has come in for attack, not because they find dressing up embarrassing but simply because it is ersatz. The same criticism is made of similar projects in America, especially in inner cities. One academic condemned a turn-of-the-century scheme for San Francisco's rundown Pier 39 as 'Corn, Kitsch, Schlock, Honky-tonk, Dreck, Schmaltz, Pseudo-Victorian junk . . . an ersatz San Francisco that never was.'

Added to that there is a worry about what is portrayed or preserved. In cities it is often the very kind of industrialization which socialism emerged to fight.

The heritage which inner cities have to sell, like their dock or waterfront areas, is usually industrial. Yet some of this heritage was, in its day, hardly attractive. Birmingham has protected its last remaining back-to-back slums, and the Calderdale Industrial Museum in Halifax proudly advertizes its exhibits about the 'sweated labour' of mill workers. Some critics feel that the industrialism of the old kind should be scrapped completely, and remembered with horror rather than nostalgia.

The debate extends into the architecture. Developers watched with fascination the progress of the Milton Keynes exhibition of the homes of the future in 1981. Builders from all over the world were invited to build examples of future styles, and the visitors were asked to vote on the style they preferred. When the public voted overwhelmingly for the neo-Tudor, with half timbering and diamond-paned windows, many of the developers abandoned plans and commissioned Tudor and cottage designs instead.

Architects like Quinlan Terry have emerged as champions of a new 'conservationist' classical style, enthusiastically supported by Prince Charles. Terry had been 'suspect' as far as radicals were concerned since 1975, when he designed an ornamental pillar for Lord McAlpine, who had in Latin round the base: 'This monument was built with a large sum of money, which would otherwise have fallen, sooner or later, into the hands of the tax-gatherers'. When Quinlan's neo-classical facade, Richmond Riverside, was opened in 1988 the antagonism from some architects about this style, which blends in neatly with the past, was apparent from the remarks of Richard Meier, who claimed that it 'ransacks the past, robs the present and obliterates the future'.[5]

What has happened to our view of ourselves, cried the historian Raphael Samuel, accusing the National Trust of turning into a 'gigantic system of outdoor relief for decayed gentlefolk'[6]? But if you can market products from food to books by referring to their heritage, why not the parts of cities that nobody used to be able to sell to anyone?

IV

The heritage industry, it is said, is pedalling false visions of the past, encouraging us to look backward instead of thinking ahead. Some heritage promotions are little more than Hollywood style snapshots of history, with muffin men and jolly Victorian gentlemen behaving like a cross between Santa Claus and the Laughing Policeman. Granted, there probably is little of educational value in some of the heritage 'experiences' like Royal Britian – but there is a range on offer from the Victoria & Albert Museum to the Catherine Cookson tours of the north east. Not all heritage is the same.

English heritage has also been criticized as escapist. But if people are not encouraged to escape into the history books, there are many far less attractive alternatives that might claim them – like the American businessmen who spend weekends screaming death cries during their leisure 'war games', on the unlikely basis that it makes them milder during the rest of the week.

There is a puritanical streak in the broader British establishment, especially among the people whose views determine ours. The fear of turning Britain into a vast theme park for the Americans stems from an interesting mixture of this puritanism and xenophobia. But dismissing heritage entirely is like throwing the baby out with the bathwater. Understanding history is vital for us if we are to understand our own time, and if the picture presented is wrong, then we must put it right.

The final reason given for discouraging heritage is the claim that we are refusing to face up to a changing world. Why can't we create new architecture, new ideas, and progress – rather than dreaming of a bygone rural idyll? Certainly, people are looking to the past in the face of the enormous changes in society. But they are also looking back in response to the failure of a functional and streamlined view of the future that promised so much to the last generation but failed so dismally to deliver it. A good look back at the past may be just what we need before we can stride forward again.

But in many ways the 1980s in Britain has been a time of unprecedented new thinking, and that is partly the theme of this book.

Architecture is less earth-shattering and streamlined, but more human – which is progress in itself – for as John Betjeman said, human-scale is the 'shape God made the World'. People who say we are looking backwards are often saying simply that nobody is adopting their own idea of progress.

As inner city areas battle for a foothold so that they can earn a livelihood, using the untapped asset of heritage may be just what they need to force their way onto the economic map. But another pitfall is the sheer drawing power of an inner city area after the heritage 'treatment'. It can be a hindrance as much as it is a help, by changing a neighbourhood out of all recognition – almost as finally as demolition would have done.

Award-winning Covent Garden, a much-vaunted achievement of the late Greater London Council, is a rehabilitated Georgian building, surrounded by cobblestones, iron lamp-posts and restaurants in the best English 'heritage' style. It has been trumpeted as an enormous economic success. But is it?

Covent Garden was a fruit, vegetable and flower market for 300 years before it was closed in 1974. It was by then the scene of one of the most effective local campaigns against a GLC redevelopment plan. The campaigners won, and a scheme to surround the famous piazza with offices was dropped. An alternative 'conservationist' scheme, with small shops and eating places opened in 1980, and became a symbol that 'planning' had changed. Yet, although the buildings of Eliza Doolittle's day are still there, she may well not have recognized it. What was a working class area has become a haunt of artists and designers, filled with their expensive flats and offices. The drawbacks of creating a 'heritage' in the hope that it will benefit the worse-off are clear from even a short visit to Covent Garden. 'There's nowhere to buy a pint of milk,' cartoonist Michael Heath told a meeting to discuss the inner cities organized by *Designer* magazine. 'You can't *eat* denim.'[7]

After the shops close and the restaurants shoo out their customers, Covent Garden becomes a different place. Residents complain of muggings and children urinating through their letter boxes after dark.

The 'success' of Covent Garden has forced land and property prices so high that projects which would genuinely benefit the community are made unviable. The Covent Garden Community Association, which first led the battle to save the district through the 1970s, is now swamped with prospective development, little of which they want. The abortive 'heritage' plans by the Royal Opera House, abandoned when they were leaked by *The Guardian* at the beginning of 1989, included a Mozart cafe with 'an ambience reminiscent of old Vienna', a 20s speakeasy saloon, a Victorian ice cream parlour, and a San Francisco cable car. At least in the docklands they have kept some rusty cranes as a real link with the past.

The sad truth is that investing in heritage often prices inner city people out of an area, scattering the community. The architect and activist Brian Anson, an early organizer of the Covent Garden campaign, did an experiment with older people who had lived there all their lives, drawing lines on a map to represent the various places that were significant to them in the years before.

'We concluded the exercise by turning to an empty plan and asking Sam to draw his Neal Street of 1974,' wrote Anson. 'He drew one line, from outside the area to his home on the third floor of Nottingham House. There was nothing there for him any more. Neal Street was no longer *his* home, but just a place to walk through on his way to and from work. He no longer peered into the shops nor stopped for a quick chat with a neighbour. The culture of the street was alien, representing the richer side of his own unequal society.

'The tragic irony was that the Covent Garden Community Association had saved Neal Street from the bulldozers, and Sam had been in the vanguard of that struggle. But he had saved it for others, not for his own kind.'[8]

Worse, once a city is locked into marketing itself as a heritage attraction it may be unwilling to discuss these kind of problems at all. Pennine Heritage chairman David Fletcher warned a major conference to promote a 'Mersey-Humber Strategy' for the north that no amount of complaining would help them. 'It is more likely to be counter-productive, merely serving to reinforce the stereotype view of the region which cannot get its act together,' said Fletcher. 'When has anyone ever wanted to invest in defeatism?'

A heritage success in one part of the city may take years to spread its effects in jobs and income to other deprived areas. Yet they do have a symbolic value that makes tackling other intractable inner city problems just a little bit easier. It provides the will.

'The restoration of shop fronts or the refurbishment of the covered market are not to be sneered at as cosmetic,' said Civic Trust director Martin Bradshaw, in defence of their efforts in Halifax. 'They are seen as a symbol of change and if the evident buoyancy of the town centre is not yet reflected elsewhere, at least a start has been made'.

V

Britain has massive resources of heritage which are used to fuel the international tourism that is now one of our highest earners. Yet almost none of the most visited attractions are in inner city areas. Of those that attract over 200,000 visitors a year, only four could conceivably be considered anywhere near an inner city. Interestingly, they are all on waterfronts: the Cutty Sark, Tower Bridge and HMS Belfast in London and HMS Victory in Portsmouth.

Why should this be? Why not other areas, which are sometimes in the oldest parts of cities?

Climbing on the heritage bandwagon means that inner city heritage must be about marketing assets that have been forgotten, like the Maritime Quarter in Swansea or Little Germany in Bradford. It means having the imagination to see places in different ways. But finding the assets has to be a job for the locals. No Whitehall quango using a set of guidelines, however clear, can possibly discover the forgotten gems lost in the heart of a city.

A local authority sold on heritage is also much more likely to protect and improve the environment, keeping familiar buildings and protecting streets as places for people rather than motorized highways. But good heritage is also good PR for urban living. 'Conservation of the heritage is not first a physical matter about buildings, but a social matter about people,' says architect Patrick Nuttgens. 'Urban life can be good and rich and wonderful'.

The most important point about heritage is that identikit urban life is not rich and wonderful at all. If it feels the same in every inner city from Hackney to Halifax, the effect is utterly deadening.

The kind of heritage that works is about what makes places *different* from each other: it means developing what makes them special. Just as history encourages a sense of identity for the nation, using heritage in a city can bring with it a sense of identity and pride in its inhabitants. Pride does not pay for the groceries, but it certainly provides an inspiration.

Heritage need not be about country houses, statues and cathedrals, but about what we value in any neighbourhood. 'Everyday heritage gives us our sense of place, continuity and stability,' said environment minister Virginia Bottomley in Halifax in 1988. 'Our surroundings are a focus of identity. They help us to generate pride and a sense of worth.'[10]

Precisely so. But Mrs Bottomley's understanding that neighbourhoods should have this kind of control over their surroundings is years ahead of her own government's. She went on to praise the importance to heritage of city parks, many of which look set to be in the way of new motorway proposals.

Another problem is that the roots of many inner city people are actually in other countries, as they always have been in inner city history. How does heritage tackle multi-racial culture, as it must do if it is to bring in many of the people who live nearby?

This is beginning to be faced in the USA, where, for example, the AT&T Foundation has recently paid to expand the museum town of Colonial Williamsburg so that it includes black history as well as white. We need this kind of heritage in British cities, history that recognizes that a mixture of people has been moving in and out of the centre of cities through the centuries, and recognizes that black and ethnic minorities are part of it. There is some Jewish heritage in the London East End, but most of our popular heritage now is too English and too aristocractic.

It may be that inner cities have been left out in the past because, deep down, we tend to think of heritage as rural. It's an attitude that puts country living above city living, and allows urban areas to be filled with high density flats to protect the countryside around the green belt. Of all the heritage an ancient country like Britain has to choose from, it is the countryside that the establishment tends to hold dear. But when nearly 80 per cent of the population actually lives in towns and cities, there should be an urban 'myth' in our imaginations to balance the rural one – one that includes urban ideals together with rural ones.

We need to find urban heritage that is about life and excitement, something that celebrates the vitality and diversity of cities. Then maybe we can begin to feel that city living can also be healthy, idyllic and sophisticated. We have a great tradition, from Dick Whittington to the Blitz, that can bring out the best of city living and this may be the link between heritage and inner city success.

6

THE CULTURAL REVOLUTION

The resources of civilization are not yet exhausted.
W. E. Gladstone, 1881

Carrying a rubber duck and wearing a striped Edwardian bathing costume, Mayor William Schaefer climbed into Baltimore's new aquarium, surrounded by the press and some surprized-looking fish. Mayor Schaefer had promised in 1980 that if the $22 million aquarium did not open on time, he would swim in the tanks himself. It was a promise he felt it best to keep, though the aquarium opened six weeks later in the summer of 1981.

Schaefer is now Governor of Maryland. He was one of the civic leaders in America who came to power in the aftermath of their race riots in the late 60s – and one of a handful who have succeeded in finding new solutions to the old problems of inner city decline.

Elected Mayor of Baltimore in 1971, Schaefer set about organizing a 'downtown' festival to get people back visiting parts of the city which had become almost deserted since the riots. His fair was the first of a series of free concerts, theatre happenings and fireworks displays which were aimed at bringing people back into the city. It attracted a stunning 180,000 people.

'We did it initially for one real reason – school spirit,' said one of the organizers, Sandra S. Hillman. 'We wanted Baltimoreans to begin to feel good about themselves, so that they would feel good about their city.'

The process of turning Baltimore round, not by trying to attract jobs and industry in the traditional way – but by changing the atmosphere of the city – was a long process. The National Aquarium was simply the latest stage. Schaefer was so successful at pulling the different interests and ideas together that he became symbolic of the whole process. When the senior vice-president of one large corporation which moved there was asked his reasons for chosing Baltimore, he said simply: 'Mayor Schaefer'.

In fact there were many others involved. The origins of the rescue of Baltimore's inner city and run-down harbour go back to 1954, when local businessmen decided they had to take responsibility for the decaying areas of the city. They formed the 'Committee for Downtown' and drew up a detailed strategy to revamp the area, using new and exciting architecture, culture and public space. The plan cost $225,000 just to draw up and there were fears that the then mayor would reject their ideas as impertinent. But when they took the plans round to his home late one night in 1954, the mayor sat down and began to draw up the necessary legislation that very moment.

The result was an early example of a word that is now becoming so familiar in planning circles: 'leverage'. The city spent $35 million, and managed to attract another $175 million from the private sector.

The rotting docks of Baltimore had not been used since the war, and they might have disappeared altogether in the 1960s had community groups not battled successfully against the Interstate 95 motorway which was to have ploughed right through. Instead a plan emerged for the docks which was to be called 'Harborplace' – not for new industry as traditional planning would have assumed, but as a new asset for central Baltimore to make it a better place to live and work.

The harbour must be a 'people place', said Schaefer. What emerged there, organized by the local developer James Rouse, was a mixture of new architecture, cultural facilities and eating places – next to the masts of the preserved USF *Constellation*, the first warship in the US Navy.

Harborplace was successful from the start, attracting more than 18m people in its first year of operation – more than Disney World in Florida. An annual city fair now attracts a further one to two million more, and the rates revenue for the city receives a tremendous boost. Unemployment for Baltimore dropped nearly four percentage points between 1982 and 1984.

Rouse had cut his teeth developing the new town of Columbia in Maryland, one of America's few successful examples of the genre. Baltimore's Harborplace made him one of the most sought after developers in the world, and his concept of 'festival market place' in great demand. New York, Boston and Sydney all took advice from Rouse, whose approach to 'downtown' areas is becoming a new orthodoxy.

Rouse demonstrated that redeveloping inner city areas was not necessarily about rebuilding, or factories or even about exploiting the untapped heritage. It was about *life*, and about creating new assets that made an exciting and diverse mixture, so that living there or visiting was an exciting experience. 'The only legitimate purpose of a city is to provide for the life and growth of its people,' Rouse told the *Sunday Times* on a visit to the UK.

Rouse has unusual principles of development, which can be summed up in the words 'attention to detail'. The retailers for his developments are carefully selected for the atmosphere they can bring, rather than simply for profit. The style of the development is based on what is unique about a city, not on some pre-recorded blueprint that can be found anywhere. In this way you bring out some of the city's assets which they have often forgotten all about. 'Every city in America has some specific resources that it is not using,' Rouse emphasized.

What made the English Tourist Board invite Rouse to the UK in 1987, on a special tour of Manchester, was that he was obviously able to put these ideas into practice and make them work – and also make a profit at the same time. Together with his Australian partners Merlin International he put together an outline scheme that filled in some of the widest gaps between other rebuildings in Manchester. They included speciality shops, restaurants and open air places. People had been talking about the renaissance of the city for some years, but Rouse seemed to be able to make it a reality.

The word 'renaissance' conjures up pictures of stately architecture, light and civilization, and above all the arts, which are beginning to play an important, if unofficial, role in the revival of cities. But what had 'renaissance' to do with the deep problems of inner cities?

The old solutions to 'downtown' problems were simply not working. It was clear that industrial cities had almost completely lost their old-fashioned role as a base for manufacturing industry. The idea that cities should attract more factories to survive – what Americans called 'traditional smokestack hunting' – seemed to be deepening their problems: while civic leaders were trying to remake inner cities in their 19th century image, the workforce just mouldered away on the dole. All over Europe, similar problems of industrial collapse and population decline were hitting similar kinds of cities. Once economists began talking about abandoning some northern British cities to their fate, without regional aid or subsidies, the search for different kinds of assets became urgent.

If cities were to be born again, they had to set different goals – and these tended to be more intangible ones to do with making their inner areas better to live in and visit. Some entrepreneurial cities are beginning to look to the arts, sports, restaurants or shops, not as fripperies for overspenders – but as solutions to their economic problems. After all, bringing life and excitement – even temporarily – back to rundown central areas, is an easier goal than turning round the industrial base and rehousing the slum-dwellers.

The renaissance solution is a mix of the different approaches. It includes restaurants – and there are plans on both sides of the Atlantic to create new Chinatowns – which are known for being especially vibrant and dynamic once they had emerged as a result of the US Chinese Exclusion Act of 1882, which forced the Chinese to live in restricted areas.

It also includes sports. Sheffield as drawn up plans to promote itself as the 'City of Life', a concept that includes home renewal, education, conservation of the local heritage, better shopping and leisure facilities, a good environment and a 'human' city centre – which they sum up in the words 'vibrant and dynamic'.

Sheffield is making special efforts to make itself a sporting centre, hosting the World Snooker Championships every year in the Crucible Theatre, and the World Student Games in 1996 – which will mean millions of pounds' worth of stadiums, pools and velodromes for cycling. It has also meant clearing some of their most notorious blocks of flats, like the massive Hyde Park block, which became famous when tenants began dumping old televisions by throwing them out of the window at night. Hyde Park

The Cultural Revolution

and other blocks will be refurbished for the athletes, which demonstrates the political dangers with this kind of project. The dividing line between asset-building and asset-stripping is very thin, and it is quite possible to pass over the continuing needs of locals in the rush to promote the cities to the world outside.

This new interest in sports has had Manchester making a £83 million bid for the Olympic Games in 1996, after Birmingham's bid for the Barcelona Olympics was considered so seriously by the International Olympic Committee.

The Birmingham Campaign cost £2.3 million, inspired by the knowledge that the Los Angeles Olympics had made nearly 100 times that amount for the city. Winning the games would have meant 16,000 man years of jobs for the city. And once experts began to study the area they discovered that Birmingham had a number of sporting assets which they never realized they had: there was even a site for international archery next to Stoneleigh Abbey on the River Avon. They discovered that Birmingham had more trees than any other city in Western Europe, and had more canals than Venice[2]: these assets could be useful even if the bid failed. By the end of the campaign, three times as many companies were contacting the city asking for details about moving there.

Birmingham was following the path of Indianapolis, which set about turning itself into the amateur sports capital of the USA as a way of tackling the city's decline. In 1982 they organized the National Sports Festival, and found that the US army's Soldier's Physical Fitness Centre moved to the city shortly afterwards. Now they have a sports centre, a velodrome for cycle racing, the fastest swimming pool in the world, and the Hooster Stadium.

'Renaissance' includes not just what assets a city has but what it feels like to go there – which means that the design of urban areas is another crucial ingredient. If visitors are to be attracted back into inner cities for pleasure, design must be interesting and on a human scale. The New Yorker William Whyte discovered what made some spaces in cities popular. 'What attracts people is other people,' he said.[3] He worked this out after spending years in the 1950s and 60s using time lapse film of spaces in the city, watching the bustle, the people eating lunch and all the other comings and goings, and found that people liked something happening, and somewhere to sit nearby. His findings formed the basis of the New York Open Space Zoning Provisions of 1975.

Francis Tibbalds, the urban design enthusiast elected president of the Royal Town Planning Institute in 1988, recognized that 'the physical design of the public domain is an organic, human-scale, attractive environment, and is the over-riding task of the urban designer.'[4]

The organic is at the centre of Rouse's developments. Something of that atmosphere of hustle and bustle is being incorporated into the design of many new buildings, where puritanical clean lines and blank walls are giving way to a more exuberant and detailed environment. The new shopping centre at Dalston Cross, in Hackney, was able to promote itself on the basis of its 'craftsmanship and detailing' – unheard of a decade ago – with designs inspired by the Italian Renaissance.

The problem with some of these 'renaissance' schemes in Britain is that they tend to be aimed at city centres more than inner cities. Sports centres, even in inner areas like Islington, find that they attract a predominantly middle class clientele. And relying on shopping, sports and big companies for regeneration may mean a sameness creeping into all inner city developments – with every shopping centre offering much the same shops and much the same design. Since 1982, there have been 20 major takeovers of retailers, and the groceries market share of the top five (Sainsbury's, Tesco, Dee, Asda and Argyll) has risen from 38 per cent in 1985 to 52 per cent.

On the other hand, bringing any kind of activity back to declining cities means that the economy can begin to reverse the decline by bringing in visitors. Their spending power brings jobs in their wake.

The real challenge is to attract people, not as visitors but as residents. That means bringing their employers. With the impact of information technology on work, companies are much more able to choose the location they want for their headquarters – rather than being forced into one because of the necessity of transport for their manufactured goods. They will tend to go where their employees want to live.

'Jobs increasingly follow people', the Rand Corporation told the USA in 1977: if a rundown city can be the kind of place where well-educated people *want* to live, the employment will follow to find them.

This makes the intangible 'quality of life' *the* vital ingredient to rescuing cities. It will include a good mix of 'heritage' attractions, shopping, restaurants, culture and exciting buildings, but probably also includes a great deal more besides which contributes to making somewhere a happy and fulfilling place to live.

II

When the authorities in Stuttgart commissioned a British architect to build their new art gallery they were hoping for a building that would be well-known all over Europe. They got more than that. Soon after opening, the Staatsgallerie had become the most visited gallery in West Germany, massively boosting the economy of the city.

The idea that exciting, innovative architecture could put a place on the map was the message of an exhibition at the Royal Academy in London in 1986. The exhibition was called 'New Architecture', and it featured the work of three of Britain's leading architects: Richard Rogers, Norman Foster and James Stirling. Both Rogers and Foster were known for their 'high-tech' style, with atriums of light, glass towers, and lifts and other equipment stuck on the outside. James Stirling, famous for his controversial work in Oxford and Cambridge in the 60s and 70s, was the creator of the Stuttgart Staatsgallerie – the high point of Post Modernist architecture at the time, with coloured stone walls, and historic 'jokes', like the piles of great stones lying in imitation of 18th century picturesque ruins.

The New Architecture exhibition opened with great celebrations and unprecented private sector sponsorship. Each of the three rooms included one built or planned project in London and one abroad, and both the official launch and press conference were told of the economic importance of allowing architects to be exciting. Here were three British architects, fêted around the world, but – like prophets – almost without honour in their own country. Yet building an art gallery in Stuttgart had changed the pattern of visitors in West Germany.

But there was a note of criticism at the press conference when the *London Evening Standard*'s property correspondent Mira Bar-Hillel launched into the exhibition organizers. The British equivalent of Stuttgart was not London at all, she said – it was Rotherham. Why was there no talk of putting their theory to the test by building an art gallery in Rotherham?

'I hardly think anyone is going to want to build an art gallery in Rotherham,' Stirling replied. There was a polite titter at the ridiculousness of the idea from the Royal Academy audience.

The New Architecture exhibition did not travel the country and the concentration on London and abroad – as if they were the only theatres for great architecture – seemed to demonstrate a certain snobbery towards Britain's provincial cities. London was the centre of life and culture, and the rest of the country was beating a path to its door. Whoever heard of anyone suggesting that if a man was tired of Rotherham he was tired of life? The idea was laughable. Still, there were people who believed that encouraging culture outside London might bring a better quality of life with it. This was why Michael Heseltine battled successfully to open the Tate Gallery for the North in Liverpool's restored Albert Dock.

The New Architecture exhibition coincided with a reawakened interest in public monuments because of the interest and excitement they could bring to places. The architect Theo Crosby published plans to build a massive £30 million monument for the Battle of Britain, with a circling Spitfire, a tall column and Churchill's 'we shall fight them on the beaches' speech around the bottom.

Applying the same principles to an inner city area, Leeds proposed to go one further, planning a 120 ft figure of a man in bricks on wasteland near the railway line to London. Sculptor Anthony Gormley made sure his design was 10 cubits higher than the original Colossus of Rhodes, though the plan does not look like happening.

Exciting, though not entirely the stuff of urban romance. The same problem emerged in Oxford when local cinema owner Bill Heine constructed a 30 foot shark, diving through the roof of his terraced house, arguing that it was a 'statement about the danger of nuclear oblivion'. The council was desperate to avoid confrontation, and suggested that Heine gave up the shark so that they could put it on top of the local swimming pool. In the meantime, his small home became one of the most photographed and visited terraced houses in the country.

Public authorities hit back in New York, insisting that a 120 foot rusty steel wall, commissioned in 1979 for a public square, should be taken down. The sculptor Richard Serra took out a $30 million damages suit against the US General Services Administration, arguing that his wall was 'site specific art', and the authorities were violating his right of free speech. The judge ruled that passers-by were also losing some of their rights – and noted that

4,500 complaints had been received.[5]

The concrete cows in Milton Keynes belong to a different kind of public art. Nobody needs a university degree to be able to understand them, and there is a quirky – almost cynical – amusement about them. This is not art for experts, but something that everyone can enjoy. The same is true of British Rail's life size sculptures of commuters in bronze recently erected at Brixton Station. They add something to the life around them. In the US, artists are now working closely with urban designers in what they call 'place-making', renewing and building new public places.

But can they add something to the economy as well?

III

Sheffield is encouraging community arts as a deliberate policy, because – organized properly – they can involve the young people who are otherwise drinking from beer cans in the city centre. Stirling, near Edinburgh, has done the same thing, and another experiment in downtown New York is trying to woo disaffected youth via the arts. The Hub Community Centre in the Bronx are successfully persuading graffiti artists to agree to stop their activities for three months in exchange for canvas, paints and a studio. For many, it was the first time anyone had regarded them as serious artists, and some of them have begun to make a living by selling their work.[6]

The importance of the arts has grown enormously in the debate about cities during the 80s. In the USA, economists have found that both sports and the arts bring in a great deal more money to cities than they cost. The New York Port Authority tried to quantify this in 1983, and calculated that the arts brought $5.6 billion to the New York City–New Jersey area. As well as the tickets and admission charges, every 'cultural' visitor to New York City spends an average of $126 per person on meals, drinks, hotels, taxis and transport.[7]

The figures have excited some of the biggest corporate bosses – like Wendell Cherry of Humana Inc, which now sponsors the Humana Festival of New American Plays every year in Louisville. 'No city ever got to greatness by filling potholes,' Cherry declared.

In Britain it was Bradford that took the lead, restoring their Alhambra Theatre – surrounded by derelict buildings – at a cost of over £8 million in 1986. It now attracts a regular audience of 90 per cent capacity. They also organized the Bradford Festival in 1987 and began working to attract touring visits from the National Theatre. Their first Bradford season paid for restoring and re-opening the old Turkish baths under the theatre. There is talk of the Victoria & Albert Museum's Indian Collection finding a home in the city, possibly in the recently derelict Salt's Mill, Saltaire, which was bought by a local entrepreneur and used for a successful exhibition by the Bradford-born artist David Hockney.

A year later, they commissioned a new ballet from the London Festival Ballet at a cost of £100,000: it will be performed around the world as part of the company's repertoire, and the first performance was a major event for the city and a source of pride from the mayor to the taxi drivers. In 1987, Bradford managed to spend £8.69 per head of population on the arts – compared to Harrow at the other end of the scale, at 15p.

After losing the Militants, Liverpool's new administration resurrected the arts as a major plank of policy: their project City Beat spots local pop talent, and they have also launched a £5 million media centre scheme. 32-year-old Keith Hackett, who went from community arts worker to chairman of Liverpool's finance committee in just one year, explained the theory: 'There is a pattern here of producing artists of some quality,' he told the *Sunday Times*. 'But once they have made it they have to move on – usually to London. The question is, how can we reverse this so that the money they generate comes back to the city?'

Bristol meanwhile is reaping the benefits of using deserted dockside warehouses for the Arnolfini gallery and other arts projects. Sunderland has refurbished its Empire Theatre, and Cardiff is busy promoting itself as 'Media City'. In Birmingham many believe that Simon Rattle, the young conductor of the City of Birmingham Symphony Orchestra, has done more than anyone else to speed the city's revival, giving Birmingham's music an international reputation.

Glasgow's rehabilitation has been built on the arts. The 700,000 tourists they attracted in 1984 has now grown to a massive 4 million and many are visiting the Burrell Collection of paintings and sculpture opened by the Queen in 1983 in the city's leafy Pollok Park. When Burrell died in 1958 he left his collection to Glasgow, on the condition that it was not housed in the city – where the atmosphere was too dirty and polluted. By the time the council managed to decide what to do with his bequest, which has done so much to rescue them from decline, it was the mid 1970s, and

The Cultural Revolution

smokeless zones – combined with industrial collapse – had made the air rather cleaner. They managed to overturn the condition in Burrell's will, and set up the collection in the city after all.

Glasgow's success has been crowned by the title European City of Culture 1990, for which the city has spent £200,000 commissioning new work, including two new operas. A study by the Policy Studies Institute in 1988 found that the arts were raising around £200 million for Glasgow every year, sustaining over 8,000 jobs directly and another 6,000 indirectly – or 2.25 per cent of the workforce. What's more the cost of creating each job turned out to be £1,361 – compared to over £2,200 for jobs created through the government's Community Programme.

But the argument that the arts are good for economic revival was not easy for the government to accept. A report commissioned from National Film Theatre official Paul Collard for the Office of Arts and Libraries entitled *Arts in the inner cities* – which found a link with economic revival – was put on ice by the government in 1987. 'Let's face it. They just don't believe it,' said Collard. This was partly because of environment secretary Nicholas Ridley's objections to Collard's conclusion that local authorities had a key role to play in encouraging the arts.

By the following year, organizations involved in the arts and sports feared that the government was about to close down their main activities in cities. Ridley wanted to close some of the loopholes in capital spending controls that allowed councils to do 'barter' deals with developers – offering them land or planning permission in exchange for arts or sports facilities. Faced with the new rules, Coventry had to abandon £40 million worth of deals, which was to have paid their maintenance bills.

By April, the Department of the Environment had softened. There would be exceptions: councils could exchange land for land, or replace council assets with others for similar uses, and so on. Sports facilities, though, would still have to be put out to private tender.

By now the link between the arts and urban regeneration was being firmly made by the Arts Council, under the chairmanship of Sir William Rees-Mogg, the former editor of the *Times*. More powerful evidence, published the same year, came from academic John Myerscough and his team at the Policy Studies Institute. The arts in Britain in 1985/6 had turned over £10 billion, employing 2.1 per cent of the workforce and accounting for over a quarter of all earnings from tourists. Over two thirds of all adults had visited some arts event in the previous 12 months – which meant an enormous 251 million bottoms on seats, as they say in the arts world. And that did not take account of arts spin-offs in the fields of fashion, architecture, design, printing, advertizing and catering.

Myerscough and his reports arrived 'like cavalry over the hill for a besieged arts world.'[8] By the middle of 1988, the *Sunday Times* was able to call the economic advantages of the arts to cities 'received wisdom', and Glasgow played host to a major international conference on the subject in October.

But opposition from ministers, who could not believe something so ethereal could make any real difference, was matched by those who did not like the idea of using the arts in this way. Might economics not undermine the arts in the long run? If opera suddenly stopped attracting people and money, would that mean closing the whole thing down?

These are important warnings. Yet the arts, together with other cultural and sporting assets of cities, have helped give a crucial economic boost to the cities themselves. This is not just because of new money earned and new visitors attracted, but because of the importance of culture to senior executives. Myerscough found they put it equal in importance to more tangible assets like education and housing. Senior managers put it second only to a pleasant countryside nearby. The arts are becoming a new factor in the battle to attract companies into inner cities, simply because they make 'decision-makers' want to live there. As Virginia Bottomley told the Council of Europe conference in 1988, companies will move to places where 'lively people want to live.'

What can attract them to one city rather than another can be summed up in three already over-used words, 'quality of life'.

In 1986 the mayors of America's 16 most 'liveable' cities came together in Washington DC. President Reagan had sent a message of support to the mayors, representing places which proved that the quality of life in their cities went hand in hand with good economics. The awards ceremony had been organized by a successful alliance of charities, pressure groups and community projects known as Partners for Liveable Places, which in the USA has been leading the argument that 'quality of life', culture, sports and heritage, comes before the old ideas of hard-nosed industry.

The Partners approach is based on what the Americans call

The Cultural Revolution

'liveability' – those assets that can be used by a city to make it a better place to live, encouraging pride and commitment and attracting investment. Liveability comes from whatever makes places special and exciting. It is a growing concept in the USA – and is the reverse of the old method of demolishing inner city areas and building an identical nationwide formula of homes and shopping centres and car parks. This kind of liveability makes places different. 'Cookie cut-out approaches that 15 years ago dropped the same pedestrian mall into dozens of cities around the country will not work,' said the liveability guru Robert McNulty,[9] echoing James Rouse's thesis that 'every city has some special resources that it is not using'. It is whatever is *special* that is important here.

Partners – with McNulty as President – has been working to help rundown cities find those assets and use them to lift themselves out of their cycles of decline. The organization was set up in 1977 with a grant from the National Endowment for the Arts, and now has 1,200 member groups. The original aim was to design a method of measuring how good a place cities were to live in, but this soon proved too small a goal to aim at.

They decided to evaluate the positive projects that were happening, and show how these were related to the success of the different cities. Giving awards to the cities doing the right things was a way of encouraging good practices and discouraging the bad ones, so that instead of mass demolition, cities would look to their forgotten assets of riversides, theatres, zoos or parks, and develop them. A liveability award for a city seeking investment was also a powerful political weapon for the mayors to continue their programmes.

Equally, Partners could force the losers to start looking at themselves critically. There should be an award for 'Places That Really Known How To Ruin A Good Thing', said a Philadelphia paper, when it became clear that the city was not on the winning list. Getting a centre for the arts in Philadelphia, the article went on, was 'like pulling hens teeth, getting blood from a turnip and bringing horses to water and getting them to drink all at the same time'.[10]

Also raising awareness about which cities were nicer to live in – was the American Rand McNally Corporation. Their *Places Rated Almanac* became an unexpected best seller when it first appeared in 1981, listing 277 American cities in order of their quality of life.

Building Futures

This was worked out according to a complicated formula bringing in schools, transport, the arts, health care and so on. Atlanta, in Georgia, came top the first time, though Pittsburgh toppled them in the next edition. Number 277 was Lawrence in Massachusetts. Others around the bottom considered suing Rand McNally – which might have had problems justifying their rather ad hoc ratings system.

Scottish researchers tried to go one better, by organizing a wide public opinion survey of what people thought were most important aspects of living in a city. Then they were able to 'weight' the assets people wanted most in their survey. Crime and health came top – rated important by 93 per cent – which meant that Britain's most liveable city was Edinburgh, followed by Aberdeen. Plymouth, which has low crime rates, came 4th, and Birmingham came bottom of the list at 38th, together with most of the biggest cities with inner city problems. Glasgow was still struggling at No 25.

But the UK still has a long way to go towards making use of this information. American cities are 20 years ahead thinking in terms of arts and quality – rather than factories and quantity – for their inner cities.

A generation ago, Seattle lawyer Jim Ellis was representing a community next to a polluted part of Lake Washington, where raw sewage had covered the lake in an unpleasant green algae. He realized that if the problem was to be solved, political differences would have to be put aside across a wide area. He was able to set up the METRO organization to begin to tackle the problem, and succeeded in creating a sewage system for the city and surrounding area.

And if people could be brought together to tackle algae and sewage – why not for other problems as well? Ellis put the proposition to the local Rotary Club in 1965, warning that unless the city invested in parks and public transport, any economic growth would undermine the city's attractive way of life. People from all areas of the city's life were drawn together to work out what to do, and to put together a plan for the future called 'Forward Thrust'. It began with a warning: 'Metropolitan communities must work together and think ahead or face worsening survival options.'[11]

When Forward Thrust was put to a local referendum, Seattle citizens turned out to vote in greater numbers than they did later that same year to choose between Nixon and Humphrey as President. There followed hundreds of projects, valued at over $5 billion, paid for partly by local bond issues, including 100 neighbourhood parks. It remains a demonstration of the power a simple vision has to unite.

The plan was firmly based on voluntary effort. People would be encouraged to 'adopt-a-park', and donate time to maintaining it. By 1983, nearly 11,000 hours were being donated to the city. As the years went by, Ellis constantly warned against the dangers of replacing volunteers with full-time employees – though he reckoned his own time donated to the city in one year, when he was planning a convention centre, would have cost them $250,000.

St Louis was another pioneer, this time concentrating on attracting culture to their city, which in 1980 had been the 'most distressed big city' in the USA, losing half their population over the previous 30 years. This time the agent for change was the university, which found itself stuck in what had become a surrounding sea of inner city decline. The Chancellor, Father Paul Reinart SJ, realized that they could either move and make it worse, or stay and concentrate on revitalizing their neighbourhood. 'This area must return to what it had been,' said Reinart. 'It has to be the entertainment centre of metropolitan St Louis'.[12]

Reinart's New Town/St Louis Inc was set up as non-profit-making organization, and began to revitalize 600 downtown blocks with the help of the Kellogg's organization. The area had another boost when local entrepreneur Leon Strauss bought the old Fox Theatre for $2million, did it up, and found that it took $11 million in its first year of operation. The developer James Rouse took on the old railway station in a $135 million project, and St Louis now has the second largest shopping mall in the USA.

Partners called these different ideas about urban revitalization the 'New Civics'. Their first task was to promote the idea and make sure other cities knew of the possibilities. It soon became clear that there were other factors involved in some cities' success. A formula for resurrecting a rundown city and its worst inner city areas had to include the kind of leadership that could unite diverse sections of the city with a common view of what things could be like. They called this 'Beyond Confrontation'.

Finding new ways out of the traditional confrontations between the usual points of conflict – on race or public spending – meant that the old battles of local government had to be set aside. It was vital that enough common ground could be provided for cities to start believing in themselves again.

'People realize the ox is in the ditch and we have to work together to get him out,' said Mayor Gene Roberts of Chattanooga. 'We've got our work cut out to catch up with the times, but I think we are in better shape and condition than most of us know or think. Chattanooga can be the most attractive city in the country'.

Chattanooga was made famous by the 40s song 'Chattanooga Choo-Choo'. Before that it was remembered simply for the railway and some important battles with the Indians. A detailed report on the state of the city in 1980 found that, apart from the lack of attractions in the inner city areas, there was a communication gap between the civic leaders and the people. Roberts began by attracting people to downtown festivals, then developed new parks and an arts and garden festival in the old station. The new downtown park would 'only bring in the winos', the city was told – in fact it has been the catalyst for $300 million growth in the surrounding area.

When Partners for Liveable Places gives awards for civic leadership, it is for the places that tackle old intractable problems in new ways – the cities that can find a new language to unite different sides. San Antonio mayor Henry Cisneros, for example, has aimed at tackling poverty – but has rejected welfare payments as the answer, because welfare 'produces no permanent change towards self-reliance'. But he refuses to rely on the British government's favourite 'trickle down' theory either. So when the city bought a $1.2 million computer, it was on condition that the company they bought it from employed 400 San Antonians.

Memphis is going beyond that with a radical programme to reduce the number of people on welfare by three quarters by the year 2000. Mayor William Morris set up a programme to boost schools, which would double as adult education centres and day care centres, and employ local people in home and school building.

McNulty and his Partners organization finds it is more effective to give awards for 'effort' than to cities that have nothing left to achieve, and are just sitting back and relaxing. Awards tend to go to cities that are making the most progress, sometimes from a low base.

Pittsburgh was after all the city where, 30 years ago, the air was so polluted that street lights had to be kept on all day. When the

The Cultural Revolution

great architect Frank Lloyd Wright was asked what to do with Pittsburgh, his reply was 'abandon it'.

The idea that Pittsburgh could make a success of life was a challenge in itself. The problem was, as one commentator put it, that Pittsburgh suffered from 'paralysing fear and deeply nurtured self doubt.' Yet since the start of the decade, Pittsburgh has won the accolade of being America's most liveable city, and has attracted 185 companies to relocate there. The city has redeveloped the old steel mills, revamped its theatre, and has 160 tennis courts.

Beating cynicism often means involving people in the process of turning round a city or a neighbourhood. In Fort Wayne, Indiana, involvement was so successful that when the city was threatened by disastrous floods in 1982, 35,000 volunteers were mobilized to line the river with sandbags and evacuate the elderly. People in St Paul, Minnesota, could also identify with the success of their city. After a year's work paid off and St Paul had won the designation for the state's World Trade Centre in 1984, the reaction was tremendous with people openly celebrating in the streets.

Pride in the city is a powerful force, and in Britain we have become embarrassed by it. Mayors in Britain are slightly ridiculous figures, playing a very different role than they do in the USA, but their British equivalents, the leaders of councils, are usually anonymous, unfamiliar people. Part of this difference stems from the powerlessness of local government in Britain. Councillors are seen as causing petty irritations while important issues carry on without them. The public does not tend to understand the divisions of powers in local government, nor why local government exertions are carried on in such narrow fields. Even within the town halls, the idea of stepping outside departmental boundaries and tackling people's problems as a whole is still too rare in the UK.

'Quality of life', on the other hand, is a concept that seems to take in everything – which is why political activists are using it more. It allows politicians and officials to think about inner city problems right across the board – not just under separate headings like 'housing' or 'recreation'. Using the quality of life of inner city people as a yardstick of success is a valuable safeguard against people running away with enthusiasm over some half-baked blueprint aimed at solving inner city problems at a stroke.

One thing is absolutely vital. No city can continue to be successful indefinitely if a large section of the population is excluded from that success. Using the quality of life of the city as a whole is at least one way of reminding politicians that there must be results from their prestige developments. In the long term, only cities that can unite all the very different elements of their population, and find solutions for the problems of their most depressed areas, will be able to keep that success running. Otherwise divisions will tear apart the loose alliances that have been forged.

V

The lead set by American cities has pitfalls, both political and practical. A number of things can go wrong if any of the different elements that go to make up 'liveability' are emphasized more than others.

Enthusiastic cities may find that new 'amenities' are just a recipe for sameness. How many waterfront developments can be supported by one nation, and how many marinas? There is a danger that if a formula works in one place, it will be slavishly copied by others.

The point is that blueprint or downmarket solutions will not work. Amenities are about what makes cities different, not what makes them the same. Dropping standards or adopting the same solutions everywhere will undermine any success that has been achieved. This is a new argument for the UK, where most of us believe at the bottom of our hearts that things are bound to get tackier and tackier. It is also a useful lesson in a country where nearly every modern shopping mall has the same features – arranged differently, maybe – and the same Next, Benetton, Body Shop and McDonalds.

Second, there is a danger in thinking too big. In fact, thinking big was one of the problems that led Britain's inner cities down such a wrong turning in the 60s and 70s. Thinking small, dealing with one derelict spot at a time, together with the local neighbourhood, is often a more effective approach. The bigger the projects, the less local people can be involved in their organization.

Another problem arises from the pro-city approach which encourages people to start living in inner cities again. What about the quality of life for the people who still want to live somewhere else? A recent survey found that 41 per cent of Londoners would prefer to live somewhere else. And unless help is given, it will continue to be only the better-off who can afford to get out. What is more, the quality of life of a city probably *depends* on some of them going.

Finally, there is the familiar objection that concentrating on orchestras and zoos is not tackling directly the real problems of poverty and powerlessness in the inner cities. Places like Easterhouse in Glasgow, where 40,000 people live in an area without any assets that could possibly be recognized as amenities – need assistance as a priority. And there is a danger that they will be ignored by the well-heeled as they flock into other parts of the city to spend their money. Glasgow now has art galleries, and a new opera house, yet elderly people are still living in badly-maintained flats, coping with fungal growth on the walls and electricity bills of up to £200 a quarter because of the poor insulation. And should the largest ever European Commission grant – £125 million for Birmingham – have been spent on an International Convention Centre? People living in sub-standard council accommodation remain to be convinced.

The same problems are there in the US cities. Baltimore won a liveability award in 1986 with its aquarium and Harborplace, but still has enormous problems. 'There are a lot of Baltimoreans for whom it is not liveable, for whom it is dangerous, for whom the schools are not good, where there is enormous drug-dealing,' said the director of a Baltimore charity. 'You and I wouldn't want to live in those ugly neighbourhoods'. Equally British waterfront developments can be traced back to St Katherine's Dock in the 1970s, which replaced rundown homes with a luxury marina – even the original dock had itself replaced thousands of homes for the poor in the early 19th century.

This is why organizations like Partners for Liveable Places in the USA are stressing that quality of life is not a goal, towards which cities can strive – it is a process. They discovered early on that liveability was more a guide to how hard neighbourhoods and cities were prepared to work to improve themselves. It was not a measurement of status quo, but of how much people were prepared to change. 'We are a Pollyanna group in a sense,' said McNulty. 'We've found that cities that don't dwell on the negative things can get things done.'[13]

The idea that liveability is a process that never reaches its goal is much more radical, and far more relevant to the UK. No more blueprints and artists impressions of the City of the Future – regeneration has become an ongoing process, hence the emphasis on 'participation'.

Investing in culture to save cities may just be an alternative version of Mrs Thatcher's shift from welfare-based solutions to wealth creation. Yet only part of the US lesson is popular with the government in the UK, who are generally very open to ideas from across the Atlantic. The lesson they are missing almost completely is the importance of local pride – which means that local civic leaders and institutions are vital.

This is not a happy idea for ministers who have been battling to suppress local government ever since the conservatives were elected in 1979. It is hard to imagine them accepting the freedom of action used by civic leaders such as Mayor Schaefer in Baltimore. Yet this freedom is necessary if there is to be any hope of developing the civic pride that sustains regeneration. In fact, as McNulty says: 'The quality of a city's leadership . . . may well be the factor that separates the successful from the unsuccessful cities'.

There are two lessons here for the government, if they are prepared to take them. The first is that they must stop thinking of 'public-private partnerships' as things that go on between big companies and the government, which then informs cities what is expected of them. The kind of partnerships that are effective in the USA are between local government and local or regional business. These kinds of partnerships are crucial for building up momentum in a city, and the city council must have something they can contribute to the relationship. It is interesting to note that the government's latest efforts to stop cities getting involved were roundly condemned at a major private sector conference on 'Enterprise and the Inner Cities' held at the Barbican in 1988. Unless the government learns to trust city leaders to have pride in their own cities, they cannot expect local business leaders or a city's inhabitants to have much pride either. Unless the government starts to get 'beyond confrontation' themselves in their dealings with councils there is little chance of the growth of civic pride and independence.

The second lesson is the importance of local knowledge. Central government officials are simply not able to search out those forgotten assets: local people need to be involved. The alternative is that blueprint solutions will be imposed from the centre, because outsiders cannot understand what makes a place unique and what assets can be used to good effect. Americans are beginning to learn that it is the distinctiveness of cities that will help them prosper, but city centre redevelopment in the UK still tends to be the same old designs plonked down anywhere from Aberdare to Aberdeen.

Another lesson for Britain is the involvement of local business. This is a good deal easier in the USA than it is over here, because big companies tend to feel they belong to particular cities – and they realize that it is in their interest to help regenerate their home towns. Not so in Britain, where years of tax advantages have led to head offices being predominantly sited in London. Regional companies' enlightened schemes for the common good – like Cadbury's model houses in Birmingham and the building of Port Sunlight by Lever Brothers – have all but disappeared.

Probably this is as much the fault of the companies themselves as it is of successive centralizing governments. As the *Economist* pointed out in a leader column on the inner cities, it is a shortsightedness that has damaged the companies as well: 'Companies might reflect that one of the reasons corporation life became unattractive as a career for the bright young in so many countries in the 1960s and 1970s was that it so often seemed to be about money-making and not much else'.[14]

The *Economist* leader writer suggested that firms like the Norwich Union or the Halifax Building Society should make links with cities and take an interest in local arts, sport and education. One way they might start to do this is to copy the Boston schools compact – where local firms promise jobs to school-leavers who have reached an agreed level of attendance and ability.

There are other lessons in the US experience. They show that cities need new goals to strive towards, which can unite the disparate forces that divide them: the political debate must move on from the old-fashioned issues of whether or not public spending is a good thing or not, or the pros and cons of public ownership. With more local autonomy and power, local action might be able to go beyond the symbolic gestures we have become so used to from inner city authorities.

Another lesson from the liveability experts is to beware of snobbery – not the old-fashioned class kind, but of a more pervasive feeling in the British establishment that London is where things happen, and that the 'provincial cities' will never be as exciting. Rotherham is 'hardly' a place for a new art gallery, yet Bradford now has a ballet, Liverpool a Tate Gallery, and when the

BUILDING FUTURES

Royal Shakespeare Company visited Middlesborough for a month in 1988 all 5,000 tickets sold out within 24 hours. The arts can be developed in other cities, and can provide the backbone for a revival.

Finally, the lesson is the need for inspiration in the rundown areas – as James Ellis reported to Seattle a generation ago: 'We have the means and talent to create the city we want within our time,' he said. And then, echoing President Kennedy: 'Young men and women looking for a cause beyond self can find it here.'

That call for involvement in city life is all the more relevant now. It is a call for activity, not only in small ways like planting flowers on wasteground, but for getting involved in formulating common plans that consider all aspects of city life.

It is also a call for new political alliances across the old divisions, which can unite a variety of communities across one city for its common good. It is an alternative to repeating the nation's divisions at local level, which has led to such a stalemate in the cities.

7

FROM TRICKLE DOWN TO BOTTOM UP

What is the city but the people?
William Shakespeare, *Coriolanus*

Tower Hamlets mayor Brian Williams was adamant that the first meeting of the newly-elected council was over. All the committees had been abolished, the borough had been split up into seven 'neighbourhoods' and the chief officers – who had spent careers specializing in areas like housing or social services – had been sent off to run new local town halls, each covering a run-down area of 20,000 people.

A revolutionary scheme to attack inefficiency and cynicism in one of Britain's poorest inner cities was being forced into effect by the new councillors just days after taking control on behalf of the Liberal Party in 1986. Inner city local government was to be brought closer to local people, who could be more involved in decisions affecting their lives. The new standing orders, despatched to councillors 48 hours before, were now being read to them in the council chamber.

Opposition councillors complained about the short notice: voices raised, disorder grew, and half way through they were standing on seats shouting for the meeting to be abandoned. Many said they did not hear when the mayor called for a vote. The meeting broke up in chaos, but the new experiment was in place.

The advice of council officials was less easy to brush off for the new leaders. Many advised that it was impossible to run a borough split into seven neighbourhoods and local town halls. The aim was laudable enough, they said: councillors would be encouraged to put local needs above the more distant ones of the borough, people would be involved in decisions affecting them, information would be better, experiments easier – but what about efficiency, co-ordination, professional demarkation, strategy, everything local government had been bred to hold dear? The scheme was all the more controversial in a borough with 9,000 homeless families on the waiting list, spending more on bed and breakfast accommodation than any other area of the UK.

Under the new leadership of Eric Flounders, an aggressive and enthusiastic public relations expert, Tower Hamlets was attempting the most ambitious decentralizing of power ever risked in an inner city. And risk was what it was all about. They were risking bureaucratic collapse to shift the balance of decision-making away from the paternalism that has stultified efforts to reverse inner city decline.

Decentralization was the Tower Hamlets' Liberals 'big idea'. A couple of miles up the Thames at Westminster, even Liberal leader David Steel was worried about the implications: because decentralization, self-government and self-help were ideas that had gone firmly to sleep after the war, only to begin the long process of waking up in recent years. But it was facing a great deal of suspicion.

'If the Lewisham Labour group has a fault, it is the conviction that if a thing is worth doing at all, it is worth the council doing it for you'. That was the verdict of a Lewisham borough architect, persuading councillors that local homeless families should be allowed to build their own homes.

Nor were Labour councillors the only offenders. The 'managerial' and professional view, that public servants were there to provide houses *for* people, to improve the environment and set up jobs *for* people, grew in strength through the 50s, 60s and 70s. The consequences for the inner cities – that nobody felt qualified to help either themselves or their neighbourhood – are increasingly apparent, and the official attitude remains. Professor Peter Hall has catalogued the mistakes of distant bureaucracy in his book *Great Planning Disasters*. All the resources channelled through professional architects, planners and officials to rebuild the slums,

From Trickle Down to Bottom Up

have left us – in the end – worse off than before.

The backlash against this paternalism took a long time coming. The idea that things might be better done if officials stepped back – and used the special knowledge of the people who knew the neighbourhood better than they did – emerged slowly from the work of various different people.

There were those who simply wanted to make things happen where officials were failing: practical people, like Rod Hackney, whose success with Black Road has been described earlier. Then there were those who were suspicious of organization by nature: the theoreticians. Among these was the writer Colin Ward, the editor of *Anarchy* and later *Bulletin of Environmental Education*. His questions cast doubts on the efficiency and humanity of the big organizational management of people and their housing in particular.

'I was present myself,' said Ward, 'at a meeting to discuss one councillor's very mild proposals for tenant involvement in housing management in a north London borough, when the outraged representative of one of the local government unions got to his feet and said, "We're not going to be dictated to by a bunch of tenants".'[2]

It was Ward who helped popularize the thinking of other doubters, like the Dutch architect Nicholas John Habraken who believed that 'mass housing reduces the dwelling to a consumer article and the dweller to a consumer'. According to Habraken and Ward, people should take part in the process of providing their homes, each making an individual contribution as an expert on their own needs. Nor was this a new idea to Britain, as Ward showed in his book *Arcadia for All*, which described how hundreds of the poorest families from the East End in the 20s and 30s had been able to build their own homes on the coast or in what we now know as the green belt.

For those who could cope with his impenetrable prose, the former Roman Catholic priest Ivan Illich – who coined the phrase 'Deschooling Society' – was busy raising the same fundamental questions, and showing how the wrong kind of development in the third world could undermine ordinary people's ability to live. 'The presence of a new school, a paved road and a glass-and-steel police station defines the professionally built house as the functional unit,' he wrote. It 'stamps the self-built home as a shanty.'[3]

Illich lives in Latin America, and it was from there that another argument for self help emerged. The English architect John Turner was among the first to look at the growing squatter camps – created by their own inhabitants sometimes in the face of bulldozers from the authorities – and see something other than human degradation. Although the officials and the local middle class linked the camps with delinquency, crime and prostitution, in fact – Turner found – the worst crime was usually no worse than petty thieving. Turner's observations about the success of self-build housing led to the United Nations backing the idea of providing sites, with drains, water and power, where people could build the rest – instead of designing third world homes in the old way, in Western architects' offices. Since then tens of thousands of families in squatter camps like Orangi outside Karachi in Pakistan have built their own shacks and have provided themselves with new plots, schools, and clinics.

And in the developed West, community groups were emerging who believed they should also have a say in the management of their housing.

II

'Local authorities of both political parties have been painfully slow in associating tenants in the management of their own homes.'

So the journalist MP for Romford Dick Leonard informed the House of Commons as long ago as 1971, as he unsuccessfully tried to persuade them to pass his Council Housing (Tenants Representation) Bill. The decade that followed was the decade of 'corporate management', of local authorities run by committees of chief officers, of 'efficiency' and centralization.

Leonard's inspiration – and the inspiration for most of those interested in more risky forms of management – grew out of an experiment on the massive new Byker estate in Newcastle. The gold-medal winning architect Ralph Erskine had been appointed for the rehousing scheme in 1969, setting up his office in a disused funeral parlour, and working on the design with a large staff of architects and a series of new residents committees. It was, according to Alison Ravetz, 'possibly the most brilliant solution to the problem of urban mass housing',[4] emerging from the Newcastle planners' rare objectives of public participation and keeping the community together.

As the scheme developed, a series of voluntary groups emerged run by the people who would live in the flats, from tenants' associations to the community newspaper the *Byker Phoenix*. The local clergy organized a Byker Liasion Committee so that the views of these groups could be fed to councillors and officials: it lasted eight years.

Their progress was not without problems. As the years went by, the number of tenants involved began to drop, often because they had managed to get rehoused in one of the homes they had helped design and had therefore achieved their main objectives. Studies later emphasized that the committees had no real powers to take decisions, and so people saw little reason to spend time on them.

Nonetheless Byker was an important forerunner of the community architecture movement. Another precedent came in the late 70s as south London councillors battled over the principle of allowing their council tenants to build their own homes. Planning committee chairman Nicholas Taylor eventually squeezed through agreement just to 'explore the possibility' by one vote in 1976. By the end of that year the families had been chosen, most of them living in tower blocks or deck access council estates elsewhere in south London.

It was not for over two years of bureaucratic delays – including approval for the timberframe building system designed by architect Walter Segal – that they were able to start work on site. But once they did it was clear that the results would be exciting. A system was devised so that the families could work together on their homes, the women alongside the men – on previous self-building schemes wives had been banished to the coffee and biscuits. Each family could also work as fast as they liked, and they formed an informal support group to help each other out by exchanging tools. 'No-one will be able to tell me that I cannot do something — anything – ever again', said one of the self-builders after the experience. The designs were so flexible that one family was able to build an extension for a child over three weekends for just £1,200.

The 'working classes cannot be trusted to undertake this sort of thing', one GLC official was reported to have commented, joking that they would keep chickens, pigs and rabbits in the houses.[5] The GLC was then firmly in the hands of the Conservatives, but Socialists too were throwing up their hands in horror at the prospect of ordinary people becoming 'little capitalists'. But despite disapproval from both political camps, this and other neighbourhood activities formed some of the few shafts of light in inner city areas.

In Liverpool this shaft of light was being provided by new experimental housing co-operatives, led by the Weller Street Co-op in 1976, when their terraced homes were earmarked for clearance by the council. Residents had been under threat of a redevelopment scheme for 20 years, which had blighted their homes and made repairs difficult and improvements impossible. Six years later, 61 of the households were living in new homes which they had designed themselves and which they now manage together.

The co-op was born out of frustration and anger at the city council, and their determination not to be scattered out to anonymous outlying estates. They learnt the hard way that nothing was going to come to them easily. When the homes were built, the city engineer's department even tried to reject the name 'Weller Way' they had given to their main road.

The co-op chairman is still asked by journalists how the usual system helped them. 'The system didn't give us anything,' he says. 'We had to wring everything out of them'.[6] This 'wringing out' often took the form of aggressive confrontations with officials on their own ground, culminating in the invasion of a private dinner party held by the Housing Corporation chairman Hugh Cubitt at the Atlantic Tower Hotel. Eight co-op members piled in at the soup-serving stage, and one of them put their finger in it. 'You won't eat that, will you? It's contaminated,' he told Cubitt. 'That's what our places are: contaminated'.[7] Since then the Housing Corporation has refused to fund any other projects for Weller Street; but in spite of all the aggression an official study in 1984 found that Weller Street tenants are far more satisfied with their homes than almost all council tenants.

Other co-ops faced smothering at birth when the Militants took over Liverpool City Council in 1983. One of their first acts was to withdraw funding from eight co-ops, which had been preparing new homes for more than two years, and the city's direct labour organization was told it must not tender for housing association contracts. The new council was opposed to co-ops partly because they had had the enthusiastic support of the outgoing Liberals and partly for more ideological reasons. Co-ops were 'part of a deliberate and calculated attack on municipal housing' according to their 1984 housing policy statement.

From Trickle Down to Bottom Up

'All they want is a good house,' said the council's new besuited spokesman, deputy leader Derek Hatton. 'When we can offer them good housing, all that support for a co-op will melt away?'

In Glasgow the Labour council's attitude was very different. Their tenant grant scheme for rehabilitating homes, as an alternative to waiting for the council to organize it for them, was an enormous success and was taken up by 10,000 city tenants.

In London, the long planning battle over the future of the Coin Street site on the South Bank resulted in another model of cooperative housing, designed and managed by the local homeless. A second public inquiry for the site gave permission to two opposing schemes: one a conventional project of tall offices, the other prepared by the Association of Waterloo Groups which included workshops, houses for rent and a park. But it was only when the GLC stepped in to sell the site to Coin Street Community Builders for a nominal £1 that the co-op could go ahead: sky-high land prices have usually defeated most ambitious projects at an early stage.

But the local projects which have gone ahead have given confidence to people about their own power and ability, after decades of receiving handouts from remote 'decision-makers'. 'I never thought I'd have the confidence to chair a meeting,' said Theresa, who was involved in setting up a youth club, playscheme and elderly visiting project at Garfield Community Centre, Battersea. 'I found that chairing the meetings taught me to listen to what other people say as well as giving my own views. It gave me the confidence to apply for the job I've got now, as a superviser in a hospital.'[8]

Even on Broadwater Farm, small-scale projects had been going on since 1981. After the riot, they approached local contractors about employing local people on local projects – and, by the middle of 1987 about 70 had been taken on to set up a launderette, greengrocer, hairdresser and photo workshop.

The next stage was to move from specific schemes to helping local people take responsibility for their own areas. Neighbourhood councils, as a local balance to borough or city councils, have been backed by governments as far back as the 1960s. Derek Senior, the *Guardian* writer appointed as a member of the Redcliffe-Maud Commission, suggested a series of 'common councils' to channel local feelings and provide other services in what he called 'recognizable communites' – in other words real neighbourhoods. This approach was used a generation later by the GLC, which chose a series of embattled communities – from Southwark to Fitzrovia – to protect them from office developers and to boost their economies.

The Maud report was one of a series of commissions and administrative revolutions that hit Britain in the late 60s. It also coincided with a change of government, and the structure for local councils underwent a series of startling political changes before the Local Government Act of 1972 set them in concrete.

Included in the Act was the possibility of giving parish council powers to city areas – as long as they were outside London, and requested by the local communities. Councils had to review the boundaries of parishes in their areas starting in 1978. But leaving the onus on the local authorities meant that many reviews never took place. By 1984 there had been only 100 proposals for changes to urban parishes in England – and only a handful for new parishes. The Association of Neighbourhood Councils found that many chief executives did not know that they had to have reviews if they did not have any parish councils.

A series of private members bills – none of which have made it to the statute book – tried to improve the situation. Liberal MPs Graham Tope and David Alton and Lord Avebury have all tried, and so has the Labour peer Lord McIntosh, the man Ken Livingstone ousted as leader of the GLC.

'For the life of me I cannot understand why . . . it has been so difficult to persuade a government of either complexion . . . to carry out what seems to me this minimum act of justice and to make this provision for local democracy,' McIntosh told the House of Lords. 'The only suspicion I can have is that the power of the existing bureaucracies and of the existing oligarchies in local government – the councillors and the officers – is in some way threatened by legislation of this kind'.[9]

Urban parishes seem to have reached a brick wall. But there was no shortage of the role they could play: the Town and Country Planning Association's 1986 report on the inner cities *Whose Responsibility?* called for 'Community Planning Zones', where local groups could run their own environment according to guidelines agreed with the planning authority. It was adopted by the Labour Party in the following year's general election, and by the Democrats in their planning policy in 1988. The problem was that the existing neighbourhood groups in inner cities had no power.

Often 'participation' simply meant that officials would draw up plans and announce them at public meetings armed with glossy brochures: 'consultation' had taken place, but the local people were alienated by the often furious meetings, and there was even more mutual distrust.

What could be done to get the two sides closer and stop all the wasted effort?

III

An alternative approach was emerging to alter the balance of the borough's powers, either by splitting them up so that offices are nearer the tenants and other people who need them – or, as in Tower Hamlets, splitting up the committees so that decisions are taken for the good of the neighbourhood, rather than the good of the borough.

Stockport was the first in 1970, setting up a series of area management committees, arguing that it would lead to better management and better information. But the committees were given few powers, and the pattern was not widely copied. Ten years later a new breed of Labour councillors took over Walsall Borough Council in May 1980, and began to crank the handle of local government away from corporate management, towards organizing their services locally. The manifesto promised to give the borough a human 'face' to break down barriers and involve people more. Their solution was to open 33 local housing offices, based in Portakabins within walking distance of the council estates. Tenants no longer had to travel to the town hall and queue to see an official, who usually had little knowledge of their area.

Walsall also changed the way officials worked. Housing staff had to reapply for their jobs, and in the new structure there were only two job descriptions, rather than the orchestra of careful gradings so beloved of local government. This led to a confrontation with the members of NALGO, and to a strike over Christmas of 1980.

There was opposition too from some of the Labour councillors: 'they felt their traditional identity as councillors and "fixers" was under threat,' one of the neighbourhood officers, Mike Beazley, remembered. 'They often relied on the mystique of how local government worked and on the alienation between the officers and people for . . . We have all heard how that Councillor A managed to get Mrs B's daughter a house when she got married as she was getting nowhere with those awful housing people.'

The new leadership knew that the changes had to be organized fast. Their majority was slim, and the commitment of the new neighbourhood officers was vital. The following year battle was joined with the social services department, and social workers were included in the new offices.

By the end of 1981, all 33 offices were open. A 34th was lost the next May, when – as predicted – Labour lost control. But the system was by this stage so popular that decentralized offices stayed. Walsall's lead was followed by another Labour borough, this time in London – and this time, Portakabins were not enough. When Islington decentralized its services, it had to be to architect-designed bricks-and-mortar 'neighbourhood' offices.

The decentralization project was the brainchild of a newly-elected councillor Maurice Barnes. 'Instead of having to traipse around the borough as they did, they can pay their rent, request a housing transfer, ask about local improvements, get repairs seen to, speak to a social worker, get advice on welfare benefits, or find out about getting a home help,'[10] he wrote triumphantly at the end of their first four-year term. There were to be 24 local offices in the 'Going Local' programme, with £10 million spent on building 16 of them. They would cover everything from rent to housing benefit, and each office would also have a repair team attached.

It was an approach that was bound to bring trouble. The council's trade unions made it clear that they would accept no redundancies, no departures from existing codes of practice, no compulsory changes in job descriptions, no pilot schemes, no changes in opening hours and no sharing the premises with other organizations like the Citizens Advice Bureau. There followed a long series of negotiations until 1984.

The next stage was to delegate the management of the neighbourhood offices to the public who lived in the area. Local councillors were put on the management committees, but they could not vote unless they lived there as well. Objections emerged straight away. Black and ethnic minority groups, which played a leading role in Islington's policies, were afraid that local committees would mean they would not be directly involved. Councillors were worried at the idea of actually transferring power. And – more reasonably – tenants' associations were worried about people who were not tenants taking decisions about council housing. There were also deep disagreements in the decentralization team.

Such are the complications when democracy starts getting serious. The only solution was to press ahead and show that it works, and that was what Barnes did. He was able to claim after the first year that waiting times for repairs had been cut, and in one neighbourhood the number of empty council houses had been halved. The next stage was to experiment with local budgets and local decisions – but by then a massive shift in the balance of power was taking place a few miles away in Tower Hamlets.

By the end of the first Tower Hamlets meeting after the 1986 elections, the only central departments left included accountants, some social services – because of a legal requirement – some architects and the Direct Labour Organization. The new neighbourhoods, with their mini-town halls, were run by the councillors which covered their area. Apart from throwing a bold plan into gear at breakneck speed, the new Liberal administration was taking another major risk. After ten years of trying to defeat the ruling Labour councillors, decentralization meant that Wapping, Stepney and Isle of Dogs neighbourhoods were promptly handed back to Labour control – because there happened to be more Labour councillors elected in those areas.

'This decentralization of political control is revolutionary', bragged the new council leader Eric Flounders. 'Nowhere else has an opposition party been given so much control.' One of the Labour-controlled neighbourhoods, the Isle of Dogs, voted not to meet at all.

The original idea for decentralizing Tower Hamlets had emerged during a discussion one evening in the Liberal Party's run up to the 1978 elections. Why not go back to the old boroughs, it was suggested: Bethnal Green, Stepney and Poplar, whose borough councils had been merged to form Tower Hamlets in 1965. In 1986 it was the key to Eric Flounders' strategy for tackling the bad communication and the lack of purpose which beset what was one of Britain's poorest boroughs, where only four per cent of people owned their own homes. Splitting up the borough was not going to be a matter of negotiations this time.

The day after the result gave the Liberals a one vote majority, their plan for decentralization was handed to the chief executive. Soon the neighbourhoods each had a chief officer and a couple of staff. 'First-stop shops, were set up straight away where people could be helped in one place, instead of being shunted between different departments, and Portakabin town halls soon appeared. A year – and two chief executives – later the first phase was over. The number of empty council houses was already dropping. People were reporting them as soon as they were empty – and, more importantly, turning up for the neighbourhood council meetings, which they had never done for the old borough-wide committees. Two years later, the total of empty homes was down by 1,000 – and the equivalent of an extra council estate had been added to the council's stock.

'Decentralization was not an end in itself,' warned Peter Hughes, appointed by the council to see the project through from the political side. 'In the long run it is intended to lead to much better government'. Some of the problems faced by the council may have even helped the neighbourhood councils get off the ground. In spite of having a bed and breakfast bill of £18 million to house the homeless, Tower Hamlets was rate-capped – the only Liberal-SDP Alliance council to earn the distinction. This meant that the local committees were forced to experiment to find new ways of raising funds, including selling blocks to pay for new council houses with gardens, matching luxury flat developments with low cost homes so that the profits from one could feed the other. The Bow neighbourhood was divided further into 18 smaller forums of local representatives, and by 1988, 85 per cent of home repairs were being done within a fortnight.

No other inner city local authority has yet followed the pioneering Tower Hamlets example – perhaps because its very success can prove a problem. People's hopes are raised: they believe their problems will be tackled, and that means that the full extent of the problems become clearer. There is less cynical 'grinning and bearing' if there is a chance that the council might act. Consequently the demand for repairs in Walsall rose by nearly 500 per cent in the first year of their decentralized offices, putting further strain on their already overstretched budgets.

In Islington repair requests doubled to 3,000 a week within two years. 'The better we do, the more we get asked to do,' said one foreman. In Lambeth the implications became clear when requests for council house repairs shot up by 20 per cent.

Here is the problem of decentralization in a nutshell. As local hopes rose, Lambeth was busy coping with a serious financial crisis, and cut-backs were necessary to fill a budget gap of £60 million in 1988/9. The decentralization committee was forced to close 12 of its 32 new offices, and organizers confessed later that 'we have often felt – in spite of a strong commitment towards this type of organization – a great deal of frustration, a fair amount of anger and occasional disillusionment.'[11]

Raising hopes can often mean disillusionment, and that makes people angry. At least one local office in London has had to employ security guards as the council staff became the 'meat in the sandwich' between government squeeze on local government and the individuals affected.

But real decentralization of power is about taking risks – which is why the more embattled councils have steered clear of the idea, while others are testing it more gently. For if you risk giving power to local people, there is more than a risk that the wrong decisions will be made. People will not always stick to the party line, and there will sometimes be financial problems that would not have happened under tight centralized control. But without taking the risks, there will never be any chance of giving people what they need, matching up wasted resources with local problems, and above all, allowing people pride in their achievements. Unless hopes are raised, there is no chance that the creativity and energies of the local people can be released.

There is also evidence that splitting organizations into smaller units does make them more efficient. We have come a long way since the economist E.F. Schumacher declared that 'small is beautiful'. 'Small,' as Democrats leader Paddy Ashdown said during his campaign for the leadership, 'is not only beautiful, it is also efficient, innovative, human and more accountable.'

Decentralization can make cities more efficient. But is this just a better way of coping with inner city symptoms rather than any kind of cure?

IV

If inner city people are to have their hopes raised and their energy boosted, they must be given something to do. Best of all, they should decide their own priorities – and have the power to tackle them. Neighbourhood organizations that have succeeded on both counts are the 'development trusts', which bring together local people, community groups and local businesses, working rather like urban development corporations on a very small scale, providing what all three sides want and need – as they say in the USA, a 'win-win situation'.

BUILDING FUTURES

There are now over 70 trusts, and their ability to become financially independent created sufficient government interest for a major report to be commissioned by the Department of the Environment.[12] The study found that, though the various trusts were uncategorizable, they had several things in common: they got things done with community involvement, they were independent of local government, and they were able to subsidize different projects from each other, so that social objectives could be achieved as well.

The M40 Westway flyover was the catalyst for one of the first, the North Kensington Amenity Trust. Kensington was an innovative place during the 60s: the first law centre, the first adventure playground and the first housing advice centre in the UK all opened there. When the motorway was finished in 1971, there remained 23 acres of derelict land around it – known by professionals as SLOAP or 'Space Left Over After Planning'.

Local activists Adam Ritchie and John O'Malley were the brains behind the start of the trust, which aimed at using the land in some way for education, recreation or for the good of local charities. The trustees ran into trouble when it decided to develop some of the land commercially, and were criticized as 'property speculators'. To counter this, the trust began to develop half the sites commercially and half for the community – every commercial project was 'twinned' with a social project, so that the profits from one supported the other.

This technique has now become central to the practice of development trusts. Another is 'cocktailing' – protecting each project by raising funds from a wide range of sources. The North Kensington trust is now financially self-sufficient.

In Los Angeles, the Watts Labor Community Action Committee, set up after the 1965 riots, has gone much further. They have renovated over 600 homes, own $50 million of community assets and have a 25 per cent stake in a new shopping centre. A new community trust in the outlying Wester Hailes estate in Scotland is also helping to develop their own shopping centre, which – if successful – will fund many other improvements without depending on grants from outside. But so far, no British trust has managed to come close to the achievements of Watts. But their work has been effective.

In Tower Hamlets, an environment trust has been able to forge links between local businessmen and community groups. They have set up their own technical aid centre, and are also busy promoting East End culture including the Jewish East End celebration of 1987. They have local representatives on the executive boards, which is a recognition of the fact the middle-class professionals do not have all the answers. As the DoE's development trust researchers observed: 'their strength often lies in turning those problems into opportunities: land under the Westway motorway in North Kensington, derelict land in Tower Hamlets, an empty factory in Sunderland, the decaying heritage of Ironbridge and Wirksworth.'[13]

This turning of problems onto their heads is a hallmark of decentralized revitalization, breaking out of the apparent stalemate between public spenders and their opponents that has led to such a gaping hole at the centre of political thought. Only by working with the people in a rundown area does it become clear what the real needs are, and where the wasted resources are. If it is possible to match wasted people with wasted land and buildings, suddenly a new equation has emerged.

This was the idea behind the award-winning experiment in Birkenhead based in the disused Laird School of Art (see chapter 3). The scheme was the idea of residents around Birkenhead Park, who undertook a door-to-door survey in 1983 to find out what skills and resources were unused in the neighbourhood, building up a picture of buried talent. It was pursued with the help of Dr Tony Gibson and the TCPA, which was under pressure to find an inner city equivalent for their rural new village experiment at Lightmoor – where 14 families were busy building themselves homes and livelihoods.

One disused building, the Laird School, was to become a centre for enterprises which could use the wasted skills. But like so many projects of this kind, it was beset by problems. Community Programme schemes were frozen by the government; thieves removed the roofing tiles and the snow came in. But by 1986, the Laird was in use with workshops, a pottery, a sandwich service, and won a Times/RIBA Community Enterprise Award from Prince Charles.

Just what is possible when neighbourhoods start to raise their own hopes was demonstrated by another problem-turned opportunity. This was the closure in 1980 of the Tate & Lyle factory in Liverpool, with a loss of 1,700 jobs. Instead of allowing another inner city neighbourhood to be taken apart, the local people have found they are able to provide not just new homes for themselves, but new jobs as well – and have also collected an award from Prince Charles, together with the title of Liverpool's 'Man of the Year' for former lorry driver Tony McGann, the inspiration behind the Eldonian's achievement.

Heseltine forced Tate & Lyle to transfer the site to the official English Estates, and a phone call to the chairman extracted another £400,000 towards the cost of demolition. Clearing the site for development eventually cost £2.2 million, which included dealing with the massive tar wells found there. Now the site has been reclaimed, and homes are going up, and the Eldonians are the largest new build housing co-operative in the country. Ten more acres have been bought for shops, a community centre and some of the first of 'Eldonian Enterprises'. 'Eldonians don't know the meaning of failure,' McGann says.

McGann moved to the area when his flat was demolished to make way for a tunnel under the Mersey. He first became involved with local affairs as part of a campaign to prevent the amalgamation of the local Roman Catholic parishes. But it was the council's 1978 proposal to demolish the tenement housing and rehouse the people all over the city that lit the first spark. 'Everyone seemed paralysed,' said the local priest Father Jim Dunne. 'So I mustered my most aggressive tone and asked the councillors, "who gave you authority to demolish?" ' A survey showed that 80 per cent wanted to stay, and Chris Davies, the minority Liberal administration's chairman of housing, suggested that they set up a housing co-op. By 1981 there was a community association.

Local architect Bill Halsall was among those brought in to help, though the community was not able to pay him for another four years. It was the Eldonians themselves – with Halsall's advice – who decided the layout of their new estate, the design of their homes, which homes would be at a low rent and which ones would be for the elderly.

It was at this point that the Eldonians ran into trouble with their first housing co-operative in Portland Gardens. The new Militant-dominated Labour administration which took control of the city council in 1983 was a keen opponent of the new housing co-ops. The co-op offered as a compromise to let the council nominate people for their houses when they were re-let and to let the Direct Labour Organization tender for the building work. That was not accepted, but it was agreed that the Eldonian families would be allowed to live in the homes they had designed.

That agreement was abandoned by the city council as soon as the building was finished in 1986. But the families moved in anyway, and the few remaining houses were occupied by people from the council waiting list: they aim to opt out of local authority control under the government's Housing Act.

Next they negotiated an option on part of the Tate & Lyle site for their Eldonian Village, and managed to persuade environment secretary Patrick Jenkin to fund homes for low rent. The village was to include bungalows for the elderly, scattered among the other homes so that relatives could still live near each other. For eight months an all-women design committee discussed the layout, and organized bus trips for the families to look at the way other estates were built. A complicated session with bingo cards and maps gave the families turns at choosing which of the homes would be theirs.

But the city refused planning permission for their hard-won designs. Instead of giving up the whole idea, the Eldonians appealed to the Secretary of State over their refusal, and won.

As Liverpool's financial crisis deepened in 1984, the council's deputy leader Derek Hatton had visited Patrick Jenkin to plead Liverpool's case for extra grant. He was irritated to find that the Eldonians had been in Jenkin's office the previous day, and had made sure of their funding from the Housing Corporation. When Jenkin visited the city shortly afterwards, he made a special detour to visit the Eldonians' site. To add insult to injury, the Eldonians turned up in force to their local Vauxhall ward meetings of the Labour Party, selected their own councillor, and had him elected instead of a Militant.

Meanwhile, McGann and the rest of the neighbourhood were turning their minds to improving other aspects of life in the Eldon Street area. The problems of the neighbourhood went deeper than just housing, and included a lack of training and employment – and a lack of money. How could the Eldonians, and all the others like them, keep money circulating locally, and provide a living for themselves?

An answer lay in the land. Their garden market project was able to provide training and bring money into the community. Most of the set-up money came from the Urban Programme, but local busines chipped in – Tate & Lyle refused – and a site was found over the Mersey Tunnel. The garden was a small idea, but it enabled the trainees to start tendering for landscaping work on other Eldonian projects. By 1988 they were set to take on 114 acres of derelict land next to the river – a massive undertaking for a community group – in partnership with Merseyside Development Corporation. As matters stand, the plan includes a health food warehouse, a fencing business, a metal workshop and many others.

They were given Enterprise Agency status by the government, forming themselves into a development trust together with local businessmen. Ten years before they had been laughed at: 'But they're not a laughing stock any more,' McGann told Prince Charles as he received their Community Enterprise Award in 1988.

When Liverpool's two rival Catholic and Anglican bishops published their joint autobiography, they used the Eldonian's slogan 'We do it better together' as their title. The future looked even brighter in 1987, after the Militants had been disqualified from holding office: the new housing chairman was Phil Hughes, a member of the Weller Street Housing Co-op, and there are now 40 housing co-ops in the city.

The Eldonian project has been a lesson for self help and self education. It was the project of enormous ambition by the community, determined leadership, but also enormous public subsidies from a range of sources – little was raised, certainly in the early stages, from the private sector.

Can it be repeated by other groups? And if it is, can it be protected economically once it is successful? Most important, how can groups like the Eldonians make themselves less dependent on funds from outside?

V

The straight-talking skills of Tony McGann clearly gave the Eldonians a weapon that other groups did not have: most of the exciting community projects have been forced into existence because of the persistence of articulate and energetic figures who take a leading role and refuse to give up.

McGann himself was invited to join an Anglo-American team of architects sent over to Pittsburgh to help local people get to grips with similar post-industrial problems. After the first few speeches exhorting the Pittsburgh people to 'get off their backsides', he became known as the British 'Exocet'.

FROM TRICKLE DOWN TO BOTTOM UP

American cities with their local financial institutions, are in some ways in a better position to rescue themselves. Even so, research over one year in Chicago at the end of the 1970s showed that people in one run-down neighbourhood had deposited $35 million in their banks, but received only $120,000 back in loans – because they were considered a bad risk.

How is it possible to keep local money working locally, so that it stays to be used over and over again?

The obvious solution is to keep contracts as local as possible. This is completely legal in the USA, where Washington DC requires that the city buys a quarter of its needs from local firms. In Britain now, local authorities are not allowed this kind of discretion, and must take the lowest bid – wherever it comes from. The only way of getting around the ban is to organize exhibitions of local contractors, or publish who's who of local businessmen.

Another solution is to try setting up a local currency for local transactions, which could have the added benefit of insulating the neighbourhood from any world financial disasters. More practical is local banks. There are not very many in the UK, though the Yorkshire Bank is one example. In fact over three quarters of all the venture funds in Britain are based in London and the south east.

In the 1970s, the West Midlands had the lowest investment per head of any of the old industrial regions of Europe. Those top pension funds that remained were considering withdrawing their investments completely, and it was to cope with this problem that the first enterprise board was set up there to kickstart the economy into action. The West Midlands Enterprise Board, set up in 1982, was one of five launched by Labour councils: the others were in London, West Yorkshire, Merseyside and Lancashire. By 1986, when the metropolitan county councils that had given them birth disappeared, £35 million had been invested in 200 companies – sometimes to keep jobs going, sometimes to start new ones.

This meant a new relationship between local government and local business. It meant council officers had to understand their local economies – so that the businesses they invested in could begin to support each other to keep the money flowing, and to support the livelihoods of as many people as possible. Council officers had to look at the wasted resources of buildings and begin to match them with local skills – putting in expertize and finance. When workers at a machine tool factory in Sheffield lost their jobs, discussions with council officials made them realize that their skills could be re-used to design and produce dehumidifiers to tackle dampness in council flats, and as a result they launched the Mons Co-operative to do just that.

The enterprise boards carried on after abolition, though there was a tendency to back old-style industrial business, protecting jobs rather than looking ahead. By 1987, 14,000 jobs had been protected. The government was not so keen on the idea, and minsters hoped that the top QC David Widdicombe, who they had appointed to report on local authority 'conduct', would come out against the enterprise boards. But they were disappointed: he encouraged them.

Enterprise boards were a big step forward. Before them 'local economics' had tended to mean paying a great deal of money to a London-based public relations firm, who would try and persuade companies to move to their area. This set cities competing against each other, while the government tinkered with the nation's economy, hoping that the results would eventually trickle down to the poor.

But this is no longer enough. 'People aren't very happy that you sit and wait for some benign Chancellor of the Exchequer to say that in the end it will come to you', said local economics expert David Millar. 'People don't trust central government to do that any more.'

Go-ahead local authorities have begun to see themselves as nation states which could intervene in exactly the same way. In his book, *The New City States*, David Morris wrote: 'Vulnerable to branch plant closings, cities are beginning to favour development that comes from within and relies on hundreds of small businesses rather than one or two large factories.'

Another direction has been towards the 300 new local enterprise agencies, which themselves create around 70,000 jobs every year. The organization behind them, Business in the Community (BiC), has Prince Charles as president – and with its capitalist links is not beloved of the old-fashioned left-wingers. The South London Business Initiative in Brixton, for example, has a manager from British Telecom, and staff from Sainsburys, Marks and Spencer and BAT.

Mrs Thatcher herself was busy in the same areas, as her party began to discover civic responsibility and the 'active citizen' as the answer to the accusations that she did not care. The Per Cent Club –

encouraging companies to contribute half a per cent of their pre-tax profits – was launched at a reception at 10 Downing Street.

In spite of their establishment links, BiC and similar organizations found themselves beginning to doubt the conventional economic wisdom of renewal. Links with government departments meant that these views began to infect Whitehall as well. 'It is now clear that the inner cities will not revive on their own,' Norman Perry, head of the Department of Trade and Industry inner cities unit, told BiC. 'The trickle down theory of the economy is no longer enough'.

The trickle down effect has always tended to stop short of inner cities, especially in places like the London Docklands, where the unprecedented economic explosion has hindered as much as it has helped. Often local people do not have the right skills for employment, and outsiders are brought in, so that local unemployment figures are barely dented.

One way of beginning to tackle this is by seconding staff from large companies to local organizations in order to fill the desperate need for managerial skills. The danger is that these skills may never actually be transferred to the locals, as third world governments found to their cost. On the other hand, some of the most successful schemes have meant that inner city people have been able to get for themselves the skills they need to make a living – and provide one for others locally.

One example is Giroscope Ltd, in Hull. Six young people, at the time sleeping rough after college, took out a loan to buy and renovate a terraced house, which they could then let out to the homeless. Once they had done it, they could use the house as collateral for buying others, and they now own property worth over £100,000 as well as learning managerial and development skills. The six directors' hairstyles include mohican and green, so raising the initial loan was no easy task.

The money raised by another group of young people, this time black and unemployed in St Pauls, the scene of the Bristol riots, was a greater achievement still. They formed the Zenzele housing project – Zenzele is Zulu for 'help yourself' – to build themselves a block of flats. The DHSS was prepared to accept them as 'available for work' during the building period. In the end they not only had homes, but also useful skills and experience. One of them has now set up an agency to help other young people to do the same.

These projects provided something new and important for the

Building Futures

young people involved: a means of livelihood. Inspired by this, Prince Charles predicted that the school-leaver's question 'how can I get a job?' would soon change to 'how can I make a living?'

Making a living for a run down neighbourhood was the idea behind the 'community businesses' that have been sprouting around Strathclyde in Scotland during the last decade. Community business differs from the usual kind of business in that its main purpose is not to make a profit, but to generate employment for local people. Why the idea should have been so popular around Glasgow and Edinburgh, and almost unknown in other parts of the country, is hard to understand. Perhaps it is because the idea goes back to a seminar which was at Paisley College in November 1977, when a delegate first suggested setting up a Local Enterprise Advisory Project (LEAP) to help people start community businesses. By 1978 LEAP was advising in Strathclyde and the first business – Craigmillar Festival Enterprises Ltd – had been launched as a building company in Edinburgh.

There are now nearly 4,000 jobs in Scottish community businesses, which range from community cafés to community architects, and include a live story-telling company in Inverclyde. With an investment of £193 million, Community Business Scotland has told the government they could be able to create 50,000 sustainable jobs. Since 1981, Urban Aid has been the main source of start-up funds, 75 per cent of the grants from the Scottish Office. Urban Aid is able to go to projects that are wealth-creating, and this has boosted the businesses. They also seem to be reaching people which conventional small business does not reach: one researcher found that only seven per cent of community business employees had had a job before.

Entrenched bureaucracy has not been helpful. The estates department of one local regional council tried to charge £1,500 annual insurance for an empty building – which was already covered by the council's collective insurance policy. In spite of this, most of the businesses have set up in empty schools or hard-to-let housing with the help of the local authorities – which can also support them by buying their services where possible, or at least giving them the chance to bid for council contracts.

Community business is becoming a grass-roots movement in the comparatively small area of Scotland where it is happening. It is chipping away at some of the massive problems of the Easterhouse and Drumchapel estates in Glasgow – which Billy Connolly called a 'desert with windows' – more than six miles from the city centre.

After researching the whole field, business expert Andrew McArthur believed that community business was beginning to promote a change in attitudes to economics: 'They are beginning to see that deprived areas have an internal economy of their own and an internal community structure which can be used to generate economic activity,' he told delegates to a conference in Northern Ireland. 'There is also a growing recognition that entrepreneurializm coupled with a strong social and community purpose actually does exist in depressed areas and is worth supporting.'

The new attitudes stem from the emerging new institutions. An alternative 'enterprise culture' to parallel Mrs Thatcher's vision for the conventional economy seems to be emerging in the voluntary sector. While community business is thriving in Scotland, other projects – which ten years ago would have been dependent on government grants – are now earning money in places where the conventional economy has disappeared.

I watched one representative of the Ashram Acres community vegetable business in Birmingham at a recent conference, who had all the trappings of a 60s drop-out gone legitimate. But close your eyes and listen to the talk of marketing and investment, and it could have been a child of the Thatcherite revolution talking. The distinctions between public and private, profit-making and subsidized, so important a decade ago, are now increasingly blurred.

Another business project on the Glasgow estates is the Cranhill food co-operative in Easterhouse. Taxi driver John Kerr was the inspiration behind the scheme because of his interest in the diet of his eight children. He organized a public meeting in 1981 to suggest buying good food in bulk, instead of being dependent on what the few local supermarkets stocked, and 70 people turned up. Their first purchase cost £50 at the local cash and carry, but they now spend up to £1,000 a week, and members pay 25p membership for life. 'The local schoolchildren can buy good fruit in small quantities with their coppers,' said Mr Kerr. 'Kiwi fruits are top sellers.' Cranhill are now busy organizing lunch clubs for OAPs and young mothers. They were able to break out of a system that was damaging their children's health, and begin to ensure that the more vulnerable in the neighbourhood were better fed – using their purchasing power as the only economic weapon they have.

BUILDING FUTURES

Cranhill are building on the work of the enormously successful Seikatsu food co-op in Japan, set up by a Tokyo housewife in 1965, which now covers 150,000 households and has a turnover of £160,000 a year. In the 1970s they began ordering soap powder to avoid damaging detergents, and when they found they could not buy milk without artificial additives they set up their own processing plant for organic farms, and now deliver all over the Tokyo area. With the purchasing power of half a million people they have an enormous potential impact on the market, and have even elected members onto local councils, under the slogan 'Political reform from the kitchen'.

If Seikatsu provides one model of how inner city neighbourhoods can provide themselves with more economic power, then a bank run from a motorbike in Bangladesh provides another. The Grameen Bank lends money to the poorest people to make them independent. The average size of each loan is just £35, which enables ordinary people there to buy a cow, or a rickshaw or some other small piece of equipment that can enable them to make a living. The bank was set up by economics professor Mohammed Yunis, who had criticised bankers for not doing business with Bangladesh's 80 per cent illiterate population. It now lends to 8,000 villages and manages to get 98 per cent of its loans repaid, which is considerably better than banks normally achieve.

Extending this idea widely would be expensive to organize, but it interests the US Congress, which studied the bank when it was working on the proposal of an Ohio congressman that 10 per cent of all America's foreign investment should be used for low interest loans to be repaid in foreign currencies, which would be a better way of funnelling aid than via dictators. 'I guarantee you, these programmes will work,' said former World Bank president Robert McNamara. 'The problem is how to do it . . . the administration costs are so high'.

It is a problem some banks are trying to solve in American inner cities. The foremost of these is the South Shore Bank of Chicago, which lends small sums of money in a decaying neighbourhood, primarily for rehabilitating buildings, financing small businesses or paying education fees, so that people can continue to live there. They began by lending to local businesses, but found that the state of the buildings was constantly undermining their efforts. The bank raises its money in the first place from their 'Development Deposits' which attracts investors who want their money used sensibly, and from local people's savings. It was set up 15 years ago by Ron Gryzwinski, who had reached the top of conventional banking when he became president of the Hyde Park Bank in his 30s.

'I sometimes think we're just old-fashioned good community bankers,' he told the US magazine *New Options*. 'The communities of people who've needed credit have remained essentially the same. But the banks have become international banks, and . . . can no longer relate to the neighbourhoods, because the neighbourhoods' needs aren't for billions of dollars. They're for tens or hundreds of thousands of dollars per deal.'

Like the Grameen Bank, the default rate is less than two per cent. Other schemes, like the Bank for Social Responsibility in New York, are following in South Shore's footsteps.

San Jose, in California, took a similar step towards financial independence when they realized that the nearest source of fire insurance was 3,000 miles away. So they set up their own insurance company. Not only did it give them greater flexibility, but the $25 million that the city was paying in insurance stayed within the local economy to be used again.

One of the first and most successful of the local banks was the Caja Laboral Popular, in the distressed area of Mondragon in northern Spain. The bank and the co-operative businesses that fed off it, were the life's work of a Jesuit priest, Father José Maria Arizmendiarretta, who arrived in Mondragon as a curate in 1941 when unemployment was around 50 per cent.

His first step was to organize a new technical college. By 1955, the first co-op was launched, making stoves. Now over 20,000 people work in a string of co-ops, set up with capital from the bank, which has £70 million in assets and 133 branches. There are 4,000 co-ops, and amazingly – such was the nurturing by the Caja Laboral – only three of them were ever failed.[14]

In Britain, local banking is taking the form of credit unions. There are now over 100, and the fastest growth has been in the Birmingham council estates, where almost the only remaining economic activities involve social security and the money-lenders who come round every week to collect their repayments – with interest of up to 3,000 per cent. The Birmingham Money Advice Centre is helping people to save instead through a credit union which they control, and from which they can borrow at reasonable rates of interest. There are now 10 credit unions in the city.

The co-ops, banks, credit unions and community businesses are all symptoms of a shifting perception of what economics is all about. They are different ways of reassessing the assets of local communities. Looked at in the old way, inner city neighbourhoods have only the social security payments of the unemployed and their families. Looked at again, they might have their combined purchasing power, or combined saving power, or a multitude of half-forgotten skills that might be brought to bear on local problems. Not very many neighbourhoods have used this knowledge yet, compared to the vast scale of the problem, but new 'home-grown' economies are emerging, where the goal is more than simply making a profit. Sometimes it is to employ people, sometimes to make them fulfilled, sometimes it is to learn.

The more people look to the hidden assets in their community, the more diverse the activities become. And the more money is kept flowing locally, the more they can begin to move outside the great necessities of the national economy – with its slumps and occasional recoveries – then the more they can start to build a healthy local economy to make their lives more liveable.

Local self reliance is the key to revival. Alternative economist Paul Ekins puts it like this: 'It is only when people, communities or countries can meet their needs from their own resources that they can take an independent stand in the world, and not only determine their own development path, but make their own contribution to the common good as they define it'.[15]

VI

So far, decentralization of power and economics to inner city communities has been achieved only on a very small scale. Over one million homes are still unfit to live in. How can this small-scale series of enthusiastic schemes ever hope to overturn these problems of centuries?

The schemes will remain mere drops in the ocean as long as governments and institutions believe they can be no more than that. Resources have been pumped into experimental schemes, or scraped together by charities and local groups, demonstrating that helping people to do things for themselves is tough – but possible. Organizations as diverse as ACTAC or Community Business Scotland have put forward plans for massively increasing the number of local groups they can reach and support. Maybe it is time they were tested.

From Trickle Down to Bottom Up

Officials are also suspicious of anything that might diminish their professional standing. For many years tackling problems meant high levels of public spending on big projects, co-ordinated from the top. The idea that salvation might lie in setting up and supporting a very large number of self-help projects is still strange to those brought up in public services or big corporations. Many officials are still unused to their new role as 'facilitators' for other people's decisions.

There is a different role for the professional architects and planners. The future may find them employed *by* neighbourhoods, not just employed on their behalf, and matching their expertize with that of the locals. But doing this means backing communities, making resources available with the minimum of what Prince Charles called the 'cat's cradle of red tape'. It means a revolution in inner city education, part of which comes from local people getting involved in the first place. Neighbourhood development and self help, as Tony McGann of the Eldonians said, is 'the best adult education you could give anyone'.

Yet the government shows a strange and contradictory attitude towards self-help. On the one hand they are encouraging and enthusiastic, with talk of the Victorian values of independence. On the other hand, their running battle with local councils who want to be entrepreneurs, or who show imagination of nearly any kind, constantly stops it from happening. Projects nearly always mean public spending of some kind in their early stages – often through local authorities – and this tends to close the collective government mind.

'It is essential that national policies for economic growth are nurtured at local level,' said government under secretary Christopher Chope, launching a report on local economic development, 'and that the public sector assists this process to take place.' It sounds promising, but the promises have not been fulfilled.

Another major objection raised against self-help is that it lets the government 'off the hook'. This is the argument of a frustrated socialist, implying that there is something intrinsically good about centralized public spending. Yet if public authorities are unable to cope, there must be a fundamental right for people to do it themselves: the alternative is the apathetic hopelessness of people trapped in appalling conditions. But there is a proviso: the government must remain responsible for making sure health, education, housing and other essential services are accessible to everyone. They cannot wash their hands of the responsibility, any more than inner city councillors should when they tie self-help projects up in red tape because they fear the government's job is being done for them.

There are two fundamental problems with decentralization that must be faced. One is how these projects can become self-sustaining.

The vast majority of local projects remain dependent on grants or hand-outs from one source or another. If they are to escape from the whims of government or local authorities, they must be economically independent, and a great deal more work will need to be done to find ways of achieving this. 'Local people need a stake in the ownership of the scheme,' Prince Charles told the Per Cent Club. 'Company patronage, or gifts and legacies, no matter how generous, from outsiders will not have the desired effect if the community has not been actively involved'.

The converse side of the problem is that community businesses must be protected from outside interference. There is a danger that the moment they become successful, they will be eyed greedily by conventional businessmen. What starts as a community business, ploughing its efforts back into local people, must be defensible.

Another path towards self-sufficiency may be by using land values to raise resources. When a community gives planning permission for a development which might even damage local people's interests the site can shoot up in value by up to ten times over. As it is, most of the profit – known as 'betterment' – goes to the developer. Agreements between developers and planners about whether walks or community centres ought to be provided in recompense are, at the moment, the only way that locals can benefit from this rise in values. Creaming off some of it would provide one way for neighbourhoods to tap into and use the value of their own land.

Finally there is the problem of the word 'community'. It is, as Tony Gibson has said, a 'fly-blown' word. 'Community' as a prefix in the 80s, as 'social' was in the 70s, is a guarantee that people will regard the idea as exciting and new. Often it is nothing of the kind; local people can be as wrong as anybody, especially when decisions affect individuals. As people are trusted to take their own decisions, relying increasingly on informal social pressure to keep each other in order or pay back their debts, we are in danger of letting loose a new parochialism, or an unhealthy interest in what the rest of the community is doing. Neighbourhood Watch may become more than the feared 'licence for snoopers'.

Not everyone warms to the idea of 'community spirit' – which expects them always to be mucking in and organizing festivals. Neighbourhood development is as much about learning to live with neighbours, and understanding that people rely increasingly on the good will of each other, and the honesty of our neighbours. But there will always be those who simply do not want to play.

Humanity is far from perfectible, and no amount of trusting some people with responsibility will make them so. But it is a risk worth taking. A decentralized society can solve problems, because it brings out hidden talents and resources in a way that a centralized state is simply unable to do. It may be our only way forward. We must still take care that we do not unleash a monster of social disapproval at the same time. And we must be careful that in two generations time, a backlash of young hawks who want to remould society in another way does not emerge to take us back where we started.

There is also a danger that these initiatives, adopted when government officials ignored the cities, might be pushed aside once the recession is over and 'mainstream' solutions take over again. But as one commentator said: 'Any idea which manages to combine Thatcherite self help with Marxist power to the people, and win royal approval, must surely have something going for it.'[16]

The last word should go to Alan McDonald, from his book about the Weller Street Housing Co-op. 'Lightning didn't strike a small corner of Liverpool one starry night and spark genius in a dozen homes. Talent likes theirs is buried in council blocks, in offices and on the shop floor, in the under-achievers at school and the under-employed in the dole queue. The co-op happens to have been a rare opportunity for a group of working class people to demonstrate what society is burying.'

In fact some of the alternatives being developed go way beyond either Thatcherism or Marxism – and they suffer from the usual uncertainties and hurdles of pioneering ideas. It is far from clear, even, how local self-help can be encouraged. If officials intervene with support too early or too late, or in the wrong way, people's hopes or motivations can be swept away, leaving them with the same hopeless resignation. There is still a long way to go.

8

MEET ME IN ST LOUIS

*And dream of London, small and white and clean,
The clear Thames bordered by its gardens green.*

William Morris

'Modern architecture died in St Louis, Missouri, on July 15 1972 at 3.30pm (or thereabouts).' So concluded the influential architectural critic Charles Jencks, with a precision reminiscent of Archbishop Ussher's calculation for the moment of Creation. What actually happened at the fateful moment was the spectacular explosion of part of the massive Pruitt-Igoe flats, which had been so widely praised for their design when they became home for 3,000 families in the 1950s.

It is a satisfactorily symbolic moment for what was in fact a very long process, spreading over more than 20 years: a process that is the background to many of the possibilities outlined in this book.

Pruitt-Igoe, named after a leading Democrat politician (Pruitt) and a black fighter pilot (Igoe), was 11-storeys of 'deck access' housing, with the clean square lines beloved of the powerful 'modernist' school of design. 'Modern'-style flats transformed the post-war inner cities. In Britain they filled the empty bomb-sites and later replaced district after district of run-down terraced homes. The demolition of Pruitt-Igoe in 1972 marked the end of a style which dominated inner city housing 'solutions' for a generation.

Before it reached the age of 15, Pruitt-Igoe was half empty and in such bad repair that some blocks had water flowing down the stairs. The original dream of Pruitt-Igoe as a community of mixed classes had long been abandoned, and the flats had become a 'sink' estate for anyone who could not afford anywhere else. When a general meeting of tenants was called in 1971, they begun chanting 'Blow It Up!' as soon as it began. After the remaining flats were cleared from the site in 1976, St Louis' city authorities still had $60m to pay for the original building and the repairs.

High rise and 'modern' flats were intended to put an end to deprivation once and for all, and they have failed. Worse, both the designs and the attitudes that went with them are now central to inner city problems 20 years later.

Modernism began with the work of the German architect Walter Gropius, who opened his Bauhaus school in Weimar in 1919. He stood for simplicity, clean lines, and above all – in a new generation struggling to transcend the destruction of the First World War – he stood for honesty. There was to be no more pretending that life was something it was not. Houses were, as the French modernist Le Corbusier put it, no more and no less than 'machines for living in'.

The style had won through so completely by the 1950s that it was taught to the exclusion of any other in western architectural schools. This was the age of the expert and the minimalist. 'Less is more,' explained the architect Mies van der Rohe. Modernism was also the style that meant 'progress', going hand-in-hand with cheap production so that everybody could benefit. In the inner cities it meant flats designed by high-minded experts, massive blocks – known in America as 'worker housing' – like Pruitt-Igoe. The workers who were to live in the new-style flats might not like them very much, but Le Corbusier explained that they must be 're-educated'. 'The design of cities is too important to be left to citizens,' he said.

Experts believed that consulting the tenants would only water down their creations. So instead of heralding a new way of life, the blocks have often just added to the sense of alienation. 'The only people left trapped in worker housing in America today are those who don't work at all. They are on welfare,' said the writer Tom Wolfe.[1]

Meet Me in St Louis

The end of modernism had been predicted as early as 1959 by the American architectural guru Philip Johnson. It was Johnson who launched a new style 20 years later with his AT&T office block in New York, which had a Chippendale style decoration on the top as if it was an 18th century chair. By then a new 'post modernism', fun, colourful, joky and with historic allusions, was being hailed by critics like Charles Jencks, its self-appointed interpreter. 'Less,' said the architect Robert Venturi, paraphrasing Mies van der Rohe, 'is a bore'.

The shift from modernism to post-modernism is often perceived as a rather exclusive debate, confined mainly to the arts pages of newspapers and magazines. Yet its influence is enormous, and it lies behind many changes in our way of life. It also provides a parallel for the changing approaches to inner city problems described in this book.

Modernism began, like socialism, with the highest ideals. The famous British modernist Berthold Lubetkin explained in a passionate response to one of Prince Charles' broadcasts: 'The social aims of the 1918 generation were to debunk wartime bluff and those lies and deceits, that make-believe which insulted our intelligence. For us the search for truth was not a virtue but a duty.'

But by the 1960s, this truthful creed was devastating. Truth meant no fripperies or delusions. The clean designs were caricatured and mis-interpreted by cost-cutting bureaucrats, and even the better housing rarely went beyond the functional. Idealistic designers had imagined cameraderie in the new corridors and balconies or on the vast expanses of open grass around the blocks; they felt that people would live in a utopian community with each other if the building forced them together. 'We really believed, in a quasi-religious sense, in the perfectibility of human nature, in the role of architecture as a weapon of social reform,' confessed Philip Johnson. The trouble was that human nature, if it is perfectible at all, is not made any better when people are forced into each others' company. But the architects and planners clung to their idealism, and blamed the social failure of their schemes on the tenants. Meanwhile, the bonds that had sustained slum neighbourhoods throughout economic recessions had been broken.

During the 1950s and 60s – the 'great age' of modernism – professionals were regarded as the aesthetic experts: ordinary people could not be expected to understand – still less to take part in designing – the places they would inhabit, any more than they could understand the obscurities of 'modern' poetry. However, people *were* expected to enjoy the obscure symbolism they would have to live in. One Japanese architect explained that 'the family will welcome with joy not only the new dwelling, but also its elevation towards the sky, which symbolises their taking their place as members of urban society.'[2]

Modernists had started from scratch with the inner cities. There was to be no historical continuity, no consultation, no understanding, no identity at all. It was with shocked surprise that they watched the emergence of a new ideal, which was joky, cynical colourful, decorated and small-scale, firmly rooted in the past, and clearly with no intention of reforming anything.

In Bologna, a recently demolished block of 30s flats were so sorely missed that the city rebuilt it just as it had been. Philip Johnson's Chippendale style spawned a whole generation of joky pastiches, and a flurry of small brightly painted brick houses flooding into London's docklands. Artists and professionals began to see themselves not as detached observers, but as people taking part in a complex system of life, seeing it from a range of different standpoints.

This change in the way we view architecture and the inner cities has been given an extra push in Britain with the arrival of Prince Charles into the debate – which he entered like an Old Testament prophet in 1984. His views are complex, varied and interconnected, and together make up a philosphy – I'll call it 'Charlesism' for want of a better word – which is likely to have a vital long term impact on the inner cities.

Charlesism is a kind of post-modernism in a way. He talks about local identity, individual or community self-help, heritage and everybody having a say, with professional experts kept firmly in their place. Yet Charles himself is no great fan of post-modern buildings, dubbing the plan for No 1 Poultry by architect James Stirling as 'like a 1930s wireless'. Nor could anyone describe the Prince of Wales as cynical: he comes across as intense, caring and honest.

There are also distinct strands in his message and although they are linked, some of them seem downright contradictory. Protection of the environment, encouragement of classical design, and protecting the heritage all seem to fit together quite neatly. But what happens if his concern for community involvement goes against protecting the heritage? What happens if the community suddenly decides to sacrifice their environment for their livelihood?

Prince Charles' backing for the environmental movement has been one of its biggest coups of the 1980s. He was by far the most important convert to the cause before Mrs Thatcher announced that she was a 'friend of the earth' in 1988. It is said that it was Charles who first convinced her that green issues were worth pursuing. By 1987, the impact of the green movement was such that a MORI poll found that 77 per cent of Conservative voters believed that the government should give a 'much higher priority to protecting the environment'. The atmosphere was very different to the previous year, when developer Lord Northfield claimed that Charles had been 'hijacked by the loony green brigade' after he suggested that houses should be built in inner cities rather than on green fields in the countryside.

Inner cities are badly in need of a green thinking that recognizes that *everybody's* environment is important – not just the country dwellers'. Charles seems to recognize some of these contradictions in his speeches, and tries to resolve them by linking his ideas firmly to the spiritual. His BBC *Omnibus* programme in October 1988 focused on man's spiritual needs. 'The soul is irrational, unfathomable, mysterious,' he declared; if we put ourselves above God or nature, then we will suffer. 'What we really need to do is to regain the humility to understand the lessons of the past'. This is partly a technique the royal family uses when they want to say something controversial. As a future 'Defender of the Faith', Charles can wrap his sharper messages in religious hopes ,and somehow they become more acceptable. On the other hand, Charles obviously believes it. Buildings should 'raise the spirits', he said, arousing 'respect and awe for the great mystery of the natural order of the universe'.[3]

His concern for heritage supports this – and, in fact, the Prince's own Duchy of Cornwall is very good at building new projects which blend in with local pitched roofs.

The most important – and by far the most radical – of Charles' messages is that people should be involved in decisions affecting their own environment. This is the most important for the inner cities, and goes beyond what would otherwise be an abstruse debate about style. 'Having been told so firmly what was fashionable and intellectually acceptable - what was artistically correct and contemporary, most of us were cowed into feeling that we were imbeciles even to consider that what was being produced was thoroughly inhuman,' he told the Remaking Cities conference in Pittsburgh in 1988. Charles champions the belief that everyone has a right to a point of view about what buildings and places should look like: there are no 'experts'.

Inner City Aid, the fund-raising organization set up as one of the Prince's trusts in 1986, was intended to put this idea into practical terms. The Band Aid-style campaign would funnel resources through to inner city communities so that they could employ their own professionals and make their own neighbourhoods. But it was, and is, a radical message that conflicts with a whole basket-load of entrenched interests, and it was soon clear that Inner City Aid was not going to be allowed the prominence that it had expected. Rumours circulated that it had been forced by the other Prince's Trusts to delay their fund-raising.

In March 1988, the government had been seriously worried about the impact he might make with his Pittsburgh speech in US presidential election year. In spite of vigorous lobbying by the American architectural establishment, Charles still called for 'community architecture' in his Pittsburgh speech. But by the summer he was being more careful. The Civic Trust's long-awaited report on wasteland was delayed twice for the Prince to provide his promised foreword. They had to make do with one from a former chairman of the London Docklands instead.

In architecture and the environment, Prince Charles has picked a topic where he enjoys widespread public support of the populist kind that Mrs Thatcher enjoys. It is not clear that the two forces of Charles and Thatcherism are actually so opposed. Charles's remark that people will move from asking 'how can I get a job' to 'how can I make a living' is Thatchterite in tone, but looks forward to a very different kind of world.

It may be that Charles's future is not one locked in combat with the government – but, as columnist Simon Jenkins put it, he may turn out to be the 'voice of post-Thatcherism' (*Sunday Times*, 30.10.88). If that is so, we may be able to glimpse the inner city debate in his pronouncements.

It remains to be seen how the Prince's campaign will develop as he takes on more responsibility. The danger is that if inner cities become more prominent politically, Charles will have to code his messages more carefully and water them down. But we know what he thinks.

II

The 1981 riots marked a turning point in the inner city debate. People were brought face to face with the consequences of policy mistakes, and with the full horror of what would happen if they continued to be made.

Conventional thinking at the time divided neatly between the government and opposition, one favouring private finance, and the other public subsidies to lead the 'recovery'. But by the end of the decade, the debate has shifted and is no longer so clear-cut. A new interest in community architecture, 'designing out' crime, greening cities, the arts and self-help, is emerging as we look at different ways to revitalize the cities. Dour modernism is out, as are central government hand-outs. Diversity and individualism are in.

As we have seen, some of the new ideas are coming to life in inner cities all over the UK. But there is still a very long way to go if inner cities are to be put in charge of their own destinies. Fashion has turned full circle, so that the eyes of top government policy-makers are back on the inner cities. Small-scale projects that put neighbourhoods in control may be brushed aside again in the rush of government and capital in pursuit of a 'big idea' downtown. The 'alternative' approaches, which flourished when the government had little interest, could be throttled by mainstream private sector regeneration.

As time goes by the problems as well as the solutions change, and there are forces at work which could make inner cities – for better, or for worse – into very different places.

For example, people's feelings are changing about what they want out of life and the places they live. This is summed up in the term 'inner directed', coined by the market researchers who specialize in categorizing people by their attitudes rather than their class.

The fastest growing category in the UK are the people who are in control of their cravings for either the next meal or for worldly success, both of which historically brought people in their millions into the cities. This rising category of 'inner directed' people have satisfied those needs, and are looking instead for independence, health or even spirituality. These are the people who dream of self-employment rather than a new Porsche, or a small-holding in the countryside rather than a semi-detached in the suburbs. In Britain the 'inner-directeds' now account for 36 per cent of the population – and are predicted to rise to more than half the population by 2010.[4]

All this is important for the inner cities. Families like this will feel less like living in unpleasant surroundings, or bringing up children in a bad environment just for the sake of the job or the rat race. They are leaving both the inner cities and the suburbs, to a rather healthier life in the country towns. Counties like Dorset or Norfolk are growing fast, and this trend is accelerated as information technology allows more people to work from home, and more companies to move their headquarters' away from the big centres.

The redevelopment of inner cities, where it is taking place, is to a much lower density partly to cater for this. The old tenement blocks in the centre of Glasgow, which only survived because of years threatened by motorway schemes which never happened, are now being done up as private flats. But it is clear simply from walking through them, without play areas or very much space, that few families live there.

As a result of this process, inner city schools are in danger of withering away – another major obstacle in the way of creating balanced communities.

Another change is the emerging agreement in British politics. Since the riots there has been a rapid coming together, and the radical young Labour councillors of the mid-80s are now wearing suits and trying to give the impression of good management. Policy-makers in all parties are bandying around terms like 'green' and 'quality of life' to explain their new positions. Utilitarianizm is reborn, and the parties at Westminster have instead to prove each other incompetent rather than simply wrong. Suddenly everyone agrees that the environment must be protected. That means they must prove that the other parties are hypocritical, which will not make for very constructive political debate. Equally, all parties in the centre and left agree on the need to decentralize power, although they differ about the methods and extent.

The present consensus on the inner cities says that public-private partnerships are a Good Thing – though there is a debate about what kind of partnerships they should be. It also says that people ought to be 'consulted' about their neighbourhoods, without any clear idea about how this should be done. Consensus calls for house-building in the inner cities instead of in green areas, and there is growing agreement that cities have a need for green areas themselves.

Politics seems to be changing at a local level too. Councillors are learning that they must break free of the old political divisions and unite around the future of the city. Confrontation did not work for Liverpool. Co-operation may well be working for Glasgow. Equally, inner city groups are beginning to use politicians for their own benefit, rather than the other way round. The Liverpool housing co-ops, for example, regard politics as part of the system that has ignored them for so long, and are prepared to work it by playing parties off against each other. When local politicians were obstructive, the Eldonians were prepared to take over their local branch and sack them.

Other distinctions are getting blurred as well. Public-private partnerships in inner cities have confused the divisions between public and private sectors which used to so dominate the debate. Private businessmen are now involved in most major government initiatives, while public power – in the form of Urban Development Corporations – is no longer primarily on the side of the public. The involvement in inner city renewal by the private sector is probably the greatest single change in the last five years.

The problems faced by slum communities a generation ago have altered. We no longer have the Victorian slums –but we don't have the communities any more either. We have new slums, which trap their inhabitants in increasing isolation from each other, suffering from a whole gamut of social problems from drug-addiction to debt. They are trapped not just by poverty, but by the deliberate policies of 30 years, formulated by all sides of politics to protect the status quo. Ghettos of flats for the urban poor, surrounded by terraced houses deliberately kept empty in case gentrifiers moved in, have been a feature of inner city areas since the war.

Behind this lies the slow death of Labourism as a coherent political force, together with the municipal socialist dream of eradicating urban poverty. It is the same with the crisis of council housing. By 1979, municipal housing had so alienated tenants that the new Conservative government was able to offer them the chance of paying to escape council control. The years of bureaucracy, inefficiency and petty restrictions about pets, repairs and the height of hedges seem to have destroyed the dream. The years of decay and dereliction in estates which have voted Labour for years can't be entirely excused by spending controls – they go far beyond that, as if councillors preferred the propaganda value of dirty homes to doing something effective about it. Once again it was inner city people who suffered.

Meanwhile, the government has used the appalling image of local government as an excuse for winding up council housing and local democracy, without any clear idea of what can take their place, at a time when – at the present rate of progress – it will take up to 1,000 years to replace Britain's housing stock.

Partnerships between big business and centrally-imposed QUANGOs, like the London Docklands, are taking on much of the thrust of urban renewal. But they can do no more than impose blueprint solutions on areas from Liverpool to London. The resulting big redevelopment schemes often bear no relation to the needs and aspirations of local people, and could well add to their problems.

At the same time partnerships between cities and local companies which are at the centre of American success stories are being systematically undermined in Britain. As city councils have their powers whittled away, they have less and less to offer in equal partnership with local business. Equally, the new 'uniform business rate' removes one of their last remaining levers to make their area more attractive to business. Under the new rates system, businesses will pay the same wherever they are.

Local government in Britain is one of the most innovative, energetic and important forces unleashed in recent history. Using the excuse of lunacy and inefficiency to wind them up will reduce the chances of the constructive power of local pride and commitment being brought to bear in the regeneration process. It would have been far better to make councils representative by introducing a proportional voting system, properly reflecting the views of voters.

Instead the government has found a new enthusiasm, bypassing local councillors, based on construction and renewing the fabric of cities. Test that against the aim of making inner cities vote Conservative 'next time' at the general election, and it will probably be judged a successful policy. If the main objective is to tackle derelict land, it may also be a success in the end. But it must also be tested against whether it can tackle dependence and helplessness among inner city people – and by that yardstick, the policy does not offer much.

In the long run it is the visual impact that the government wants – emphasized by the new blue signs which are to appear on sites being redeveloped by them. What is to happen to the people who are priced out of their homes by policies that only cover construction? In the east London borough of Newham, for example, more houses are being built than in any other borough in Britain. But nearly all are being built for sale in the London Docklands. Newham Council, meanwhile, is stuck with more tower blocks than any other local authority and a bed and breakfast bill of £7 million.

The most frightening problem for inner city people is that there is no clear place for them to move to. Westminster made an attempt to shift problem homeless families out to temporary accommodation on the far edge of east London, and it maybe that the logical end of the government policies is to move people to new sink estates which are unlikely to find themselves gentrified in the foreseeable future. Inner city people on the edges are already in a worse predicament, without shops, land or means of livelihood. No amount of tourism or artistic excitement is likely to help the people of an outer estate like Easterhouse in Glasgow.

A frightening vision of ghettos for inner city people was spelled out recently by Professor Brian Robson, a leading inner city expert. He fears that 'no-go' areas for those on welfare benefits, for the criminals and misfits and those in the poorest housing, will become part of most towns and cities, providing occasional cheap labour, work for badly-funded public services and charities, and overtime for the police. 'Those who argue it could never happen here have only to go to Belfast,' Robson warned.[5]

What will happen then? Ghettos are not containable. Their problems tend to spill out and endanger the rest of society; nor can a civilized society survive with such skeletons in its cupboard. It is one scenario that must not be allowed to happen.

III

Looking to the future, then, we have the ghetto approach, keeping people dependent and walling them in, or the alternative of helping inner city people to become more independent and in control of the assets they still possess.

Put that way, the choice seems a simple one. But rushing headlong towards self-help and local control may simply trigger some equally dangerous reactions in the opposite direction: the ideas sketched out in this book will have their drawbacks as well. After all, there will be problems for a new generation that has been brought up in communities which have responsibility for solving their own problems.

The kind of informal social controls that will emerge when neighbourhoods are responsible for budgets and decisions may be just as sharp as the bureaucratic ones. And the mistakes which *will* be made by local people with power over other people's lives may seem unforgiveable to a new generation. We must also make sure that revolutions in the inner cities are not so crude that they will be overturned in the next century. It's as well to remember that nearly every 'solution' to inner city problems has found itself turned on its head by a horrified new generation. The same will probably happen to the government's present policies, and time may even condemn ideas like community architecture or green cities, none of which can provide the whole answer.

Century after century, inner city people have suffered from the arrogance of people who thought they had the complete solution: the whole debate about inner cities is shot through with patronizing attitudes which amount to a stultifying and cynical snobbery. There is still the underlying idea that ordinary people cannot be trusted to design their own homes; that crime is endemic and natural in cities, and that nothing can be done about it. There is another idea among the intelligentsia that provincial cities would not benefit from or understand the arts. Inner city solutions are still what professionals or politicians, or property developers now, decide for inner city people.

This is not old-fashioned class snobbery, but something more subtle which is shared by people right through the political spectrum, from the Royal Academy audience who laughed at the idea of an art gallery in Rotherham, to the press who derided the idea of Birmingham staging the Olympics or Bradford attracting tourists. And from the trade unionists who would not be 'dictated to by a bunch of tenants' to the professionals who do not see that women have viewpoints about the design of underpasses or buses.

Snobbery has infected the welfare state to its core. Professor David Donnison, in his recent study of Glasgow's revival, found social security offices with 'separate waiting rooms: one courteous, relaxed, with open counters and a plentiful supply of leaflets for the majority of workers who only come to claim insurance benefits; and the other, with chairs screwed to the floor, no readily available leaflets and massive barriers between staff and public, which deals with poorer claimants who depend on means-tested supplementary benefit'.

These attitudes are deep in the political establishment, and they can be traced in one form or another throughout the history of the inner cities. They have forced people who live there deeper and deeper into powerless and sullen dependence on the state. What is provided is done by experts *for* them: solutions are what outsiders can do *for* the inner cities, which have been the subject of generations of experimental solutions imposed on them from above.

The key to the new approaches outlined in this book is to restore the latent local pride in cities and neighbourhoods by encouraging them to find their own environmental and social assets. Pride in cities has been vital to the revival of hopeless American towns, pride in neighbourhood was the key to the revival of places like Eldon Street in Liverpool. Pride can release hidden talents, skills and energies that can rescue areas. We should stop laughing patronizingly at it, and start working to release it.

To find this potential, people need to share visions of the kind of places they want their inner cities to be. What should they be for? Who should live there? What should they look like?

We no longer stare with a mixture of awe and horror at gleaming sci-fi pictures of The City of the Year 2000. We don't believe in it any more, either in the inevitability of change or of its benefits. Massive models of inner city redevelopment schemes have disappeared from council planning offices, replaced by a new kind of planning, involving leverage, partnership and long negotiations with developers.

Planning itself – the great hope of the 1940s – has taken the full blame for the disastrous development decisions of the 1960s. Planners have suffered this quite unfairly, partly because 'planner' happens to fit more neatly into headlines than does 'architect', and also because the word 'planning' now carries implications of what *They* are planning for *Us*. The word is dying out of respectable use. But what planning stands for, the management of environmental change, has never been more important or popular than it is now.

It is the *process* that concerns people, not the final goal of a 'City

2000': the slow business of small changes in the right direction. There is less agreement or common vision about the objective, the kind of inner cities we want to achieve beyond a feeling that if you organize things in a certain way, with consultation and discussions with ethnic minority groups, the change will be in the right direction. The *vision* of high rise living has given way to the *process* of community architecture.

The danger is that without any vision of how places *could* be, the passion and drive to get there are muted. Without clear agreement about the route or destination, we are even less likely to arrive.

But there is one vision that has emerged in the last few years which may well play an important role. It is a vision from the minds, not of planners or architects, but of doctors, and it looks towards inner cities where people have space, learning, green fields but – above all – health.

'To enter the city it was necessary first to pass through a tower which housed a camera obscura and what I saw within its image I could hardly believe – the central area of the city and leading away from the river, north, east and south where just 15 years before there had been dereliction and squalor, was a mass of green . . .'

Not 15 years ago, but 15 years from now. That was the way Dr John Ashton visualized a stroll through inner city Liverpool in a decade's time. Ashton and the Healthy Cities movement – under the auspices of the World Health Organization – are providing one of the few coherent visions of cities, not as they are now but as they could be in the future.

His description of walking through a pastoral version of Liverpool was in his pamphlet *Esmedune 2000* (Esmedune is Anglo-Saxon for Toxteth), one based on health and enterprize, with communal bicycles and no litter. Like William Morris' vision of London in *News from Nowhere*, published almost exactly a century ago, John Ashton had seen the future – and it was grassed over.

A World Health Organization conference in Ottawa in 1986 put together a programme for healthier cities based on community participation, reorganized medical services and learning for people about keeping healthy. Eleven cities in Europe are taking part in the project, including Glasgow, which has launched an anti-smoking campaign and a *Glasgow Good Air Guide*.

Meet Me in St Louis

The healthy cities vision is one of clean rivers and edible trout, and a less hectic, more rural, life in the heart of the city. But it carries a price with it for places like Toxteth: if they are really to have meadows and woods there must be far fewer people living there. The people who can afford to leave have been doing so for many years, and there is now talk of 'spread cities' – spread so far that they cover whole regions of the country, not with concrete, but with linked clusters of houses and small-holdings, most of them in touch with the outside world by information technology.

As the population leaves regions like the south east are becoming recognized for what they really are – vast cities with different environments ranging from concrete to cows. This trend has already gone some way in the USA, usually ahead of Europe in these matters, where half the population told Gallup pollsters in 1986 that they wanted to move to towns of less than 10,000 people.

On this side of the Atlantic, the leading geographer Professor Peter Hall believes we may be going back to the settlement patterns of the Middle Ages. 'After the rude disturbances of the industrial revolution, which dragged our ancestors from the fields into the mines and satanic mills, we return to our roots,' he said. 'The maps of population change in the 1980s are almost the precise inverse of those in the 1880.' The 'flight to the green' may be reaching its logical conclusion.

But where is the solution for inner city problems? Spread City surrounding Healthy City – on the face of it – might carry on draining resources away as the richer population leaves, leaving behind the young people to live there, and the poor. Where do the low paid and the unemployed go in this scenario?

For Spread City to be attractive as a *solution*, inner city people must be able to take part in the 'spreading' if they want to, however poor they are. And if they stay in the inner cities, they must be given the resources to build livelihoods for themselves from the extra space. Wasteland left behind does not just magic itself into woods and parks. People must be provided with the chance to find low rent or low cost housing, small-holdings or workshops – rather than given the increasingly tangled web of loopholes that such projects are fast becoming.

The spreading of cities is of great concern to the decision-makers: it means such radical changes for them. The prevailing political consensus is also against the idea, partly because of the vested interests of people who already live in rural areas, and partly because so many politicians still feel it would be better for everyone if inner city people just stayed quietly where they are.

On the other hand, the draw of small towns and rural living is obviously very strong. Policy-makers ought to take note of this, because if people with families are to remain in the inner cities of their own free will when they have the choice, something of that small town rural lifestyle must be made possible in inner cities too.

IV

So what kind of inner cities do we want? This was the question posed by the Town and Country Planning Association in their 1986 report *Whose Responsibility? Reclaiming the Inner Cities*, and the answer has been changing subtly even since then.

We seem to be moving towards a consensus for places with the atmosphere of villages but the excitement and possibilities of cities – places with mixed classes and ages, and mixed uses, integrated with the rest of the city and surrounding countryside, without pockets of poverty, however small.

Not everybody will agree even with this outline, but the real divisions are about the means to get there. The government aims to bring business back into inner areas, and with them the middle classes and entrepreneurs, in the hope that they will drag the neighbourhoods up with them.

The colourful shopping centres being built there as a result were exciting at first, but now have an air of sameness about them. This could also be said of their social policies. 'For all he tried so hard, the minister for Merseyside has left us prettier perhaps, but poorer,' Toxteth councillor Margaret Simey said about Heseltine. 'The sense of oppression and exclusion has strengthened, not weakened.'[6]

The means suggested by the other sides are very different, ranging from traditional public spending by central government to traditional public spending by local government. There are also important new ideas about economics, suggesting that we change the way city economies work so that they are 'circular' – using all the waste products and rubbish that ruin inner city environments as the raw materials for new businesses.

These kind of new economic ideas aim to insulate communities from the full effects of the world economy, so that people are able to carry on reasonably full lives in spite of the level of the stock market. But they require real political changes, giving power and resources to the local level.

In the short term, policies are easier to find. They will involve co-ordination, across government departments and professional boundaries. Inner city problems are as complex as they are deep-seated, and only a multi-sectoral approach can have a chance of getting to grips with the problem as a whole – which includes the complications of the rest of the region as well as the inner city itself.

Co-ordination is one way of cutting back bureaucracy and red tape, which as Prince Charles said, is 'strangling this country from end to end'. It must also take in areas of inner city policy which seem to be forgotten by the present government.

One of the main areas is social housing. This has become such a complex business to provide. Local authorities do not have the resources to provide it, and voluntary organizations are forced through a series of complicated legal loopholes. Behind this lies the problem of land values. The current strategy of raising the value of land in inner cities so that private developers start getting interested in it is also undermining some of the most exciting partnership projects with local groups. Methods must be found so that neighbourhoods can get access to land without having to fork out impossible commercial prices.

Then there is education. Its failure in the inner cities has deepened the cycles of decline. In London, fears about what will happen once the ILEA is abolished have driven more parents out of the inner cities for the sake of their children's education. Boston's revival as a city has been based on education – there are over 65 institutions of higher education in Greater Boston, more than in the whole of Britain – and the idea of compacts between city schools and employers was originated there.

The old compact between teachers and pupils – that if they pass exams they will get a job – has long ago broken down in British cities. Teaching must be related to their different needs, and encourage co-operation and practical independence, rather than dependence on non-existent big employers. Personal freedom is essential if people's creativity is to be released.

Finally there is energy. Cities are enormous wasters of energy, and giving city councils responsibility for it, as they have in Swedish cities, could provide the basis for a revival. Bad insulation is a source of appalling suffering for elderly people in inner city areas. District heating or combined heat and power schemes can add to energy efficiency in inner cities – as could using the acres of tarmac, or other wasted land as solar collectors.

In the long term, three directions are vital for the inner cities.

First, if they are to become pleasant places to live in, people who want to leave must be helped to do so. Without this kind of planning, the only ones left will be the young and rich and the poverty-stricken and dependent. New balanced communities, new kinds of garden cities, must be built beyond the green belt as well as inside the cities, and are vital to inner city revival. But there is a condition: that inner cities do not suffer financially as a result. Call it development tax if necessary, but some of the wealth of the new country towns must be able to be ploughed back into inner cities. The next generation of investment in garden cities must not be *instead* of inner cities, but as *well* as, and the revival by the Town and Country Planning Association of their campaign for garden cities in 1988 is an important step. We need to think about merging the best of city life with the best of the country, not just with small businesses in the countryside, but by growing crops in the cities too.

It means making inner city life more liveable, which must involve replacing some of the traffic with new kinds of efficient and dignified public transport. It is the indignities, as well as the inefficiencies, of travelling by bus, underground or train in cities that are keeping people in the jams.

Second, the principle of local control and responsibility must be established – not just for local authorities, but for the neighbourhoods within them. This is the only way of encouraging the sense of identity and the pride that is necessary for a sustainable revival. It means guaranteeing local democracy by a proportional representation system, and it means providing communities with the resources they need to tackle their own problems.

Finally, new economic tools must be developed that can cope with inner city problems. We need better methods of measuring success than the Gross National Product, which has become a hopeless blunderbuss, ignoring voluntary work or environmental damage. We need financial systems that allow inner city neighbourhoods to make use of their wasted resources – people, land, buildings, and to encourage people and companies to make use of their waste products, making some of the economics circular by using the industrial waste that has had such a disastrous impact on cities. And basic income schemes, that provide everyone with a basic wage irrespective of whether they are employed or not, could help put an end to third class citizenship.

Whether cities develop along these lines in the next few years remains to be seen. Whichever directions they take, inner cities are likely to remain as full of contradictions as before – just like the American cities that are now on the road to recovery.

St Louis, which gave birth to and demolished the Pruitt-Igoe flats, is now undergoing a well-publicized renaissance. Having been America's 'most distressed big city' in 1980, St Louis will play host to the American Institute of Architects in 1989 as a place which has 'a lot going on downtown'. Now the city faces enormous problems of gentrification, and of inner city people priced out of their neighbourhoods. Across the Mississippi, East St Louis is on the brink of bankruptcy – so that policeman sometimes even have to use their own cars.

Since Britain tends to follow American trends, it is reasonable to expect that some of the successes and problems of St Louis might be in store also for Glasgow and even Liverpool.

St Louis' renaissance came from discovering and using assets they had forgotten they possessed – the second largest cinema in the USA has been re-opened as a successful theatre, an old station has been redeveloped by James Rouse, and neighbourhood arts councils are using some of the forgotten local talents.

This book is about finding new assets like these for inner cities in Britain. Recent history demonstrates that simply throwing public or private money at inner city problems is worse than useless, though money is desperately needed and little can be achieved without it. Inner cities also need the clout and independence that their own assets can bring them – and they must discover them, in spite of a history of official interference which has undermined what they have. Only with their own assets, including a good environment, community skills, heritage and the arts, or local economic muscle, like the combined people's spending or savings, can inner cities find solutions that are sustainable.

What neighbourhoods have themselves will not be enough to change the future of every inner city community. But it may still provide the chance of a better future for some of them. They can be helped or hindered: the choice is ours.

NOTES
TO THE TEXT

INTRODUCTION
1. 'Looking for the Inner City', *Town & Country Planning*, October 1988.
2. Church of England Commission on Urban Priority Areas, *Faith in the City: a call for action by Church and nation*, London 1985.

CHAPTER 1
1. *The People of the Abyss*, quoted in Peter J. Keating, *Into Unknown England 1866–1913: selections from the social explorers*, Manchester University Press 1976, p.224.
2. Ian Archer, forthcoming book *The Achievement of Stability/ Social Relations in later 16th Century London*.
3. Raymond Williams, *The Country and the City*, Chatto 1973, p. 221.
4. Quoted in Michael Hebbert, *Inner City Problems in Historical Context*, Social Science Research Council 1980.
5. *Past and Present*, London 1843.
6. (ed.) G. K. Clark, *Portrait of an Age: Victorian England*, OUP 1977, p. 20.
7. E. D. Simon and J, Inman, *The Rebuilding of Manchester*, Longmans 1935.
8. Friedrich Engels, *Condition of the Working Class in England in 1844*.

9. Michael Hebbert, op cit, p. 29.
10. *Town & Country Planning*, October 1938.
11. (ed.) J. Wood, *Still to Decide*, quoted in Martin Walker, *The National Front*, Fontana 1977.
12. Quoted in Julian Critchley, *Heseltine: the unauthorised biography*, Deustch 1987, p. 60.

CHAPTER 2
1. *The Times*, 10 July 1981.
2. *The Scarman Report: the Brixton Disorders 10–12 April 1981*, Penguin 1982.
3. Speech to the National Housing and Town Planning Council November 1982.
4. *The Times*, 15 July 1982.
5. Michael Heseltine, *Where there's a Will*, Hutchinson 1987, p. 143.
6. Ibid., p. 133.
7. Dockland News 11.
8. Roger Tym & Partners, *Monitoring Enterprise Zones: Year Three Report*, 1984.
9. Anne Jacobs, *50,000 Bluebells: the story of Liverpool's Garden Festival*, Windward 1984.
10. *The Times*, 14 April 1982.
11. *The Sunday Times*, 20 February 1983.
12. Francis Wheen, *The Battle for London*, Pluto Press 1985.
13. *Financial Times*, 11 March 1985.
14. *The Times*, 2 October 1985.
15. Ibid, 8 October 1985.
16. *Whose Responsibility? Reclaiming the Inner Cities*, Town and Country Planning Association 1986.
17. *Estates Times*, April 1987.
18. Alan Pike, *Financial Times*, 8 March 1988.
19. Colin Ward, *When we Build Again*, Pluto Press 1985.
20. (ed.) David Donnison and Alan Middleton, *Regenerating the Inner City: Glasgow's Experience*, RKP 1987.
21. Stuart Cosgrove and Denis Campbell, Behind the Wee Smile, *New Statesman and Society*, 16 February 1988.
22. *New Society*, 8 January 1988.
23. Nigel Pollit, 'Gerrymandering the Tory Vote', *Roof*, November/December 1988.

24. Brian Robson, *Those Inner Cities: Reconciling the social and economic aims of urban policy*, OUP 1988.
25. *Blueprint*, June 1988.

CHAPTER 3
1. Mary Tuck and Peter Southgate, *Ethnic Minorities, Crime and Policing*, Home Office Research Study 70, HMSO 1981.
2. Geoffrey Pearson, *Hooligan: a history of respectable fears*, Macmillan 1988.
3. Sir Robert Mark, *In the Office of Constable*, Collins 1978.
4. Quoted in J. J. Tobias, *Crime and Police in England 1700–1900*, Gill & Macmillan 1979.
5. T. A. Critchley, *A History of the Police in England and Wales 1900–1966*, Constable 1967.
6. Margaret Drabble, *A Writer's Britain: landscape in literature*, Thames & Hudson 1979.
7. Colin Buchanan, *The State of Britain*, Faber & Faber 1972.
8. Jane Jacobs, *The Death and Life of the Great American Cities: the failure of town planning*, Penguin, 1961.
9. Sam Webb, *Housing & Town Planning Review*, February 1987.
10. See Keith Tompson, *Under Siege: Racial Violence in Britain Today*, Penguin 1988.
11. *Deck Access Disaster: the Hulme Conference 22 February 1985*, Manchester City Council 1985.
12. John Alderson, *Policing Freedom: a commentary on the dilemma of policing in Western democracies*, Macdonald & Evans 1979.
13. Alice Coleman etc, *Utopia on Trial: vision and reality in Planned housing*, Hilary Shipman 1985.
14. Action for Cities press release, 3 November 1988.
15. *Town & Country Planning*, June 1986.
16. Quoted in Nick Wates and Charles Knevitt, *Community Architecture: how people are creating their own environment*, Penguin 1987.
17. 'Community Architecture', *Urban Design Quarterly*, September 1988.
18. Eugene Silke, 'Cultivating a Community down on the farm', *The Surveyor*, 17 November 1988.
19. Tony Gibson, *Counterweight: the neighbourhood option*,

BUILDING FUTURES

TCPA and Education for Neighbourhood Change 1984.

CHAPTER 4
1. Ebenezer Howard, *Garden Cities of Tomorrow*, London 1898.
2. Ibid.
3. Dennis Hardy, 'Setting light the spark of garden cities', *Town & Country Planning*, February 1987.
4. George Orwell, *The Road to Wigan Pier*, Left Book Club, Gollancz 1937, Penguin Secker & Warburg 1962.
5. Tony Champion, 'Momentous revival in London's population', *Town & Country Planning*, March 1987.
6. *Derelict Land*, Department of the Environment 1986.
7. David Nicholson-Lord, *The Greening of the Cities*, RKP 1987.
8. Jane Jacobs, *The Death and Life of the Great American Cities: the failure of town planning*, Penguin 1961.
9. See Chris Baines, *The Wild Side of Town*, BBC Publications 1986.
10. See Bob Smyth, *City Wildspace*, Hilary Shipman 1987.
11. Ibid.
12. Ibid.
13. W. G. Teagle, *The Endless Village*, Nature Conservancy Council.
14. Quoted in Bob Smyth, 'Wildlife winning inquiry battles', *Town & Country Planning*, May 1987.
15. Tony Gibson, *Counterweight: the neighbourhood option*, TCPA and Education for Neighbourhood Change 1984.
16. Tom Woolley and Steve Sharples, 'Community Technical Aid', report for the DoE, Strathclyde University 1987.
17. Quoted in Charles Knevitt and Nick Wates, *Community Architecture: how people are creating their own environment*, Penguin 1987.
18. 'Community Architecture: Design Goes Local', *Going Local*, July 1986.
19. Quoted in Knevitt and Wates, op cit.
20. *Planning for Wildlife in Metropolitan Areas*, Halcrow Fox & Associates/Nature Conservancy Council 1987.
21. Comparison of the Performance of firms in new towns, CIFC report to the Department of the Environment 1976.
22. Gerald Dawe, 'Fruit and veg from derelict land', *Town &*

Country Planning, February 1987.
23. Gill Cressey, 'Ashram Acres: where nothing is wasted', *Town & Country Planning*, April 1988.
24. Joan Davidson, *How Green is Your City? Pioneering approaches to environmental education*, Bedford Square Press 1988.

CHAPTER 5
1. *Town & Country Planning*, March 1987.
2. Keith Waterhouse, 'My Country Right or Wrong', *Sunday Telegraph Magazine*, 14 August 1988.
3. J. B. Priestley, *English Journey*, Heinemann 1934.
4. Robert Hewison, *The Heritage Industry: Britain in a Climate of Decline*, Methuen 1987.
5. *Architects Journal,* 2 November 1988.
6. 'Little Englandism Today', *New Statesman and Society*, 21 October 1988.
7. *Town & Country Planning*, February 1988.
8. Brian Anson, *I'll Fight you for it: Behind the struggle for Covent Garden*, Jonathan Cape 1981.
9. David Fletcher, 'A new definition of the north', *Town & Country Planning*, December 1987.
10. Speech to Council of Europe conference, 28 October 1988.

CHAPTER 6
1. Quoted in Robert McNulty etc, *The Economics of Amenity*, Partners for Liveable Places 1985.
2. Richard Collicot, 'The Birmingham Olympic Bid' in (ed.) David McDowell and David Leslie, *Planning for Tourism and Leisure*, University of Ulster 1988.
3. Quoted in Robert McNulty, op cit.
4. *The Planner* mid month supplement, October 1988.
5. *Place*, January/February 1988.
6. *New Economics*, Winter 1988.
7. Kevin V. Mulcahy, 'The Arts and the urban economy', *Town & Country Planning,* October 1988.
8. *New Statesman and Society*, 19 August 1988.
9. Robert McNulty, *The Return of the Liveable City,*, Atlantis 1988.
10. *Philadelphia City Paper*, 24 October 1986.
11. Quoted in Michael Middleton, *Man Made the Town*,

Bodley Head 1987.
12. *The Return of the Liveable City*, op. cit.
13. *Washington Post*, 18 November 1986.
14. *The Economist*, 16 January 1988.

CHAPTER 7
1. Quoted in Colin Ward, 'A Small Triumph in Lewisham', *Town & Country Planning*, March 1981.
2. Colin Ward, *When we Build Again*, Pluto Press 1985.
3. Ivan Illich, *Tools for Conviviality*, Penguin 1973.
4. *Architects Journal*, April 1976.
5. Ibid. 17 December 1980.
6. Quoted in Alan McDonald, *The Weller Way: the story of the Weller Streets housing co-operative*, Faber & Faber 1986.
7. Ibid.
8. *Releasing Enterprise*, National Council for Voluntary Organizations 1988.
9. Quoted in Joan Perrin, *Democratically Elected Councils at Neighbourhood Level in Urban Areas*, Association of Neighbourhood Councils 1986.
10. *Going Local: decentralization in practice,* Islington Borough Council 1986.
11. Wendy Hayhurst and Mark Howarth, 'Decentralization in Lambeth', *Going Local*, February 1988.
12. Diane Warburton and David Wilcox, *Creating Development Trusts: good practice in urban regeneration*, HMSO 1988.
13. David Wilcox and Diana Warburton, *A Guide to Development Trusts,* Partnership Ltd 1987.
14. See Mark Lutz and Kenneth Lux, *Humanistic Economics*, Bootstrap Press (USA] 1988.
15. Talk to the Entropy Society, Ryukoko University, Japan, 22 November 1987. See also (ed.) Ekins *The Living Economy*, RKP 1986.
16. Michael Delahaye, 'A small solution to a big housing problem', *The Listener*, 11 February 1988.

CHAPTER 8
1. Tom Wolfe, *From Bauhaus to Our House*, 1981.
2. Quoted in Gabriele Scimemi in (ed.) Dieter Frick, *The*

NOTES TO THE TEXT

    Quality of Urban Life, de Gruyter (USA, 1986).
3. Speech to European Year of the Environment, 22 March 1988.
4. Peter Large, 'Britain's new people are top of the world', *The Guardian*, 7 February 1986.
5. Brian Robson, *Those Inner Cities*, OUP 1988.
6. Margaret Simey, *Government by Consent*, Bedford Square Press 1985.

INDEX

Action for Cities, 53–4, 59
Air pollution, 8, 23, 140
Amsterdam, 105
Architecture, 65–6, 101–5,
    117–18, 119, 130, 131–2,
    177–80
Art, 132–6
Ashram Acres, 106, 169
Ashton, Dr John, 190
Association of Community
    Technical Aid Centres
    (ACTAC), 101, 104

Baines, Chris, 94, 95
Baker, Kenneth, 44, 51, 61, 76
Baltimore, 37, 125–7, 143
Banks, 165, 170–2
Beamish Open Air Museum, 115
Belfast, 75, 114, 115
Birkenhead, 86, 161
Birmingham, 18, 27, 29, 34, 48,
    60, 105, 106, 117, 129, 134,
    138, 171
Black Road, Macclesfield, 65,
    102
Booth, Charles, 13–14, 16, 19
Booth, General William, 13

Boston (USA), 110, 145, 193
Bottomley, Virginia, 122, 136
Bradford, 62, 112, 113, 133–4
Bristol, 32, 134, 167
British Urban Development, 59
Brixton riots, 31–4, 45, 48, 71
Broadwater Farm estate, 48–50,
    79, 85, 153
Buchanan, Sir Colin, 71
Business in the Community (BIC),
    166–7
Byker estate, Newcastle, 101,
    150–1

CASE, 103
Chadwick, Edwin, 17–18
Chamberlain, Neville, 21
Charles, Prince, 70, 77, 84, 86,
    87, 99, 101, 102, 103, 108, 117,
    164, 166, 168, 173, 174, 179
    and environmental debate,
        180–2
    RIBA speech, 65–6
Chattanooga, 140
Chicago, 165, 170
Church of England, 2, 16, 50
City Action Teams (CAT's), 51–2,

54, 60
City farms, 90–1, 106–7
City Grant, 54
City Technology Colleges, 54
Civic Trust, 108, 116, 121, 182
Coin Street site, 40, 153
Coleman, Professor Alice, 66, 77–85
Community architecture, 101–5, 151
Community arts, 133–6
Community businesses, 167–70
Community Development Programme (CDP), 26–7
Community policing, 48, 78
Community Urban Design Assistance Team (CUDAT), 102–3
Conservation, 110, 111, 117, 121
Conservative Party, 4–5, 29, 30, 38
Council house sales, 55
Covent Garden, 12, 110, 119–20
Cranhill food co-operative, 169–70
Credit unions, 171–2
Crime, 9, 66–70, 76, 77–80, 82–3, 87

Decentralization, 147–8, 155–9, 174
Development trusts, 159–61, 164
Dickens, Charles, 9, 14–15
Disease, 10, 11, 12, 18
Divis Flats, Belfast, 75
Docklands, 29, 39–42, 58, 60, 61, 167, 187
Dudley Enterprise Zone, 42

Ecological parks, 96
Edinburgh, 138, 168
Education, 193
Educational Priority Areas, 26
Eldonians, 162–4, 185
Energy, 193–4

Engels, Friedrich, 8, 18, 19, 20
Enterprise boards, 165–6
Enterprise Zones, 41–2
Environment, Department of, 28, 37, 53, 78, 81, 83, 86, 101, 135, 160, 161
Ethnic minorities, 67, 76

Fairbrother, Nan, 95
Faith in the City, 2, 16, 50–1
Fielding, Henry, 9, 68–9
Finance, 37, 54, 165–7, 170–2, 194
Financial Initiatives Group (FIG), 37
Fort Wayne, Indiana, 141
Foster, Norman, 131

Garden cities, 20–1, 92–4, 194
Garden festivals, 42–3, 98–9
Gateshead, 115
Gibson, Dr Tony, 85–6
Giroscope Ltd, 167
Glasgow, 1, 27, 51, 56–8, 60, 74, 86, 87, 98, 114, 138, 143, 153, 168, 169, 184, 185, 187, 188, 190
  art and culture, 134–5, 136
  GEAR project, 28, 57, 62
Gloucester Grove estate, Peckham, 2–3
Grameen Bank, 170
Grants, 54
Greater London Council, 39, 40, 44–6, 71, 97, 119, 151, 153, 154
Green belt, 21, 23
Greensight Project, 97

Hackney, Rod, 99, 102, 103, 149
Halifax, 115–16, 117, 121, 122
Hall, John, 59, 115
Hall, Professor Peter, 41, 148, 191
Handsworth riot, 48, 50

Index

Harvey, Jonah, 8
Hatton, Derek, 46, 47, 153, 163
Health, 190–1
Heritage industry, 110–23
Heseltine, Michael, 29, 31, 35–44, 52, 54, 74, 98, 132, 162, 192
High-rise flats, 23, 24, 27, 50, 71–5, 177–8, 187
Homelessness, 24, 39, 41, 54, 61, 71, 73
Hooliganism, 68, 69
Housing, 19, 20–1, 23, 24, 27, 38–41, 54–6, 58, 61, 71–6, 150–1, 185, 193
   co-ops, 152
   and crime, 66, 76, 77–80, 82–3
   decentralization, 148–9, 155–9
Housing Action Trusts (HAT's), 55–6
Housing design, 80–6
Howard, Ebenezer, 20–1, 91–4
Hulme estate, Manchester, 56, 67

Illich, Ivan, 104, 149
Immigration, 25–6
Indianapolis, 129
Inner Area Studies, 27
Inner City Aid, 104, 182
Inner City Enterprises, 37
Inner City Trust, 102
Inner London Education Authority, 45, 193
Inner Urban Act (1978), 29
Investment, local, 165–7
Isle of Dogs, 41–2, 59, 84, 157
Islington, 156, 158

Jacobs, Jane, 79, 83, 93, 107–8
Jencks, Charles, 177, 179
Jenkin, Patrick, 44, 46, 163
Johnson, Philip, 179, 180
Joseph, Sir Keith, 45, 81

Kensington, 160
Kentish Town City Farm, 90–1, 100, 107
Kiffin, Dolly, 49–50
Kinnock, Neil, 46, 47
Knevitt, Charles, 102, 103, 104

Labour Party, 23, 28, 29, 30, 45, 46–7, 148, 154–5, 156, 163, 185–6
Laird School of Art, 87, 161
Lambeth, 27, 29, 47, 50, 158
Land Use Consultants, 96
Landlife – *see* Rural Preservation Association
Le Corbusier, 178
Lea View House, Hackney, 84
Leeds, 132
Liberal Party, 148, 157
Lightmoor, 161
Liverpool, 15, 24, 27, 29, 30, 36–8, 39, 55, 56, 62, 74, 81, 87, 93, 94, 97, 100, 101, 132, 134
   crime, 67
   garden festival, 42–3
   rates rebellion, 46–7
   self-help housing, 152, 161–4
   Toxteth riot, 33, 36
Livingstone, Ken, 44, 45, 47
Local authorities, 37, 38, 39, 44–7, 52, 54, 55
   and private sector, 59–61, 144–5, 165
Local Enterprise Advisory Project (LEAP), 168
Local government, 27, 141, 144, 194
   attack on, 186
   decentralization, 147–8
   growth of, 18
   politics, 184–5
   reorganization, 44–6, 154
Local Government Finance Act

(1982), 39
London, 2, 3, 29, 39, 45, 59, 62–3, 109
  East End, 7–8, 14, 19, 20, 23, 161
  growth of, 9–13
  homelessness, 54–5
London, Jack, 7–8
London Docklands Development Corporation (LDDC), 39–41, 61
Longbenton estate, Tyneside, 82
Lowell (USA), 112–13

McGann, Tony, 162–4, 173
Macmillan, Harold, 23, 24, 65, 77
Management Improvement, 78–9
Manchester, 13, 17, 18, 24, 34, 51, 54, 56, 67–8, 69, 94, 101, 113, 127, 129
Maud Report, 154
Mayhew, Henry, 14
Memphis, 140
Merseyside Development Corporation, 39, 40, 42, 54
Merseyside Task Force, 37–8
Metropolitan county councils, 44, 45, 62
Militant Tendency, 46, 47, 152, 162–4
Milton Keynes, 106, 117, 133
Modernism, 177–80
Mondragon co-operative, 171
Motorways, 70–1
Mozart estate, Paddington, 76, 82
Museums, 112, 113, 114, 115, 117

National Community Partnership (NCP), 101, 103, 104
National Planning Aid Unit, 100
Nature Conservancy Council, 95, 105

Neighbourhood councils, 153–4
Neighbourhood watch schemes, 87
New towns, 22–3, 24, 93, 105
New York, 79, 106, 129, 132, 133
Newham, 72–4, 76, 187
Newman, Oscar, 79–80
North Bergen, New Jersey, 98
Northern Ireland, 75–6

Orwell, George, 22, 93, 116
Osborn, Sir Frederic, 21, 22
Oxford, 131, 132

Partners for Liveable Places, 136–7, 140, 143
Pearson, Geoffrey, 68, 69
Per Cent Club, 166
Pittsburgh, 103, 140–1, 164, 182
Planning, 127–8, 189–90
  community, 99–102, 154
Planning for Real, 86
Police, 48, 49
Pollution, 8, 140
Population, 20, 59, 109–10, 191
Poverty, 8, 9, 10, 12, 14–19, 20, 22, 83, 143, 185
Powell, Enoch, 25–6, 33
Power, Anne, 78–9, 81, 83
Priority Estates Project (PEP), 78–9, 83, 85
Private sector, 37, 54, 58–60, 144–5, 165–7, 185, 186
Pruitt-Igoe flats, 177–8
Public spending, 173–4

Race riots, 24–5
Racial discrimination, 34, 49, 76
Rand McNally Corporation, 137–8
Ratecapping, 39, 46–7
RIBA, 65–6, 87, 99, 101, 102, 104
Ridley, Nicholas, 52, 53, 56, 60, 81, 135
Riots, 24–5, 31–4, 35–6, 47–51,

INDEX

69
Robson, Professor Brian, 61, 62, 187
Rogers, Richard, 131
Rohe, Mies van der, 178, 179
Ronan Point, 72–4
Rotherham, 131–2
Rouse, James, 126–7, 130, 137, 139, 195
Royston Hill estate, 74
Rural heritage, 122
Rural Preservation Association, 97, 100

St Louis, Missouri, 139, 177–8, 195
St Paul, Minnesota, 141
St Paul's riot, Bristol, 32
San Jose, California, 171
Scarman, Lord, 32–3, 34, 36, 99
School-industry compacts, 54, 145, 193
Scottish Development Agency, 57, 62
Seattle, 138–9
Seikatsu food co-operative, 170
Self-help schemes, 149–51, 159–64, 173–5
Sheffield, 13, 47, 54, 128–9, 133, 165–6
Shopping centres, 130, 139
Shore, Peter, 28, 62
Social Science Research Council, 1, 29
Socialism, 19, 185
Southall riots, 33
Southwark, 4, 11, 12, 20, 46
Sport, 128–9, 130, 133
Stead, W. T., 16
Stirling, James, 131, 180
Stockbridge Village Trust, 56
Stockport, 155
Strathclyde, 168
Stuttgart, 131

Tate and Lyle, 161–3
Technical aid, 100–4
Teeside UDC, 52
Thatcher, Margaret, 4–5, 24, 26, 29, 30, 32, 33, 34, 38, 44, 51, 52, 53, 54, 81, 166, 169, 181, 182
Tibbalds, Francis, 83–4, 130
Tottenham riot, 48–9
Tourism, 110–23
Tower blocks – *see* High-rise flats
Tower Hamlets, 147–8, 155, 157–8, 160–1
Town and Country Planning Association, 94, 100, 101, 154, 161, 192, 194
Town planning movement, 20–1
Toxteth riot, 33, 36
Traffic, 70–1
Turner, John, 150

UK 2000, 97
Unemployment, 21–2, 41, 48, 167
United States, 34, 37, 54, 60, 79, 98, 106, 112–13, 122, 125–7, 129, 132, 133, 143–6, 165, 170
city revival, 136–41
Urban development corporations, 39, 52, 58, 60, 61, 62, 185
Urban Development Grants, 37, 54
Urban Programme, 1, 26, 29, 51, 60, 100, 163
Utopia On Trial, 66, 77, 79, 80, 81, 83

Vandalism, 82, 83, 85
Voluntary sector, 54, 101

Walsall, 155–6, 158
Ward, Colin, 1, 55, 149
Watts, 160

Webb, Beatrice, 19
Webb, Sam, 73, 74
Weller Street Co-operative, 97, 102, 152, 175
West Midlands Enterprise Board, 165
Wester Hailes estate, Edinburgh, 160
Westminster City Council, 61, 62, 187
Wigan, 116
Wildlife, urban, 94–6, 108
William Curtis Ecological Park, 96
Wilson, Harold, 23, 26, 72

York, 113–14
Young, Lord, 52, 53